FROM PANIC TO POWER
The Positive Use of Stress

FROM PANIC TO POWER
The Positive Use of Stress

JOHN J. PARRINO, Ph.D

Private Practice
   and
Consultant, Behavioral Systems, Inc., Atlanta

JOHN WILEY & SONS
New York   Chichester   Brisbane   Toronto

Library of Congress Cataloging in Publication Data

Parrino, John J   1941
 From panic to power.

 Bibliography: p.
 Includes index.
1   1. Stress (Psychology.   2.   Biofeedback training.
I. Title.
BF575.S75P33   158'.1   79-12027
ISBN 0-471-05303-1

Printed in the United States of America

10 9 8 7 6 5 4 3 2 1

To

My parents, Angela and Joe

My brother and sister-in-law, Bob and Vini

A special person, Cindy

FOREWORD

In sports and business, as well as in daily living, one finds all too many guidelines for the management of one's own behavior. Some experts offer a steady diet of advice for increasing personal motivation and improving individual performance. Everyone has a remedy for "getting your head together." The quest for personal effectiveness can indeed be frustrating and confusing. The problem with these armchair approaches to self-management is the conspicuous absence of a scientific method for understanding and managing human behavior.

The scientific methodology that has guided the natural and biological sciences to such great heights of discovery is now available to the managers of human behavior. I have learned to deeply appreciate the value of a data-based, empirical approach to behavior management and personal effectiveness in both of my careers. As an athlete I have found my performance enhanced by the systematic application of scientifically derived principles. In my own business, Behavioral Systems, Inc. (BSI), we are using this same technology to increase the motivation and performance of workers in organizational settings.

An extremely important component of this relatively new field is the effective management of one's own behavior. *From Panic to Power* is about this process of self-management. Dr. John J. Parrino has applied the science of behavior management to the intricate workings of the Human Response System. Feedback, a principle we have used very successfully at BSI, is a central notion of this valuable book. The use of this and other tools in managing one's own behavior during stressful life events is the forte of *From Panic to Power.* I have used these tools successfully to enhance my own life. I am sure that you will find the principles of behavioral stress management of great value in your own pursuit for personal effectiveness.

FRAN TARKENTON

PREFACE

We know more about the engine that resides under the hood of our car than we know about the one that regulates our functioning every day of our lives. In our society, we have given the responsibility for our own health and emotional well-being to caretakers. When something goes wrong with our body, we visit the medical doctor. We take on the role of patient, and passively say to the doctor, "Heal me." Other professionals are identified for taking care of our minds. Mind and body are seen as separate, and individuals are left with a sense of helplessness in understanding the two.

This book does not advocate the rejection of professional help. It does, however, reject the notion of mind-and-body separatism and the relinquishing of total responsibility for one's well-being to society's caretakers.

Staunchly aligning themselves against this apathy and abdication are the *stress watchers*—all of us who are determined to gain control over our psychological and physical destinies. We are tired of suffering the assaults and abuses incurred as we function in a high-pressured and demanding environment. We refuse to sit passively and submit to nagging thoughts of self-doubt, attacks of excessive bodily arousal, and one self-destructive habit after another. We no longer wish to rationalize emotional upheavals and upsets as useful and healthy. Psychologically, we strive to become the masters of our fate, the captains of our soul. We stand ready, finally, to employ modern scientific technology in our own behalf—to build an internal psychobiological structure that ensures a new strategy for living happily, effectively, and with minimal emotional disturbance.

This should not be confused with the preambles to "Do It Yourself" therapies that pledge an allegiance to "getting your head together," no matter what the cost to yourself and to society. Many approaches to self-help dispense pat solutions to the problems of living—"Do your own thing," "Let go of your inhibitions," and "Release those pent-up emotions." You are supposed to follow this advice because the authors/helpers authoritatively state that it would be good for you. Or they have a gut feeling that the principles are sound. And finally, because the solutions worked for the authors and their small samples of clients, friends, and relatives. They advocate these behavioral imperatives without the provision of a logical rationale. These simple solutions to life's enormous problems often fail to jive with what contemporary scientists know about the complex laws of human behavior.

There is one critical difference separating the present book, *From Panic to Power,* from the plethora of self-help manuals and theories—the concept of stress is steeped in the tradition of scientific technology. It started in the physiology laboratories and is now firmly entrenched in the research camps of behavioral scientists. It is this scientific tradition that has given us the mechanism for curing the bacteria-initiated diseases of the past. The same mechanism offers real hope for coping with man's most pervasive contemporary disorder—*stress.*

From Panic to Power teaches you an in-depth knowledge of the complex workings of your Human Response System and the empirically derived principles of behavior that direct it to change in an adaptive manner. It advocates an assertive strategy for coping with the problems of living. Knowledge of the results of one's own human responses and the use of these data (feedback) is critical to effective personal functioning. This book's major objective is to help you integrate and utilize at a practical level the concepts of feedback, self-regulation, and self-control. It is an attempt to teach you to become acutely aware of the abundance of information you receive from your human response system—the tiny bits of human data that so often get washed away from consciousness by the numerous distractions of contemporary existence.

Awareness for what, you may ask? Not simply for the sake of awareness, but for the discrimination of healthy from unhealthy responses, for feedback and reinforcement toward maximizing habit change in a desirable direction, and for self-regulation and control of critical human responses that determine your daily moods and feelings of well-being. Through the use of a personal feedback system, *From Panic to Power* helps you strive towards a self-determined strategy for living happily, effectively, with a minimal amount of emotional disturbance. In this manner, you can retrieve a portion of the responsibility for monitoring, evaluating, and altering the functioning of your Human Response System.

JOHN J. PARRINO

Atlanta, Georgia
February 1979

ACKNOWLEDGMENTS

Many scientists and clinical practitioners have influenced me through their research activities and writings. Their names pervade the pages of this book, so I do not formally acknowledge them here. I wish to use this space to express my gratitude to the friends and colleagues who assisted me through their personal help and contact in the first ten years of my professional life.

The friend and colleague that has influenced me the most during this period is Dr. Aubrey Daniels. He plucked me from the throes of a non-scientific orientation, shaped and molded me into a behavioral scientist, and provided me with opportunity, support, and reinforcement to make my own unique contribution to the science of human behavior. Two other associates who were helpful in the early stages of my transformation were Drs. Ross Grumet and Douglas Slavin.

A special thanks is extended to a protégé turned mentor, Dr. Dennis Herendeen, who listened and learned and then accompanied me in my investigation of the intimate connection between covert and overt behavior.

In my capacity as a consultant I have received the aid of a number of people. The most noteworthy are Larry Miller, Executive Vice President of Behavioral Systems, Inc., who served as a good model for the writing and work behaviors that were necessary for the completion of this project; Jesse Watson, Senior Vice President of Behavioral Systems, Inc., who allowed me to apply my stress management model in a variety of situations and locations; and, Francis Tarkenton, Chairman of the Board of Behavioral Systems, Inc., who provided me with both tangible and nontangible reinforcement for my work.

Two people helped immensely in the preparation of the manuscript. Both went far beyond my requests and expectations and provided me with moral support, positive feedback, and personal sensitivity. They are Diane DeFrancis, who worked with me in the early stages of the book, and Mary Mansour, who revised the manuscript several times and helped me prepare the final copy. Along these same lines I would like to thank Debbie Hall for working diligently on the illustrations and Jeanne Bradbury for her assistance in the last stages of the preparation of the book. Also, Ed O'Donnell, who read the manuscript and provided me with invaluable feedback that served as a stimulus for numerous revisions.

Numerous friends provided me with the support, humor, and personal interactions that enabled me to make it through a difficult project in an adaptive manner. Fred and Mary Wesson gave me sustenance. Jerry Pounds and Perry Nelson listened to my woes, made me laugh, and shared their lives with me.

J. J. P.

CONTENTS

INTRODUCTION: STRESS AND YOU   1

CHAPTER 1:   THE CASE OF PAUL: A SEVERE STRESS
             REACTION   6

Hospitalization   8
Near Death   10
A Critical Decision to Treat   11
Treatment   12
A Dramtic Recovery   14

CHAPTER 2:   STRESS AND FEEDBACK   19

Case of Paul Revisited   20
What Is Stress?   24
Feats of Self-Control   27
Behavior Modifiers   29
Feedback   32
Personal Feedback: System Gone Astray Versus Self-Control   34

CHAPTER 3:   THE HUMAN RESPONSE SYSTEM   37

Emotions   38
Thoughts, Physiological Responses and Behavior   40
Summary   44

CHAPTER 4:   EMOTIONS   46

Emotions: Results of Thinking, Physiological Responses, and
   Behavior   47
Anxiety, Depression, and Anger: The Stress Emotions   48
Emotions and Feedback: What Are Your Emotions Telling You?   50
Three Stages of Emotional Reactions: The Case of Paul   54
The Various Faces of Emotional Upset   55
Emotions and Stressful Life Events   58

CHAPTER 5:   HUMAN RESPONSE SYSTEM:
              PHYSIOLOGY   66

The Stress Response   67
Common Examples of Physiological Arousal in Humans   72
The General Stress Response: The Alarm and Resistance
    Reactions   76
Hypertension, Coronary Artery Disease, and Sudden Death:
    Potential Consequences of a Chronic Stress Reaction   77
The Stress Response: Summary   83
Muscle Tension: A Common Example of a Disruption in
    Homeostasis   84
The Breakdown of Feedback: A Unifying Concept   90

CHAPTER 6:   SELF-REGULATION: PHYSIOLOGY   93

The Case of Joy   93
Muscle Tension   97
Relaxation   98
Applications of Relaxation: General Use and High Blood
    Pressure   100
Feedback and Relaxation   111

CHAPTER 7:   HUMAN RESPONSE SYSTEM: THINKING   114

The Brain   115
Thinking and the Environment: The Silent Dialogue   118
The Case of Dr. T   121
Disordered Thinking   122
Summary   130

CHAPTER 8:   SELF-REGULATION: THINKING   132

Counteracting the "Dangerous Environment" Hypothesis   134
Counteracting Thought Distractions and Increasing
    Concentration   139
Counteracting Irrational Thinking   145
Counteracting Disordered Thinking: Summary   151
Self-Regulation of Thinking and Feedback   154

CHAPTER 9:   HUMAN RESPONSE SYSTEM: BEHAVIOR   157

The Case of James: A Phobic Behavior Pattern   159
Principles of Learning   163
Learned Maladaptive Behavior Patterns: Avoidance and
    Hyperresponsiveness   167
Creatures of Habit   169
Other Learned Behaviors   171
Maladaptive Habits of Living: The Breakdown of Feedback   173

CHAPTER 10:   SELF-REGULATION: BEHAVIOR   176

The Case of Richard   176
The "Dangerous Environment" Hypothesis Revisited   179
Adaptive Exposure or Taking Another Look: Counteracting the
    "Dangerous Environment" Hypothesis   179
Altering the Hyporesponsive Behavior Pattern: Adaptive Coping in a
    Depressed Individual   182
Altering the Hyperresponsive Behavior Pattern: Adaptive Coping in
    the Type A Individual   186
The "Safe-Environment" Hypothesis: Risk-Taking and
    Assertiveness   190
Adaptive Exposure, Risk-Taking and Assertiveness: The Case of
    James   196
Summary: Feedback and Behavior Change   202

CHAPTER 11:   HUMAN RESPONSE SYSTEM: FEEDBACK   204

Feedback and the Human Response System   206
Feedback and Interpersonal Relations   209
Feedback, Learning, and Human Behavior   209
Personal Feedback System   211

CHAPTER 12:   SELF-REGULATION: PERSONAL
                FEEDBACK   213

The Case of Joseph   213
Self-Management Project   222
Uses of Self-Monitoring   228
The Second Stage of Personal Feedback: Use of Other
    Feedback-Facilitating Techniques   230
A Personal Feedback System: The Final Stage—A New Strategy for
    Living Happily, Effectively, and with a Minimum of Emotional
    Upset   231
The Case of Dorian: The Profound Effects of a Personal Feedback
    System   232

APPENDIX I: Results of Maladaptive Coping   238

APPENDIX II: The Muscular Relaxation Response   244

APPENDIX III: Behavior Profile   249

REFERENCES   252

INDEX   255

FROM PANIC TO POWER
The Positive Use of Stress

to the subtle manifestations of annoying thoughts, bodily malfunctions, and addictive behaviors such as alcoholism. The prolonged repetition of these stress responses eventually take their toll. All of the dangerous consequences to the human system have not been identified. Investigators agree that the list of pathological conditions attributed to stress is growing longer. Conditions such as obsessions (thought preoccupations), severe anxiety and depression, muscular tension, tension headaches, migraines, constipation, diarrhea, ulcers, colitis, and lower back pain are often directly associated with stress. Stress has been indirectly implicated in a variety of other serious problems such as coronary artery disease, angina, heart disease, arthritis, high blood pressure, and even cancer.

Although the ultimate consequences of stress are readily observable, its early effects on the response system are very subtle. Unlike infections and other direct assaults on the system, the symptoms of.the stress response are difficult to watch. Early warning signals such as excessive worrying, depression, and insomnia may be attributed to other causes. As a result, the alterations in coping responses that are necessary for inhibiting the development of a severe stress reaction may not be initiated.

Stress is democratic. It does not discriminate between the housewife and the executive, the hourly employee and the company president, or the high school dropout and the college graduate. It levies its assault regardless of age, sex, occupation, ethnic background, and economic level. As humans, we appear to be uniquely susceptible to the consequences of maladaptive coping.

Stress is not necessarily unhealthy. The machinery that powers the adjustments we make in coping with life's demands is equally capable of returning the system to a state of equilibrium and adaptive functioning. The cyclical nature of the stress response—arousing the system to meet the demands of a situation and relaxing it when the task is accomplished—is a very natural and healthy characteristic of a biological organism that is striving for survival. Stress becomes unhealthy when we ignore the system's signals to return to this state of rest and equilibrium. Unfortunately, the depressed housewife, the overachieving college student, and the hurried executive are prone to ignore this information simply by virtue of the habits they have acquired for coping with their environments.

Stress can be the stimulus that motivates you to change in a positive direction. You are uniquely capable of learning the intricate workings of your response system, observing the information that it provides to you on a regular basis throughout your life, and using these data for self-regulation and self-management. Becoming aware of one's own unique stress reactions can be a very enlightening and exciting experience. Utilizing this information for your own behalf can provide the sense of control that is the basis for a profound feeling of self-confidence. Constructing a personal feedback system can provide a strategy of living that minimizes emotional upset and increases a long lasting sense of happiness and well-being.

The subsequent chapters of this book provide you with the ammunition necessary for stress watching and the construction of a personal feedback system. You will become intimately aware of the intricate workings of your Human Response System. Various questions you have about this complex system are answered: How do my thoughts contribute to my stress-related problems? Are my physiological reactions completely out of my control? How do my behaviors become habitual and resistant to change? The major human emotions are analyzed. You will learn that they provide valuable bits of information for evaluating the adaptiveness of your current coping strategy. Scientifically derived behavioral techniques such as relaxation, desensitization, and biofeedback are provided as change strategies for each component of the Human Response System.

The book relies heavily on the intimate details of the lives of individuals who have been the victims of stress. Through their own personal efforts and work with me, they have become successful stress watchers and managers of stress. I share these cases with you because I hope they will provide you with a model for increasing your awareness and personal effectiveness. There is no intent on my part to imply that you will experience the same kind of stress reaction as the individuals whose lives are placed before you. I chose these cases from hundreds of others because they most clearly display the workings of the Human Response System. The exaggerated nature of some of these problems will help you identify the more subtle manifestations of stress in yourself.

The case presented in Chapter 1 exemplifies the very basic characteristics of the Human Response System. It illustrates the deep trouble people can experience when confronted with excessive environmental pressures. It also reveals the immense human potential for change. Caught in the most profound depths of a personal crisis, this individual showed the courage and stamina to lift himself from near death, to once again confront an extremely frustrating series of life events. I share this case with you with his blessings in the hope that you will learn from his personal crisis and triumph.

I wish to make one strong point about self-help. A major objective of this book is to help people take on more responsibility for their own emotional well-being and happiness. I am thoroughly convinced that we can become masters of our fate. Many individuals can help themselves through reading, learning and self-discovery. That does not preclude the seeking of professional medical and/or psychological help for others. It may have just the opposite effect. Through the process of watching your stress reactions, you may uncover a long-lasting problem that necessitates professional assistance. After reading this book you will be in a better position to become an enlightened participant in the helping process.

1 THE CASE OF PAUL
A Severe Stress Reaction

By January of 1969 Paul had interviewed many of the major political figures and personalities of this country. Richard Nixon and Robert Kennedy were perhaps the most famous participants of "Dialogue," a short talk show that was getting Paul national recognition. At the age of 36 he had reached the pinnacle of local television. As anchorman of the 6:00 PM News and Director of the Newsroom, Paul had achieved popularity and recognition. This was an enviable position for any young television personality. In addition to enjoying the unusual combination of position and local fame, his current status could eventually materialize into a network position. Like other local newsmen from major cities Paul hoped to be a Cronkite, a Huntley, or a Brinkley. There were even political aspirations in the back of Paul's mind. Due to his popularity in the area he was seriously considering a campaign for a major position in the city or perhaps even a statewide political seat.

In September of 1969 Paul was admitted to a state hospital with the diagnosis of Creutzfeldt-Jakob Syndrome. The diagnosis originated from a reputable neurologist at a well-known medical center. It was terminal. Paul had a neurological disease and was given nine months to live.

The events that transpired between January and September were astonishing. These months were filled with confusion and agony. During this period most of the information about Paul's life was obtained from friends and relatives. Paul could not recall a single experience. An almost complete loss of memory was one of the first symptoms of his illness. Friends and colleagues at the television station remembered the initial stage of his deterioration. They stated that Paul began forgetting the small events of the day. He became repetitious and failed to remember facts and stories *that he had related to them in earlier conversations. He forgot appointments. Even names and faces of people at the television station were difficult for him to recognize.*

Employees at the station observed subtle changes in his behavior. "Paul is not the same person that he used to be," was a statement often heard from people who knew him well. In fact Paul was not the same! He was tense, confused, and disorganized. Socializing was a strain. He became detached and isolated from the remainder of the employee group. Smiles, vigorous laughter, and humorous story-telling were common social responses from Paul in the past. They were replaced with grimaces, nervous gestures, and a generally tense manner of relating.

Paul experienced his first grand mal seizure in March, 1969. It is the type of seizure that involves a temporary loss of consciousness and muscular control. The seizure victim falls to the ground and experiences rapid, jerky movements of the entire body. The abnormal muscular response is sometimes accompanied by biting of the tongue and excessive flowing of saliva from the mouth. The seizure is followed by a period of unconsciousness and sleep. Although it is frightening to observe someone having a grand mal seizure, it is an amazingly innocuous event. Unless the individual is hurt by the fall there are often no harmful effects to the brain or remainder of the body.

Paul was admitted to a general hospital for examination. The examination proved to be fruitless. The physicians were confused by the presence of neurological symptoms in view of the absence of significant evidence for the existence of a neurological disease. He was discharged from the hospital after a short period of time and returned to work.

Reports from friends regarding Paul's profound loss of memory and confusion were becoming more frequent. They were becoming alarmed about his condition. Shortly after this time he experienced his second seizure. He was transferred out of state to a very reputable hospital for an expert opinion. An exhaustive neurological workup at this hospital proved equally frustrating. There were numerous disturbing symptoms but no definitive neurological abnormalities. The diagnosis was finally made on the basis of the following findings:

1. Complaints of failure of recent memory.
2. Profound confusion.
3. Several grand mal seizures.
4. Right-sided twitches of the body and transient loss of balance.
5. An electroencephalogram (EEG) that showed diffuse abnormality (the EEG is a record of brain waves which reflects the electrical activity of the brain).

On the strength of these findings Paul was granted disability benefits, indicating the expectation that he would be totally and permanently disabled or terminal.

HOSPITALIZATION

I first became aware of Paul's case several weeks after his admission to the hospital where I was working as a clinical psychologist. It was quite common for community organizations, local playhouses, and professional athletic teams to donate tickets to the hospital so that our patients could attend outside activities. The first time I saw Paul was at one of these functions, which I had attended as an escort for the patients.

Paul was not watching the play. He was slumped over in his seat and staring at the floor. I nudged the nurse sitting next to me and asked her about the distinguished man sitting several seats down from us. He appeared to be half asleep. As she recalled his name I remembered hearing it around the hospital. Rumors around the hospital focused on the well-known television personality who was transferred from a very reputable medical center. Staff members from various psychiatric units stated that there was no hope for this patient. He had a terminal neurological disease, and his condition should deteriorate progressively until death.

Why send someone to a psychiatric institution who is going to die of a neurological disease? Many of us asked this question. There was no clear answer. Some said it was because he was a well-known personality, and he should have access to the relatively plush surroundings of our hospital for his remaining months. Others said that a 36-year-old individual was too young to be placed in a nursing home and would live too long to remain at a general hospital. The only alternative was to place him in a long-term hospital setting.

The hospital where Paul resided is the major psychiatric institution for a large metropolitan area. Admissions include psychiatric patients who need 24-hour long-term treatment. Paul was placed on one of our inpatient units to reside with a variety of psychiatric patients. No specific treatment was recommended at this time. He had a terminal neurological disease. "We can't do anything about that." That's what the staff understood from the physicians at the medical center. The doctors at our hospital corroborated that conclusion.

Paul was placed on our general token economy (a treatment technique used at the hospital for managing large groups of patients in a community living arrangement) so that he could be on an equal status with other patients on the unit. The token economy allows patients to earn tokens for behaving in a manner compatible with community living. Tokens are earned for behaviors such as getting up on time, attending important meetings, participating in recreational activities, and getting along with other people. These tokens are spent for special privileges: access to the token store (where items donated by individuals and community organizations are purchased), special activities outside of the hospital, and other reinforcers.

Paul did well on the token economy and in community living in general. He was well-liked by the staff and the patients. His week consisted of attending scheduled activities, socializing with patients and outside visitors, and special weekend functions. Paul's mood was comparable to our most depressed patients. It was very low and fluctuated very little throughout the day. His seizures occurred on a regular basis. Unlike the grand mal type that occurred in the earlier stage of his illness, they did not precipitate a complete state of unconsciousness. The seizures took place while he was in a standing position and included a temporary loss of consciousness, jerky movements of one side of his body, and a transient loss of balance.

I vividly remember the first time I was introduced to Paul. He reached for my hand and at that moment experienced gross, jerky movements of the left side of his body. His face turned abruptly to the left. His left arm and leg jerked, and he moved in a dancelike fashion while grasping my arm. A few seconds later he was back to normal. We shook hands and spoke for a short while. During the *conversation Paul experienced several of these brief seizures. A subsequent count of them by the hospital staff revealed an average frequency of 58 per day, ranging from a low of 22 to a high of 95.*

The general symptom picture for Paul was severe depression followed by short periods of mood elevation. Regular episodes of seizure activity were observed on a daily basis. When he wasn't depressed and withdrawn he communicated fairly well. His recall of past events was extremely poor, and memory for current events was fair. Although the neurological tests administered at the medical center were inconclusive, it was easy to see why Paul was diagnosed as having a neurological disease. Neurological functioning was very low, and Paul's condition appeared to be steadily deteriorating.

NEAR DEATH

None of us doubted the diagnosis. We sadly awaited the progressive deterioration in functioning that typically accompanies a terminal condition. Our expectations were fully realized one afternoon when Paul went into a burst of uncontrollable seizure activity. The seizures were unaffected by medication or other medical procedures. The physicians had warned us that neurologically disordered patients sometimes experience this burst of seizure activity before they expire from the disease. Paul was transferred to the emergency room of a general hospital. The staff felt that he was close to the end of his life. Preparations were made for his death and funeral.

The gravity of the situation was expressed by an article written around this time, dealing with Paul's prolific contribution to the Catholic church. A scholarship fund was started in his name. The following excerpt was taken from an editorial written by the editor of the Catholic newspaper.

The Paul . . . Scholarship Award has been established at St. Joseph's High School to honor the Catholic layman of the same name who is critically ill of a rare brain disease.

The establishment of this fund is a fitting tribute to a man who seemed always to give more than he took.

In a business where vanity is not uncommon, he didn't absorb it, but used his communicative talents not only to earn a living, but to further his church, his fellow man and his newspaper.

Many will be saddened by his illness, because he touched the lives of many in meaningful ways.

He was especially interested in youth, thus the scholarship fund at the school where he frequently talked to students.

Approximately one week later Paul was back at our hospital. An amazing transition had taken place. His general mood and appearance was improved in comparison to his pre-emergency status. His memory was still very poor, and the seizures were still occurring at a high frequency. But something was different about him. His overall condition had improved. The information surrounding these events remains unclear to this day. No one really knew what happened during and after the emergency. Paul couldn't remember the events, and no one documented the week's activities. It happened so quickly that there was little chance to prepare for his transfer to the emergency unit.

A few pieces of information were gathered by staff members who were involved in the crisis. They explained that Paul was taken immediately to the emergency room. He was treated and sent to a hospital room. While he was there Paul was visited by friends from the television station and by his wife. She had only visited him sporadically during the months of his hospitalization. No other information was available. The outcome of this period was definitive. There was a change in the nature of his symptomatology and an improvement in his condition.

A CRITICAL DECISION TO TREAT

I was attending a staff meeting when Paul returned to the hospital. The staff was obviously confused about the events surrounding the emergency and the subsequent change in his status. We discussed the situation at length. This was the first time in his stay at the hospital that the unit staff and I questioned the neurological diagnosis: "If he was dying of a neurological disease," we asked, "why did his condition improve?" He was still very confused. His memory was poor and he continued to experience seizures at a high rate. Yet his overall condition was improved. Paul was not deteriorating.

Speculations were rampant during that staff meeting. Was this a temporary state of remission that would be followed by the full course of the disease? Did the neurologists fail to make the appropriate diagnosis? Perhaps it was another disease that had an unpredictable course of action. Numerous ideas were considered. Each led to the same conclusion: the original diagnosis and prognosis had not materialized, and arriving at another equally unverified conclusion would not help Paul.

By the end of that meeting we had arrived at a course of action. The staff decided and I concurred that therapy was warranted in this case. I was a consultant to various units at the hospital and often took particularly difficult cases that demanded an extra opinion or special help. I decided to take the case and use the assessment tools and behavior therapy techniques that were my specialty. It was an ambitious undertaking, but Paul had nothing to lose and perhaps everything to gain from the endeavor.

TREATMENT

I began working with Paul in June 1970, nine months after his admission to the hospital. My first task was to do an assessment of his problem. I took the stance that I was dealing with a psychiatric problem and assessed the situation from that standpoint. Very little evidence from specific medical tests was available. In view of the overt, profound neurological disturbance the original diagnosis was understandable. My job was to provide a better explanation: one that would lead to a constructive treatment program.

My search through the hospital records for evidence of emotional triggers to Paul's problem was not productive. The most helpful information came from two sources: speaking to staff members who had observed him on the unit and interviews with close friends who were aware of the early stages of his illness. The information I gathered led me to identify two major life events that could have activated a severe emotional crisis.

Paul was spreading himself too thin. He was having difficulty executing the demands and responsibilities of two major jobs at the television station. His status as director of the newsroom was being threatened. The manager of the station was considering a decision to remove Paul from this position. This move would eventually leave him with the job that he executed so well–performing for the television audience.

A second perhaps more critical event caught my attention. Paul was married and had two adopted children. During his hospitalization his wife seldom visited him. Many of his weekend visits were spent with friends. Only a few of them were spent at his own home. There were rumors of fairly long-standing marital conflicts between Paul and his wife. Further rumors among hospital staff members and the television staff suggested an ongoing affair between Paul's wife and one of his closest friends, a Catholic priest.

Paul made a vague reference about this relationship during the initial stages of his illness. He had attended a funeral with several of the staff from the television station. When asked of the whereabouts of his wife, Paul stated, "She's probably with that damned priest again." This was one of a few bits of evidence indicating that Paul had some awareness of his wife's infidelity.

The priest was the director of the church where Paul and his wife were in regular attendance. The three of them had become close friends through their association at the church. The priest was a frequent visitor at their home at the time when Paul's marital problems were becoming very pronounced. Paul and his wife were becoming progressively more detached from each other, and the relationship was deteriorating. At some level of consciousness Paul was aware of this ongoing relationship.

My initial hypothesis was that one or both of these events triggered a severe stress reaction and emotional crisis in Paul. They were so threatening and overwhelming that he had difficulty coping with them. Severe bouts of anxiety and depression began to set in. His memory began to fail him, and he became more and more detached from the responsibilities of work.

The situation became critical. His communication with his wife deteriorated even further. Paul was becoming more confused and disoriented. The severe depression, confusion, and disorientation were followed by the first grand mal seizure. Another seizure occurred in a short span of time. Something had to be done immediately. The significant people in his life followed a natural course of action. One medical examination followed another until an exasperated physician, frustrated by a confusing set of medical facts, diagnosed the condition and pronounced the expected end of his life.

The illness had not taken its expected course of action. Paul was not deteriorating. He was not going to die, at least not within the predicted period of time. My course of action was unclear. How was I going to treat Paul? If my hypothesis was correct one of my first tasks in therapy was to cautiously expose Paul to the events that triggered the emotional crisis. Only then could I teach him to confront the threatening events and memory of these events in a manner that would allow him to handle them in a more adaptive fashion.

Paul needed desperately to acquire coping skills that would allow him to handle the future inevitable stress-provoking events in his life. And so with the help of the unit staff I proceeded. Paul received intensive therapy. The therapy procedures I used are described in detail in the subsequent chapters of this book.

A DRAMATIC RECOVERY

My hypothesis about Paul was correct. It was vigorously challenged by professionals who could not believe that a severe stress reaction could mimic a disease so closely. I was convinced that the process was triggered emotionally, and the evidence presented in subsequent sections of this book help document my convictions.

Paul began to show signs of improvement shortly after we began working together. He had been instructed before the initiation of treatment to count his seizures. The staff was also instructed to count the ones they observed in order to obtain a reliable and accurate measure. The seizures would be used as one barometer of his changing condition. Figure 1-1 displays the frequency of seizures before therapy and during the subsequent weeks of treatment. This graph along with a short description of the case was published in a major psychiatric journal in 1971.[1] It was one of the first cases of this nature reported in the scientific literature.

Figure 1-1 shows that Paul's seizure activity began to reduce dramatically when therapy was initiated and continued to decline throughout the treatment period. The following description of the course of treatment is taken from my article. It indicates the change in both the frequency and intensity of seizure activity.

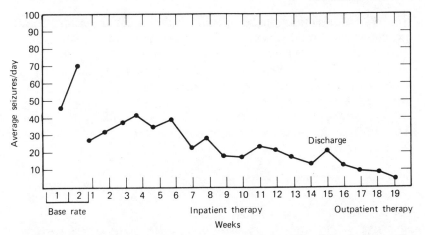

Figure 1-1. Seizure activity. (From J. J. Parrino. Reduction of seizures by desensitization. *J. Behav. Ther. Exper. Psychiatry,* 1971, 2, 215–218, by permission.)

The form of the seizures also changed significantly during therapy—from gross motor movements at the beginning to tic-like mannerisms at the termination of inpatient treatment. The response was then minimal and restricted to the facial region. The few seizures that did then occur usually went unnoticed by the casual observer. [1, p. 217]

Paul had improved dramatically during inpatient treatment. The extensive jerky movements that vibrated throughout Paul's entire body changed to mild spasms. These involuntary muscular movements were limited to one side of his face. There were significant changes in his level of depression, confusion, and memory. He became less depressed, more alert and communcative, and much less prone to forget current events. His memory for past events was still vague at points, but the situations that precipitated the crisis were more easily recalled.

Paul's improved memory of the critical events in his past provided me with more ammunition to use in a therapeutic fashion. The events leading up to the crisis became more prominent as all of the pieces of the puzzle came together through the information I obtained from Paul, his friends, and staff members from the hospital. He was becoming less sensitive to the life events that had previously devastated him. This information eventually provided him with material for his keen sense of humor.

The television station stood by Paul throughout the ordeal. They provided emotional support before his hospitalization and maintained close contact with me during treatment. During the early stages of treatment Paul expressed the desire to return to the station. It wasn't feasible at first. He was too confused and disoriented, and the seizures were occurring quite frequently. The station was ready and willing to accommodate him at any time. With the assistance of a rehabilitation counselor, Paul prepared for a return to work.

Paul was ready to return to the television station much sooner than any of us expected. His mood was changing and his memory for current events was improving. Since he had been hospitalized and away from work for an extended period of time, he was initially restricted to several hours of routine work such as script writing for other news people. The station stood by him during his illness, and they were prepared to provide him with every possible opportunity. Live camera work was too risky at this point. He was still experiencing a few daily seizures, and the stress of the live camera would likely precipitate their occurrence.

By the last few weeks of his hospitalization Paul had increased his time at the station to 20–30 hours per week. After discharge he began full-time work and was finally allowed to do some camera work. His activity was restricted to video-taped interviews that could be redone in the event of the onset of a seizure. He completed several successful taped interviews before the station managers decided to use him on live television. The station had constant contact with me during this time for advice.

I recall that all of us at the hospital were apprehensive when Paul did his first live television show. He was given the opportunity to do the Saturday noon news broadcast. Everything went well! No seizures occurred during this time. Several shows later one anxiety-provoking incident occurred. Paul paused momentarily during a brief mistake made by the camera crew. He experienced a mild seizure, but it was barely noticeable to the television audience. We continued to be courageous during this critical time period. He got progressively better and more at ease on the live camera. Paul had returned, and judging from the phone calls and letters that were received from the television audience, it was a happy event for everyone.

A RETURN TO A STABLE LIFESTYLE

Paul is currently the anchorman for the daily noon show. He has held this position for several years and continues to obtain high ratings for this local television production. His seizures diminished altogether, and he remained free of them for approximately three to four years. Two years ago he experienced several grand mal seizures over a period of two weeks. He returned to me for treatment at this time.

Paul had been experiencing an extraordinary amount of stress in his life during this time. We worked together for a few short sessions, reviewing the behavioral techniques and practicing the coping skills that had been so successful in the past. His television work was not interrupted. We learned however that he was still vulnerable, under conditions of extreme stress, to a mild version of his previous reaction. He recuperated quickly and resumed his life in a normal fashion.

Another important component in this interesting story is Paul's association with Rosalynn Carter, our First Lady. Her interest in mental health is by now well documented. The staff at the hospital feel that they helped stimulate that interest by providing Mrs. Carter with her first direct opportunity. She became a volunteer at our hospital. The director of volunteer services was Mrs. Carter's friend. She placed Rosalynn at the hospital's token store and subsequently on the alcoholism unit. Rosalynn Carter was working as a volunteer at the hospital when Paul was being treated as an outpatient. Their association during this time facilitated further contacts when Jimmy Carter changed his residence to the White House. Paul has subsequently been granted exclusive interviews with Rosalynn and Miss Lillian, the President's mother, and continues to be the main liaison between the White House and the Television station. Paul is currently quite active in the television business and his career is flourishing.

When I present this case in seminars and workshops most participants want to know about Paul's wife and the priest. They are also quite interested in his current social and marital status. I usually accommodate their interest. The story often takes on the flavor of a soap opera. Paul's wife divorced him while he was still in the hospital. There is some speculation that she confronted him with the impending divorce during the week that he was on emergency status. This confrontation may have been the stimulus that jolted him from near death to a somewhat improved condition. This datum has never been confirmed. She married the priest (who obviously left the church), and they moved away from the city with the two children.

Paul married an employee at the television station named Dale. Dale and Paul have two children and currently live in a large city in the Southeast.

As you have observed from my description of the case, Paul allows me to openly use this story in seminars, workshops, and in my writing. He also gives lectures, locally and nationally, that focus on his experiences in a mental hospital and his return to a stable life style. The title of his speech is: "I Left my Pajamas at the Undertaker's." This characterizes the lengthy road to recovery which he experienced and reflects his everpresent keen sense of humor.

Paul has recently worked with Rosalynn Carter's commission on mental health. He was assigned the duty of presenting mental health to the public through the media of television in a new, less stereotyped fashion. This was a perfect assignment for him. Paul's experiences with a severe emotional crisis, his hospitalization, and the dramatic changes in his life allow him to present a perspective on stress and mental health that few of us have experienced in our own lives.

2 STRESS AND FEEDBACK

I have presented the case of Paul to various groups in stress management seminars and workshops. I get a variety of reactions. Many individuals are alarmed about the potentially dire consequences of a chronic stress response. They are quite surprised that stress can take its toll in such a profound manner. Others feel a sense of relief. They identify with Paul's miraculous recovery and feel a sense of security in knowing that modern science is finally making inroads into the mysterious gap that existed between mind and body.

The most common reaction from individuals whose interest has been jolted by the case is captured in the following questions: What happened to Paul? How can a pattern of behavior, a strategy of coping with a difficult situation, lead to a breakdown in biological functioning? What led to his recovery? You may be asking one or more of these questions right at this moment.

The answer to these questions make up the core of this book. Your curiosity will be satisfied for the case of Paul and numerous other cases. Your inquiry will also help accomplish a major objective of this book: to teach you about your unique reactions to stress and to help you use this knowledge in altering your stress responses. I want to engage you in the process of stress watching.

Before we make any major inroads into the area of stress watching and stress management an exposure to some basic background material is necessary. In this chapter I present a brief analysis of the case of Paul and then provide you with the definition of stress that is utilized in the remainder of the book. Several very interesting areas of investigation are introduced, including the relationship between stress and heart disease, research with Eastern Indian Yogi and their tremendous feats of self-control, and a discussion of a new area of therapy that offers tremendous potential for the self-management of stress—biofeedback training.

The final thrust of this chapter is to introduce and discuss a basic principle of human behavior—feedback. This concept will help integrate many complex developments in the area of stress and provides a basis for understanding the importance of developing a personal feedback system.

CASE OF PAUL REVISITED

One can speculate about the potential number of cases of profound physical deterioration that can be justifiably explained as severe stress reactions. The case of Paul is certainly not an isolated and rare occurrence. When the case was published in a major psychiatric journal in 1971, it was somewhat unusual to find a psychologist treating a "somatic" problem. Today, one can find numerous publications that deal specifically with the application of psychological techniques to the area of total health care. The fact that my article on the case was subsequently reprinted in a book, Behavior Therapy and Health Care, *by Roger C. Katz and Steven Zlutnick,[2] is evidence that the gap between psychology and medicine is getting smaller every day.*

There is a great temptation to oversimplify the analysis of the case of Paul. The events in his life resembled those portrayed hour after hour on daytime television: Life presents an individual with a crisis. He or she responds to that crisis with one or more stereotyped strategies. A resolution of the crisis takes place and then we the audience await the next crisis. Soap operas have a way of neatly packaging life events and human responses.

In reality, life makes numerous yet very subtle demands on human resources. It is too simplistic to state that Paul was the victim of an unfaithful wife and a high-pressured job. As they unfolded in one arduous session after another, the significant activating events in his life were far more numerous and complex than any of us at the hospital first recognized. Pauls relationship with his wife provided regular doses of frustration and upset long before the development of extramarital interests on her part. The daily and weekly turmoils at work far outweighed the impact of his demotion. It was far more important to piece together his ongoing coping strategy than it was to focus on the final stage of this process: the dramatic breakdown of a Human Response System.

Since the pieces of the puzzle of Paul's past were never totally assembled, it was difficult to identify the specific series of life events, coping responses, and emotional reactions that culminated in his breakdown and hospitalization. Piecing together a life by obtaining subjective statements about the past from friends, relatives, and even Paul himself was a very difficult task. The best and most accurate way of analyzing anyone's problems of living is to observe the way they cope with everyday situations. The following brief analysis of the case of Paul was constructed by coordinating information from the past with the data collected during months of treatment. Subsequent analyses of the case are introduced throughout the book to help clarify various important concepts.

A Maladaptive Coping Strategy

Paul's seizure disorder was the final outcome of a response system that was fatigued, strained, and finally broken down by a maladaptive coping strategy. I recognized that this strategy had developed over many years, but I was particularly interested in Paul's more recent habits of living. After frequent observations of his behavior it was apparent that he consistently used two similar response strategies when confronted with the demands of life: denial and avoidance.

Paul would deny the immense pressures that pervaded his life, and he would detach himself from the problemed situation. From the very early stages of marital difficulties to the subsequent breakup of the relationship, Paul was unable to confront the situation and deal with it in a direct manner. He immersed himself in his work at the television station and failed to share his concerns with the important people in his life. The response patterns of denial and detachment were also evident in his work strategy. The events that transpired between the initial difficulties at the station and his final demotion were not addressed as significant happenings. For Paul things would always work out. He proceeded with his work activities as if nothing was wrong. He lost sight of what his environment and response system had to say to him. Communication with himself and others began to break down.

At some unknown point in the early stages of his difficulties, Paul perceived his family and work environments as threatening and dangerous. It is difficult to speculate about his thoughts at that time. Perhaps he felt incapable of dealing with these events.

Maybe he sensed an impending loss of control. The choice of response strategies was already programmed from his previous life experiences. He had responded to other threatening life events by ignoring their significance and even denying their existence. He depended on some magical process to make them disappear. Paul would deal with the current events impinging upon his life in very much the same manner.

DENIAL AND DETACHMENT ARE NOT UNCOMMON RESPONSE strategies. Richard Lazarus[3] HAS DISCUSSED several studies that document this habitual mode of coping among parents with children dying of leukemia and medical students performing autopsies. Lazarus states that these responses have a profound effect on the emotions experienced by individuals who are coping with difficult situations.

> . . . intrapsychic forms of coping such as detachment and denial are also capable of modifying, eliminating, or changing the emotion itself, including its subjective affect and bodily changes. When successful, these mechanisms not only affect the visible signs of emotion but also dampen or eliminate the entire emotional syndrome. Thus, in the well-known NIH studies of parents with children dying of leukemia (Wolff, Friedman, Hofer, and Mason, 1964),[4] by denying the fatal significance of their child's illness the NIH parents no longer felt as threatened, and in consequence they exhibited lower levels of adrenal cortical stress hormones than those parents who acknowledged the tragic implications.

> Moreover, by successfully distancing themselves from the emotional features of an autopsy, the medical students observed by Lief and Fox (1963)[5] not only behaved unemotionally but in all likelihood, if the appropriate measurements had been made, would have been shown to react with little or no affect and without the bodily disturbances that are an integral part of stress emotion.[3, p. 7. Copyright 1975 by the American Psychological Association. Reprinted by permission.]

You can observe from Lazarus' comments that coping in a detached and distancing manner is not always maladaptive. The effectiveness of each strategy depends on the situation. In the case of Paul coping in this manner removed him from problems that demanded solutions and, as such, proved to be maladaptive from the standpoint of his own emotional survival.

Paul cut himself off from an environment that seemed hostile and threatening. The early stages of this strategy resulted in regular episodes of anxiety and depression. When members of our society experience pain, even emotional pain, a visit to the physician's office is common. The hope of experiencing some immediate relief motivates this response. Paul came away from the doctor's office with tranquilizers and the hope that these pills would take care of his problems. No connection was made between his coping responses and the emotional consequences of this strategy. Little relief was forthcoming, and his emotional state began to progressively deteriorate. The frequency of anxiety attacks and depressive reactions increased dramatically. He was soon unable to function effectively at work. He was spending a great portion of his time worried, preoccupied, and depressed. Days and weeks of intense emotional disturbance failed to focus his attention toward his maladaptive strategy. Instead it forced him into further detachment.

Paul's body progressively withdrew into a detached posture. The maladaptive coping reaction began to effect his entire response system, resulting in a more intense form of detachment. The final result was a loss of memory, confusion, mental deterioration, and seizure activity.

You can observe from this brief analysis that each state of maladaptive coping resulted in its own set of warning signals. The initial stage of detachment was accompanied by the early warning signs of anxiety and depression. When this emotional state was ignored and the response strategy remained unaltered, further emotional disturbance took place. The failure of response adjustment was accompanied by the breakdown of the entire system.

It is interesting to observe that during the later stages of Paul's illness, his problems mimicked a neurological disease. The final symptom picture, in a curious way, was an exaggerated version of the initial response (escape) to a threatening set of life circumstances. Paul escaped to a world where memories, responsibilities, and coping responses were unnecessary. This was not a voluntary decision. It was the outcome of a long history of coping in a maladaptive manner.

Escape in the form of denial, detachment, and avoidance are commonly used human strategies. To one extent or another all of us use this response. Subsequent chapters will document a variety of paths used by people to escape the real and imaginary dangers that lurk in the world outside of us. Before you encounter these human responses you must obtain an acute awareness of the first signal that warns you of their presence: The Stress Response.

WHAT IS STRESS

Stress was informally defined in the introductory chapter as a response to pressures, responsibilities, and real or imaginary threats from the environment. Stress is the response that your system makes in adjusting to these demands or activating life events. It is not the event itself. The life event is referred to as the stressor.

Stress has been formally defined by a variety of scientific investigators. Dr. Hans Selye, the world-reknowned biological scientist, states that stress is the nonspecific response of the body to any demand made upon it.[6] Dr. Herbert Benson, author of *The Relaxation Response,* emphasized environmental circumstances in his definition. Stress, according to Benson, is the behavioral adjustment required by certain environmental conditions. Rapid cultural change, urbanization and migration, socioeconomic mobility, or uncertainty in the immediate environment are examples of stressful circumstances.[7]

Regardless of the focus of emphasis of a particular investigator they all agree on one basic fact: In these modern times the changes required of us are enormous and our response systems must make the necessary adjustments. Unfortunately, many people do not possess efficient coping skills for handling stressful situations and have not been trained to use their response systems to maximum efficiency. As a result we experience what Selye calls "distress"—damaging or unpleasant stress.

The stress response occurs in the totality of the Human Response System. It is not a discrete phenomenon that takes place in the mind or body: it engages the entire system. Stress is manifested in the thoughts we think, the biochemical and physiological reactions we experience, and the behaviors we emit in confronting difficult environmental circumstances. These thoughts, reactions, and behaviors occur in unison, working together to produce an effective response strategy. The working definition of stress used in this book is the following: Adjustments of the entire human response system (thoughts, physiological reactions, and behaviors) to activating life events. These adjustments become habitual. When they are adaptive they lead to effective functioning and positive emotional states. When they are maladaptive they lead to the malfunctioning of the system and to emotional and psychosomatic distress. Each component of this definition is discussed further in Chapter 3.

Type A Behavior: A Psycho-Biological Problem

The concept of stress has helped blur the distinction between mind and body that has pervaded medicine and psychology for decades. A problem in some scientific circles is no longer labeled as a medical problem or a psychological condition. It is more apt to be spoken of as a psychophysiological or psychobiological malfunctioning. Stress researchers are interested in integrating the two disciplines and are currently developing a new discipline called Behavioral Medicine.

Perhaps the most potent recent development contributing to the demise of the mind-body, medical-psychological separatism was the writing of *Type A Behavior and Your Heart* by Meyer Friedman and Ray H. Rosenman,[8] two practicing cardiologists. The book summarized in a popular style the findings of years of previous research and clinical practice by these two investigators. Their thesis was simple but revolutionary: Heart disease, traditionally held to be a product of four or five medical risk factors (high cholesterol and blood pressure, obesity, smoking, and lack of exercise) was intimately related to a behavior pattern.

The pattern of behavior that was related to heart disease was called Type A Behavior. Their studies showed that an individual's style of living, particularly work habits and interpersonal relations, was critically important in contributing, along with the medical risk factors, to the development of premature coronary artery disease. It is this disease that leads to coronary heart disease, heart attacks, and often death in men and women in the most productive years of their lives.

Type A Behavior is emitted by a person who is in a chronic struggle with his or her environment. The struggle is focused on accomplishing more recognition, money, power, and possessions in less and less time. These excessive strivings for achievement and an acute sense of time urgency are accompanied by an underlying feeling of hostility toward other people. Struggling, achievement-oriented Type As are hostile because people in their environments are perceived as potential stumbling blocks to the Type As accomplishments. The hostility is subtle, sometimes undetectable, but flares up when people stand in the way of the fast-talking, hyperresponsive overachiever.

The Type A individual is contrasted to the Type B. The Type B is an individual with an easy-going, relaxed approach to life. Type Bs have little hostility and a rational approach to achievement and recognition.

Friedman and Rosenman designed a system for rating individuals along the Type A and B dimensions. Through interviews, analysis of speech patterns, laboratory tests, and behavioral observations, they identified pure Type As and Bs and individuals at various points between these extremes. Table 2-1 summarizes some of the characteristics of the two behavior patterns.

The following excerpt from their scientific publication on the relationship between the two behavior patterns and coronary heart disease summarizes the results of their long-term Western Collaborative Group Study. The results are further summarized in Figure 2-1, which is taken from this publication.

During 8½ years of follow-up in which clinical coronary heart disease occurred in 257 initially well men, it was found that initially well subjects assessed at intake as exhibiting the Type A Behavior Pattern have been more than twice as prone to develop clinical coronary heart disease (see Figure 2-1) as the subjects originally assessed as Type B. Moreover, Type A subjects were five times more prone to have a second myocardial infarct (see Figure 2-1) than were Type B subjects during this 8½ year interval. Submission of the data to multivariate analysis indicated that, while the presence of Type A Behavior Pattern in men with other risk factors (e.g., hypertension, hypercholesterolemia, positive family history) further increased the incidence of coronary heart disease, nevertheless, Pattern A alone and independently appeared to exert a strong pathogenetic force. [9, p. 272]

The identification of these two behavior patterns and their relative vulnerability to one of the most insidious and debilitating problems of the human system documented the idea held by previous investigators that psycho-

TABLE 2–1.   Type A and B Behavior Patterns

Type A Individual	Type B Individual
Chronic struggle with the environment	Balanced interplay with environment
Hard-driving–Overachiever	Rational approach to achievement
Time urgency–hyperresponsive	Relaxed
Hostility	Positive interpersonal relations
Workaholic	Balance between work and other life events

a Most individuals fall at various points between these two extremes.

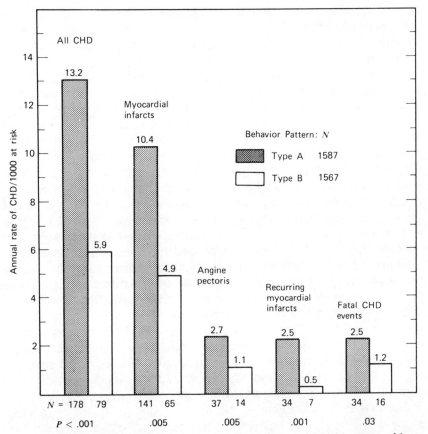

Figure 2-1. The annual rate of coronary heart disease (CHD) in 3154 subjects studied prospectively in the Western Collaborative Group study for 8½ years. The higher incidence of all expressions of coronary heart disease in the Type A subjects is shown. *N* equals number of cases. (From R. H. Rosenman, et al. The central nervous system and coronary heart disease. *Hosp. Pract.,* 1971, 6, 87−97, by permission.)

logical strategies of living must be included in the understanding and treatment of all major health problems.

FEATS OF SELF-CONTROL

At the same time that investigators were becoming more alarmed by the large numbers of pathological conditions attributed to stress, information was accumulating in other scientific circles about unusual feats of human self-control. Many of the reports of these new heights in human potential came from the studies of Eastern Indian Yogi. These studies were recently summarized by Theodore Barber at a meeting of the American Psychological Association.[10]

Barber reported the following astounding findings: Under experimental conditions, Yogi have been buried alive. They tolerated the excessive stress of those conditions by lowering their rate of oxygen consumption to one-fourth of the normal rate and remained in this state significantly longer than normally expected. Other Yogi have trained themselves to lower their heart rates. During the monitoring of this response by specialists, they have been observed to reduce their rate significantly. Some have even stopped their hearts for a brief moment. In addition, a phenomenon referred to as fire-walking has been observed. Yogi will cross a bed of intensely hot coals with no damage to the delicate tissue of the skin. These individuals who spend many hours in various meditative states exert control over physiological functions well beyond that of the ordinary individual.

Barber is well-known for his scientific approach to the study of hypnotism. Many of the previous studies that deal with feats of self-control attributed their results to the special state of hypnosis. Contrary to many other investigators of the phenomenon of hypnosis, Barber disputes the existence of a special state of consciousness that differs from the waking state.[11] He shows that the phenomena thought to be due to hypnosis are actually due to the subjects having positive attitudes in the test situation, high motivation for peak performances, and strong expectancies that they can perform unusual behaviors. When fairly untrained subjects are given instructions to "imagine, feel, think about it," and to "concentrate intensively on the task," they have performed feats such as: reducing the level of warts on their skin without medication and producing blisters on a segment of the skin where an imagined hot stimulus was placed. Other research subjects who were sensitive to poison ivy were led to believe that they would be touched by the plant. Most of them experienced the poison ivy reaction in spite of the fact that, in reality, a harmless plant was used. In this case the mere expectation that a reaction would take place produced a real change in the structure of the skin.

Other phenomenal feats have been reported through the use of intense concentration, focused thinking, and the use of positive expectations. These include the elimination of some skin diseases and even increases in breast size. Barber argues that all of these impressive phenomena are understandable given a monistic view of human behavior, one that does not separate mind and body but integrates thoughts, bodily processes, and behavior.

BEHAVIOR MODIFIERS

How can we best explain the curious fact that some individuals conduct their lives in a manner that debilitates the functioning of their human systems, whereas others seem to lead constructive, system-facilitating life styles? What critical differences exist between a system-gone-astray, exemplified by the Type A individual, and the human system that exhibits tremendous feats of self-control and regulation? Psychologists like Dr. Barber have been attempting to comprehend the psychological processes underlying these extraordinary facts for decades. In the last ten to twenty years, a subgroup of psychologists interested in the control and modification of behavior have made some impressive strides in developing principles that help explain the variety of humans' learning experiences. They are behavior modifiers, and their tools for understanding human behavior include such concepts as operant and classical conditioning, modeling, social learning, and most recently, cognitive behavior modification and biofeedback training. With these tools in hand these modifiers of behavior have been successful in understanding and changing pathological conditions that were heretofore thought to be unchangeable. These include schizophrenia, chronic depression, anxiety, problems of adolescence, obesity, smoking, and even alcoholism.

In addition to contributing to the understanding and modification of abnormal behavior, they have discovered a new horizon for human self-control: the modification of physiological responses through biofeedback training. The findings of the biofeedback specialist help justify Barber and other behavior modifiers' monistic interpretation of human behavior. Mind, body, and behavior are one integrated unit that must be studied together in order to explain the variety of human capacities for self-regulation and control.

Biofeedback

Dr. Thomas B. Mulholland, President of the Biofeedback Society of America (1970–1971) described the application of biofeedback training in the following manner:

> Biofeedback is applied to behavioral science whereby some recordable feature of a physiological process is connected by an external path to a stimulator or display which is seen, heard, or felt forming a closed loop. It is differentiated from similar developments in physiology by the inclusion of psychological processes such as perception, cognition, and voluntary control. [12]

The early use of the psychophysiological process of biofeedback focused on the electrical activity of the skin. The research was conducted by several investigators in separate laboratories including H. D. Kimmel[13] and a group from Harvard: Shapiro, Crider, and Tursky.[14] Changes in the electrical reactivity of the skin occur spontaneously at rates that vary from one person to another. These changes reflect, among other things, the amount of emotional arousal and stress an individual is experiencing. The electrical skin changes reflect the activity of the sweat glands, which reside very close to the surface of the skin. Increases and decreases in sweat gland activity are monitored by a polygraph. This instrument measures a variety of physiological responses and has been traditionally known as the lie detector.

Subjects in these studies were provided with information about their spontaneous increases and decreases in electrical reactivity. They were presented with a tone and reward each time a change in this response took place. In comparison to subjects who were not given this information, the informed subjects showed significant changes in these skin responses. These were the first studies to indicate that individuals with the aid of biofeedback could achieve voluntary control over a physiological response that was thought to be involuntary. Physiological responses could then be treated as any other behavioral responses. They were subject to self-modification and control.

These studies were duplicated many times, and the experimental approach was extended to cardiovascular functions. Control of heart rate and systolic blood pressure was achieved by the same means. The subjects were systematically fed back information about their heart rate and blood pressure and reinforced for making changes (increases and decreases) in these physiological responses. Cardiovascular activity could also be modified in a manner similar to skin potential. The magnitude and consistency of changes in these functions vary considerably, and researchers are very cautious about their conclusions. Psychologists Edward Blanchard and Leonard Epstein have recently published an exhaustive literature review of the usefulness of Clinical Biofeedback. In their conclusions, they state:

> When one surveys the wide array of clinical problems on which there is at least some evidence (admittedly of fairly poor quality in some instances) that biofeedback can be of benefit, it becomes possible to begin to believe in a "new pancea" for all psychosomatic disorders. The field continues to grow and new applications continue to be found.

> Fortunately, some investigators are beginning to conduct the hard but necessary controlled studies to determine how well biofeedback treatments compare with no-treatment or attention-placebo treatment. This latter work

will finally determine if biofeedback has a rightful place in the therapeutic world. [15, pp. 238–239]

Clinicians are vigorously pursuing this area for further documentation of the usefulness of biofeedback techniques for problems such as high blood pressure. Research and clinical work are being conducted in numerous areas including: reactivation of particular muscles in various neuromuscular disorders; control of cardiac arrhythmias, which are dependent on increases or decreases in heart rate; control of migraine headaches through the modification of blood flow to particular parts of the body; control of epileptic seizures through the facilitation and inhibition of various patterns of brain waves; and the control of asthma through changes in respiratory function.

Accompanying the optimistic outlook of biofeedback trainers is the skeptic's catastrophic fantasy: a three-hundred-pound piece of equipment is strapped to the shoulders; blinking lights and deflecting pens are constantly monitoring the internal workings of the body. The treatment seems more devastating than the disease itself. The fantasy, however, is unwarranted. A large portion of the work in clinical biofeedback training is directed toward counteracting the influence of stress through self-control, not external control. The machine, the biofeedback equipment, is viewed only as the means to the end of self-regulation and control. The ultimate goal of the biofeedback trainer is to wean the subject from the equipment as quickly as possible. The biofeedback apparatus sets up the condition under which the subject identifies internal warning signals that precipitate problems. The trainee ultimately learns to self-regulate the response without the use of the equipment.

The work of investigators interested in controlling tension headaches provides a good example of the transition from equipment-regulated to self-regulated behavior. In the case of tension headaches the subject receives information from the biofeedback equipment (the electromyograph) regarding levels of muscular activity in the forehead region. The headache sufferer attempts to lower the muscular activity and is given immediate feedback about his or her success in reducing muscular tension. The feedback reinforces the lower level of muscular responding and provides the subject with a sense of control over the headache. Subtle changes in muscle tension are detected very early in the chain of responses that ordinarily lead to a headache. Significant control of the tension-producing response is gained in this way. Soon the subject detects the changes in activity without the aid of the equipment. Self-control is then exerted to prevent the headache in environments outside the trainer's office. The results of this training have led to a new treatment alternative for victims of tension headaches.[15]

FEEDBACK

All the critical variables that account for changes in physiological responses achieved through biofeedback have not yet been identified. One finding, however, arises consistently in biofeedback research: Setting up the environment in such a manner that individuals can monitor and observe, that is, obtain knowledge of, the results of their own responses facilitates desirable changes in these responses. The process of changing a response through the increase in knowledge of results of the functioning of that response is called *feedback*.

The concept of feedback is not at all new. Every student of physiology knows that life cannot be maintained for any significant length of time without the system's ability to monitor and alter its own functioning. The physiological balance of an organism's internal environment is dependent on this feedback system. Walter Cannon, the American physiologist, coined the term "homeostasis" to describe the bodily functions that take place to assure that the internal environment of the body remains relatively constant.[16] Each system of the body (digestive, respiratory, circulatory, etc.) can be considered a structural and functional system that is working to maintain homeostasis through the communication of information about its functioning to other systems.

Stressors of all varieties (cold, heat, lack of oxygen, emotional arousal, etc.) disrupt homeostasis, and the body is forced to deviate from normal functioning. The response system makes adjustments to handle the stressful stimuli (the stress response) and then pushes the body to return to a state of equilibrium. Through the controlling effects of the nervous and endocrine systems of the body, information is constantly circulating from each organ system of the body, back and forth, to the controlling centers of the brain. In this manner the organs of the body can regulate their functioning, increasing some activities and decreasing others in order to cope with stressful events.

The circular system of information exchange that accounts for organ self-regulation is based on negative and positive feedback. If some stress, for example, causes the heartbeat to speed up and blood pressure to rise, the increased blood pressure is detected immediately. This information is fed back to the appropriate center in the brain via the nervous system and the pressure is brought back to normal by compensatory mechanisms— the slowing of the heartbeat and the widening of the diameter of various blood vessels. The feedback reverses the direction of the initial condition from a rising to a falling blood pressure and is called a negative feedback system.

Another example of this type of feedback system is the hormonal regulation of blood sugar. When the level of blood sugar goes above the normal level (e.g., by eating candy) the increase is detected and the cells of the pancreas are stimulated to secrete insulin. The blood sugar level is lowered in this manner through increased sugar consumption by body cells and the acceleration of the storage of sugar in the liver and muscles. These regulatory processes represent a small sample of the numerous feedback systems that function to maintain the internal equilibrium of the physiological responses of the human body.

Information provided by one's external environment is another important source of feedback. At the earliest stages of human development the infant engages in random interactions with its environment to obtain the necessities for survival. The infant obtains information from its environment about the adaptiveness of certain responses such as crying and smiling. This is critical to the subsequent use of these responses for meeting the infant's basic needs. The infant quickly learns that certain responses lead to predictable outcomes from the environment. A crying infant obtains a swift response from an attentive mother who is concerned about the infant's physical safety and nutritional requirements. A smiling infant is assured of plenty of warmth and approval from a parent who is concerned about the infant's psychological well-being. The infant learns very early in life to utilize the knowledge gained from this exchange with mother. Many other exchanges take place with the infant's environment so that it learns adaptive and survival-facilitating responses.

The infant's "dance of development" is discussed at length by Martin Seligman, a research psychologist interested in the phenomenon of child development, depression, and early infant deaths. In his book, *Learned Helplessness,*[17] he has documented the disastrous consequences of the deprivation of this interplay between infant and environment.

This phenomenon has been variously called anaclitic depression, hospitalism, and morasmus. It can arise from two different circumstances. One is removal of a mother who has formed a good relationship with her child of 6 to 18 months. It is interesting that, if the relationship is weak or negative, the condition tends not to develop. Alternatively it occurs when children are raised in foundling homes, lying on their backs day in and day out, with only white sheets to look at and with only minimal, mechanical, human contact. If the mother soon returns, the condition usually remits, sometimes dramatically. Without intervention, however, the prognosis is grim. Thirty-four of the ninety-one foundling-home infants observed by Spitz[18] died in the first three years; stuporous depression and idiocy resulted in other cases.

An infant deprived of stimulation is an infant thereby deprived of 'control' over stimulation. There can be no dance of development when there is no partner. How can a bottle that comes exactly every four hours regardless of what the child is doing produce a sense of synchrony between action and outcome? . . .

. . . An infant who loses his mother is an infant deprived not only of love, but of control over the most important outcomes in his life. The dance of development is improverished indeed, if the mother is not available to be the primary partner. With no mother, there is often no one to hug back when you hug. Your coos and smiles are unreturned. Cries and shrieks fall on the deaf ears of a nursery staff too busy to respond and provide you with control. Food, diaper changing, and cuddling are not usually provided in response to your demands, but in response to the demands of a clock. [17, pp. 144–145] (From *Helplessness: On Depression, Development, and Death,* by Martin E. P. Seligman, W. H. Freeman and Company, Copyright © 1975.)

The lack of response to coos, smiles, and other behaviors places the infant in a state of feedback deprivation that subsequently effects all other human responses. In the cases where the breakdown of feedback is profound, the outcome is early infant death.

The world of work offers another arena for observing the effects of an ongoing interplay between people and their environment. It is now a well-documented fact that people can profit considerably from obtaining information about their performance in the work setting.[19] The use of feedback in this environment has produced dramatic results for businesses that have attempted to increase human productivity. The systematic feeding back of information to workers about their performance by managers and frontline supervisors in a variety of industries has produced the following results: reduction in employee turnover, reduction in employee absenteeism, reduction in product waste, increases in efficiency and productivity. These employees are often given information about their performance (e.g., number of product "x" produced without error) through the use of feedback displays that are posted in the work area for public scrutiny. Maximum information dissemination to individual employees is provided in order to motivate them to improve their work functioning. In addition the constant monitoring and display of work behavior increases the opportunity for supervisors to positively reinforce their workers—a sample of human interaction that is observed at a very low frequency in work settings that have numerous employee problems.

PERSONAL FEEDBACK: SYSTEM GONE ASTRAY VERSUS SELF-CONTROL

The findings just outlined force you to stretch your imagination and step slightly beyond the scientific data. Will you ultimately be able to control and regulate any human response that is fed back to you in some manner?

Does control of all human responses ranging from the neurological firing of billions of brain cells to the tiny twitches of muscular activity await the development of technological monitoring devices that provide progressively more information about these otherwise silent responses? Imagine the possibilities!

Already the specialists in a new area of behavior modification, behavioral medicine, are making inroads into understanding and changing conditions such as essential hypertension, migraine and tension headaches, ulcers, Type A personality, pain disorders, and other psychosomatic disorders. Most of these gains have not been achieved through traditional medical treatment where the physician cures the patient and the curative effect depends on the power of the doctor and his or her medicine. Behavioral medicine involves the patient directly in his or her own treatment. The patient takes a portion of the responsibility for using information from his or her own response system in order to regulate abnormal responses. The specialist in behavioral medicine only feeds back, regulates, and reinforces until the patient is ready to take control. Self-control, then, rather than externally mediated regulation is the key concept in this new area of therapeutics. It is truly as Mahoney and Thoresen state in the title of their book: *Self-Control: Power to the Person.*[20]

The concept of feedback is critical for understanding human response change in a wide range of human functions: maintaining physiological equilibrium, child development, improving work performance, and altering "involuntary" responses. Does this concept help explain the observed wide variations in ability to self-regulate and control the human system? Research in the area of psychophysiology, biofeedback, and behavioral medicine will undoubtedly arrive at answers to this question in the near future. One highly plausible explanation, given the current state of knowledge regarding response modification, is the development of personal feedback systems.

A select group of humans by virtue of their learning experiences tend to adopt strategies of living that facilitate information exchange and feedback from their own response systems. The Yogi provide a good example of response system control and regulation achieved by meditation and long hours of intense concentration. Among other things this strategy maximizes information exchange and knowledge of response functioning. It creates the conditions necessary for the frequent occurrence of highly personal feedback.

Other human beings develop coping strategies that inhibit information exchange and feedback. At a personal level, they fail to profit from the knowledge available from their own systems. Valuable knowledge about the results of one's own actions are lost to these people. The Type A individual exemplifies this situation. The onset of premature coronary artery disease is the result of long period of failure in self-regulation and control. The Type A response system is a system-gone-astray from communicating with itself. This exchange of information is a prerequisite for personal feedback, and this feedback is a requirement for adequate functioning and response system survival.

Lodged at various intermediary points between the extreme ends of the continuum of ability to control one's own responses, the remainder of us struggle with bits and pieces of personal feedback. The increase in this knowledge of response functioning only occurs through a deep understanding of the machinery that guides our thoughts, ideas, bodily processes, and behavior. This personal feedback is important for accomplishing high degrees of self-control and regulation.

The workings of the entire apparatus, the Human Response System, are summarized in Chapter 3. The knowledge of your own response system is one major component of the personal feedback process. Thus subsequent chapters discuss each component of the system in detail. Each chapter that discusses a component of the system is followed by one explaining various techniques for altering its maladaptive responses. In this manner you will obtain an intimate knowledge of your Human Response System. You will become aware of its tendency to falter when seriously deprived of personal feedback, and its ability to flourish when saturated with knowledge of its own behavior.

3 THE HUMAN RESPONSE SYSTEM

Before pursuing a further analysis of stress and its effects on the response system it is important to construct a model for understanding the nature of human interactions with the surrounding environment. This analysis will help you understand your unique responses to specific life events. It will assist you in decifering the variables that make up your coping style and allow you to evaluate your strategy of living in terms of positive and negative emotional outcomes. The objective of this chapter is to provide you with a basic understanding of the human system and its various interacting components. The model is called the *Human Response System.*

Each of us plays a continual game with our environment to achieve the end result of biological survival. Our environment has facilitated this goal by providing us with technological advances that insure our physical safety. Biological survival is much less of a concern to us modern individuals than it was to our prehistoric ancestors. Most modern men and women are more acutely worried about achieving a state of happiness. Since happiness is a very elusive state most people are satisfied with a less absolute goal. They will strive toward increasing happiness and decreasing unhappiness.

What is happiness? Perhaps the most accurate statement one can make about happiness is that it is very difficult to define. Yet we can be assured of at least one fact in the midst of vast uncertainty: happiness is intimately related to our emotional condition at any one point in our lives. It would be unusual to encounter a human being that was seriously emotionally upset and happy at the same time. Although the absence of emotional upset and disturbance is not necessarily synonymous with happiness, it seems to be one necessary prerequisite to that end.

Understanding emotions and how to regulate them is thus an important goal for individuals who are interested in achieving personal effectiveness and a maximum amount of pleasure and happiness in their lives.

EMOTIONS

Different schools of psychological thought have varied dramatically in their understanding of emotions and the role they play in an individual's struggle with the environment. The emotion of anxiety for example is one of the most important concepts in psychoanalytic theory. According to Freudian theory anxiety is a painful emotional experience that is produced by excitations in the internal organs of the body. Its primary function is to act as a danger signal to the ego. As most students of Freudian psychology remember the ego is the executor of the personality which balances the primitive urges of the id with the moral inhibitions of the superego. In neurotic anxiety the potential danger resides in an instinctual object choice of the id. An uncontrollable urge to commit some act or think some thought makes an individual anxious because the acts or thoughts (usually sexually or aggressively oriented) can prove to be harmful. The perception of harm or danger stems from the threat of punishment of these urges.

The most classic example from Freudian theory is the "oedipal" situation. The young male child fears retaliation from the father because he experiences sexual urges toward his mother. As an adult anxiety ensues when a current life event allows this childhood fantasy to rear its ugly head. A strategy must then be developed to handle this negative emotional state.

The danger signal in the form of anxiety appears in consciousness, and the ego must institute measures to deal with the danger. According to Calvin Hall, in his book *Freudian Psychology:*

> The development of personality . . . is determined in large measure by the kinds of adaptations and mechanisms which are formed in the ego to deal with neurotic and moral anxiety. The fight against fears is one of the decisive engagements in psychological growth, the outcome of which bears so heavily upon the final character of the person. [21, p. 67]

Emotions play a causal role in psychoanalytic theory, determining the strategies for coping developed by individuals in dealing with environmental demands. According to the psychoanalyst, human responses develop as a result of the interplay between emotions and life events.

Humanistic and gestalt psychology assign an equally important causal role to emotions in the development of personality. They do not assign the exclusive and primary role to anxiety as the psychoanalysts do but focus on the entire range of feelings. These emotions include grief, depression, and on the positive side of the emotional spectrum, joy.

As the individual treads through life in childhood, adolescence, and adulthood the natural course of emotional expression comes into conflict with society's codes and standards. According to the humanists the individual responds to the threat of environmental consequences expressed by parents and other authority figures. Each person begins to build a wall, a character armour, between himself or herself and his or her emotions. The self becomes divided and the gestalt or wholeness of the person becomes disjointed. This creates a gap in communication between the person and his or her feelings.

The wall of armour was originally constructed to protect the individual from reckless expressions of potentially dangerous feelings. It begins to crumble from the pressures. The loss of emotional awareness and subsequent pent-up energy seeps into consciousness as stilted and neurotic thoughts and behavior patterns. The only hope for a return to adaptive functioning, according to the gestalt theorist, is the complete breakdown of the character defenses.

This process involves a return to emotional awareness and the bridging of communication between the divided selves. A return to the gestalt or wholeness of personality must be achieved. Human responses are seen by the Gestalt theorist as consequences of emotions. Disordered thoughts, physiological reactions, and behavior patterns stem from the chronic inhibition of emotional expression. This traditional psychological viewpoint expressed by the psychoanalysts and the gestaltists is presented in Figure 3-1.

The model proposed in this chapter stems from a view that is divergent from the two schools of thought discussed above. It does not minimize the role of emotions in the Human Response System, but attempts to place them in proper perspective. Emotions represent only one component of a system that contains a complex set of human responses. As psychologist Richard Lazarus has stated, ". . . we cannot hope to understand the emotions unless we also take into account the coping activities that affect them." [3, p. 7]

Lazarus has conducted extensive research on stress and the coping process and states that coping is a causal factor in emotion:

You will note that this analysis reverses the usual wisdom that coping always follows emotion (or is caused by it) and suggests that coping can precede emotion and influence its form or intensity. In fact, my general position requires the assertion that coping never follows emotion in anything but a temporal sense, a stand in direct opposition to the long-standing and traditional view that emotions (such as anxiety) serve as drives or motives for adaptive behavior. [3, p. 8. Copyright by the American Psychological Association. Reprinted by permission.]

In the Human Response System model, emotions do not precipitate problems. Rather problems or maladaptive responses lead to emotional upset and disturbance. Human responses such as disordered thinking habits can precipitate anger in frustrating situations. A nervous system that is easily aroused by threatening life events can produce a state of chronic anxiety and tension. Behavioral habits such as procrastination can induce deep states of depression. In summary habits of living are seen as the instigators of emotional reactions. Figure 3-1 illustrates this perspective and contrasts it to the more traditional viewpoint.

With this new perspective in mind it is important to understand each level of functioning of the Human Response System. It will help you design your assault on the negative emotional states and disturbances that inhibit your pursuit of personal effectiveness, happiness, and emotional well-being.

THOUGHTS, PHYSIOLOGICAL RESPONSES AND BEHAVIOR

In the Human Response System emotion is defined as a complex, subjective feeling state that results from the system's transactions with the environment. Although the system responds as a whole in these transactions various critical components of the Human Response System can be identified. There are *thinking responses* that include appraisals, expectations, attitudes, beliefs, ideas, and internal statements about past, present, and future environmental encounters. For example, the way an individual feels about speaking in public depends heavily on the speaker's appraisal and expectations from the group that is listening to the speaker. Such thoughts and internal statements include: "They are important people." "They will criticize me." "The consequences of poor performance are serious." These thinking responses during this life event can make a fairly calm individual nervous and upset about his or her performance.

The second major component of the Human Response System consists of *physiological responses.* These responses include physiological activities of the response system that attempt to maintain a state of equilibrium in the presence of daily demands and pressures. This component of the system is equipped to deal with emergencies that threaten bodily survival. The threat of danger triggers a series of physiological responses. This fight-flight response includes increases in heart rate, blood pressure, and oxygen consumption. These responses facilitate physical combat and/or escape as a means of protection from the threatening situation. Another series of responses reverses this arousal pattern and allows the

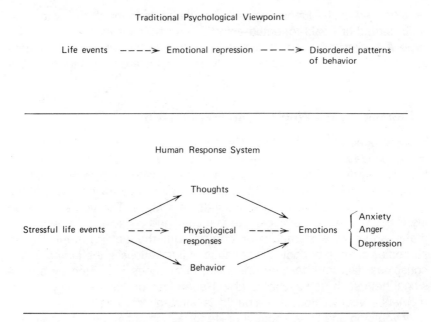

Figure 3–1.   **Comparison of the Traditional Psychological Viewpoint with the Human Response System Model**

system to recuperate and relax. This balance between arousal and relaxation is critical for healthy and adaptive functioning. The disruption or dominance of one system over another can precipitate harmful reactions.

The third major component of the Human Response System consists of *motor responses* or *overt behavior.* Thinking and physiological events cannot be readily observed; they are private events. On the other hand behavior is observable. You can hear and see a person speak. You can observe a person sit, stand, and walk. These are verbal and muscular responses. All of these overt, observable behaviors involve the use of the motor or muscular system of the body.

Two major types of behavioral responses that have been of interest to psychological investigators are adaptive and maladaptive behaviors. These researchers are interested in investigating the factors that maintain and strengthen behavior and those that weaken and extinguish behavior. The balance of adaptive and maladaptive behaviors is important for maintaining a healthy level of interaction with the environment. The inability to weaken maladaptive habits such as smoking, alcoholism, overeating, and overworking can lead to consequences that are obvious to all of us. On the other hand, the inability to strengthen adaptive behaviors such as the development of life-supporting skills, regular visits to the doctor when one is ill, and other health-oriented activities can be equally disastrous. The Type A behavior pattern is a clear example of the undesirable consequences of a disruptive balance between adaptive and maladaptive behavior.

Responding as a Whole: A Strategy for Living

The components of the Human Response System—thoughts, physiological responses, and behavior—were isolated for the sake of communication. The system is complex. To attack it as a whole would be a difficult assignment. It is necessary at this point to return to the wholeness of the system. When it copes with life, it copes as a whole. Through a myriad of learning experiences, biological tendencies, and conscious decisions humans arrive at a strategy for coping with the environment. These strategies change periodically because of fluctuations in the environment, conscious decisions to alter one's life, or changes facilitated by professional help such as psychotherapy. Regardless of this variability, at any moment in your life you have a particular strategy for living.

If you stop and think about your life for a moment you will observe that your current strategy for living is dependent on the state of your Human Response System. Your system is continually thinking, reacting physiologically, and behaving. Together these responses work to achieve the best possible coping strategy. The strategy, of course, varies from one environmental event to another so that you can experience an adaptive response to one event and a maladaptive response to another within a very short segment of your life.

An executive may cope extremely well with the pressures of a demanding job but break down from the demands of a conflictual domestic situation. Strategies may vary within one specter of life. A manager may think straight, feel relaxed, and approach colleagues and subordinates at work in a very healthy manner. On the other hand, the prospect of relating to the company executives produces disordered thoughts, an aroused response system, and a vigorous avoidance of an encounter with them. Adaptive and maladaptive strategies can thus exist within one individual who encounters numerous difficult life events with a variety of coping skills.

How does one distinguish between an adaptive and maladaptive coping strategy? Although scientists have successfully pinpointed many of the human responses that increase the prospect of adaptive coping, there are no absolute standards. Human responses can be more or less adaptive and maladaptive in their transactions with the environment. The effectiveness of this overall strategy accumulates to produce an emotional state. Concerning this self-regulatory process, Lazarus states:

> Emotion is not a constant thing, but it ebbs and flows and changes over time, as the nature of adaptive commerce and the information about it changes. . . . These shifts in intensity and quality over time reflect perceived and appraised changes in the person's relationship with the environment, based in part on feedback from the situation and from his own reactions. [3, p. 6. Copyright 1975 by the American Psychological Association. Reprinted by permission.]

Again the coping process is seen as a central feature of the emotional state. Emotions provide feedback regarding the relative merits, adaptive or maladaptive, of the response system's encounter with the environment. Pleasant feelings can provide a signal to the system that human responses and coping strategies are adaptive. Unpleasant emotions, in turn, are warning signals of a maladaptive strategy of living. Human emotions can serve as an important source of feedback for determining the effectiveness of one's strategy for coping with life events.

Life Events, Maladaptive Strategies and Emotions

The habits of the Human Response System and the emotional consequences of these habits play an extremely important role in the development of stress reactions. In a manner similar to the maintenance of biological equilbrium the system strives to continually achieve homeostasis at all response levels. The system is aroused for a short period of time to meet the demands of daily existence and relaxes towards the end of the day for the sake of recuperation. The emotional state that accompanies these responses fluctuates from the nervousness and excitement that occurs during performance encounters to the compassion and sympathy one experiences when consoling a troubled friend. It often culminates in the quiet pleasure and joy one senses while driving home to receptive family and friends. An adaptive, balanced strategy of living is accompanied and reinforced by a positive emotional state.

An entirely different set of responses may be triggered by threatening environmental encounters that result in the appearance of the stress emotions. Investigators have made vigorous attempts to identify the particular types of events that trigger maladaptive responses and stress emotions. They are highly individualized for each person and can include such diverse experiences as the changes that result from a work promotion, the assignment of a difficult school task, or simply the experience of being criticized by a close friend. Even thoughts about a future event such as an impending marriage or the anticipation of the death of a loved one can trigger maladaptive responding.

At times new and different life circumstances demand substantial and abrupt changes in habit patterns. Encountering several of these demanding events simultaneously can disrupt an otherwise balanced coping style. It is not uncommon to experience several difficult confrontations within a short span of time. For example, a change in job status, marital problems, and social pressures can rattle even the most confident and relaxed person. The abrupt change in coping style precipitated by these intense demands on the response system may be less adaptive than usual. Once the maladaptive coping strategy of the response system is set into action, emotional discomfort is experienced.

The exact content of a life event is not the critical factor in determining stress reactions. The same situation may trigger joy in one individual and apprehension in another depending upon their respective skills in coping with the event. Coping skills are developed throughout our lives. At any one point in time, we may be able to cope with one set of circumstances but unable to cope with another. The lack of coping skills for dealing with a significant life event can trigger a maladaptive strategy. A normally relaxed individual may become preoccupied with worrisome thoughts about a new promotion. A housewife who rarely loses sleep may develop insomnia because of conflicts with her spouse. These mild emotional discomforts can be used as signals to facilitate a change in coping strategies. Frequently however they go unheeded. The response system, at this point, tends to engage in cyclical behavior. Instead of facilitating awareness, the emotions contribute to an already clouded and confused strategy.

Responding continues to be maladaptive and emotional discomfort increases, often resulting in severe anxiety and sometimes panic. Unless intervention takes place at this point, either through self or professional help, the new maladaptive strategy becomes habitual. Unpleasant emotions such as anxiety and depression become pervasive. The end result of this cycle of responses includes mild emotional discomfort and severe emotional disturbance. These problems may even progress to psychosomatic disorders such as ulcers, migraine headaches, premature coronary artery disease, and a variety of other serious problems.

SUMMARY

We now have the human situation partly characterized. Life is replete with events that place major demands on the response system. These environmental events activate people to respond mildly or intensively depending on the importance of the event. The importance of an event will vary from one person to another. The activating events are those that place great demands on the response system such as difficult work, family or social encounters.

Our system provides us with feedback regarding the manner in which we are handling these activating events. The feedback comes in the form of emotions. When we are doing well, our barometer is steady. We are relaxed, joyful, and spontaneous in our actions. When we fumble around and fail to adequately take hold of demanding situations, emotional upset is the result. We are low, irritable, and somewhat tight. We lack spontaneity. We can't seem to enjoy. These are the early warning signs. When left unheeded they can become more serious. The serious side of our emotions demand attention. They refuse to be ignored for too long. They put holes in our stomach, they make our heads hurt, and they tend to break down our interpersonal relationships.

Lodged directly in the middle of the outside world and our emotions resides the Human Response System. It is the apparatus that handles the various life events that we encounter as humans. It deals with the world and all of its multi-faceted demands. It copes. In one single, coordinated action it sizes up the environment and prepares us for action. Then, like a troop of well-commanded soldiers, it marches us into battle.

The Human Response System includes all of the responses we make in coping with our environments. It generates the thoughts we have when we awaken in the morning and those that linger in our minds after a disappointing day. It charges us up when we need energy and relaxes us when we need rest. The Human Response System provides us with the unconscious reflexes necessary for executing a perfect backhand and the voluntary movements we use in communicating with the members of our family, friends, and associates. It does all of this with ease and certainty.

We must study the system to understand its strengths and weaknesses and in order to modify it for our own behalf. The following chapter on emotions initiates the in-depth look at each component of the Human Response System.

4 EMOTIONS

In medicine the clearest indication of health has traditionally been the absence of physical symptoms. Although the physician would check your temperature, blood pressure, and other vital physiological signs to determine your current level of biological functioning, health was most often defined as the absence of something—fever, cough, and so forth. Some contemporary medical researchers are attempting to alter this sickness orientation to one of health maintenance. Medical scientists have recently embarked on health maintenance and improvement programs as a defense against chronic illness and disease. The primary aim of these programs is to keep people healthy and to reveal potentially unhealthy trends before the onset of sickness.[22]

Physical symptoms and now health monitoring provide information to the physician and, subsequently, to the individual about the state of medical health. The symptom—a skin rash, a fever, or an elevated blood pressure—provides information about the adequacy of functioning of the biological system. The physician adopts a strategy for coping with the system's problems and communicates it to the patient. If the strategy is a good one, the symptom will be alleviated. These positive results are communicated to the doctor by the patient and serves as feedback regarding the effectiveness of the current strategy. If the symptom is not eliminated a new strategy is adopted.

Do people have a similar feedback mechanism for evaluating their human response system strategies? Is there a mechanism for obtaining information about how you are adapting to your environment? There is a growing body of evidence indicating that human emotions serve the same function as physical symptoms. The presence of physical symptoms often indicates the presence of an illness. Negative emotional states may provide the same kind of information about the human response system.

Emotional upset in its broadest sense is a fever of the psychological state. It can serve as a barometer of the malfunctioning of the organism. Emotions are particularly sensitive to the manner in which people are going about the business of coping with the demands of living. When the coping strategy is faltering emotional upset emerges. The absence of emotional upset is one very important signal that the response system is doing well.

EMOTIONS: RESULTS OF THINKING, PHYSIOLOGICAL RESPONSES, AND BEHAVIOR

An emotion is a very difficult experience to define. It is an extremely complex subjective state or feeling that involves all of the major components of the Human Response System—thoughts, physiological reactions, and overt behavior. In a very general manner emotions can be divided into positive and negative (pleasant and unpleasant) feeling states. The specific emotional experience, positive or negative, is partly determined by one's appraisal of current life events.

The statements you make to yourself, that is, the thoughts you generate during an activating life situation, affect both the quality and intensity of the emotion. The definition of a situation as "pleasant" or "joyful" contributes to the positive quality of the emotion. The physiological reaction, in this case, mobilizes the response system for the pleasant encounter. The overt, behavioral component of the response system carries out the actions, gestures, and impulses that contribute to the experience of joy and exhiliration. These responses occur so instantaneously and habitually that the individual experiencing the emotion has little awareness of the specific response patterns that contributed to the subjective feeling state.

Negative feeling states are generated in very much the same manner. The appraisal of a situation as "dangerous," "threatening," or potentially "damaging" contributes to the negative quality of the emotion. Actions, gestures, and impulses are emitted to fight or flee from the situation. Negative emotions follow from this particular combination of responses.

Many situations precipitate a combination of positive and negative emotions. An event that is defined as both pleasant and unpleasant will cause an individual to fluctuate from a positive to negative feeling state. For example, an event that is defined as challenging may be exhilarating at one moment and threatening the next. The specific feeling depends on the internal dialogue of the individual who is challenged (by a promotion, a new relationship, or sudden wealth) and the physiological and behavioral responses that accompany the thoughts.

Each day of a human being's life is characterized by numerous encounters with the environment. One strategy after another is employed to deal with these encounters. As a consequence emotions vary from one moment to another. They include the pleasant experiences of joy, the unpleasant vibrations of anxiety, and the feelings of ambivalence which stem from instantaneous fluctuations of joy and anxiety together.

ANXIETY, DEPRESSION, AND ANGER: THE STRESS EMOTIONS

Negative or unpleasant feelings are experienced in a variety of ways. Mild states of emotion include nervousness, sadness, and irritability. Intense emotions include severe states of panic, melancholy, and aggression. There are many levels of emotions that people experience at intermediate points falling between mild and intense states of emotional arousal. Each emotional state is a reflection of a unique style of interaction with the environment, and it is extremely difficult to identify and define all of the negative emotional states (or even positive emotional states). Unpleasant feelings however can be very generally categorized into three basic states—anxiety, depression, and anger. Each one of these emotions is the outcome of fairly specific patterns of human responses.

Anxiety is a fairly clear-cut and identifiable emotion when it is experienced in its purest form. It is that panicky feeling of apprehension you experience when confronted with a threatening situation. You can't miss it. Anxiety demands your attention and usually gets it. You feel it in your gut. It makes your stomach flutter and your heart pound. If you fell asleep at the wheel of your car on a dark, lonely highway and awakened to find yourself approaching an oncoming vehicle, you would experience anxiety in its most dramatic form.

Each component of the Human Response System plays its part in the anxiety reaction. The appraisal of the environment—the images, thoughts, and statements you make to yourself—is characterized by a perception of danger and the possibility of physical damage. The physiological counterpart to this evaluation is oriented toward preparing you for fight or flight. An entire series of bodily activities take place to help carry out a coordinated response to the environment. The behavioral component of the system executes a series of reflexes, gestures, and other muscular responses to complete the encounter.

Most of life's encounters fail to approximate the intense drama of a potential collision with an oncoming vehicle. Thus anxiety is not always experienced in its purest and most intense form. It is much more common for an individual to experience the variants of anxiety: nervousness, apprehension, and fear. The critical variable that determines the intensity of the experience of anxiety is the perception of potential danger in the environment. A mildly threatening event may produce a state of nervousness whereas an emergency situation may precipitate panic. There are literally hundreds of emotional steps between the emotions of nervousness and panic. The one common component of anxiety and its numerous variations is the evaluation of the environment as threatening, dangerous, and potentially damaging.

Anger is a very interesting emotion that occurs with varying frequencies from one individual to another. Some people are seen as chronically angry individuals, whereas others rarely display the emotion. A pure display of anger is an unmistakable event. A description of this emotion is unnecessary: the "lashing out" quality of the emotion is quite visable and clear to both the outside observer and the angered individual. Accompanying this behavior is the physiological arousal pattern of anger. Interestingly enough, this response is not readily distinguishable from the observed arousal pattern in the anxiety reaction.

The appraisal (internalized statements) in anger includes a potential struggle with the environment. The angered individual is intent on placing blame and leveling punishment for some misgiving. The angry self-dialogue often includes statements such as: "You should not have done that to me." "It is your fault, and you should be punished." "If it weren't for you, I wouldn't be in this situation. I'll get you for that."

Anger can be observed as mild irritation, subtle hostility, or intense aggression. Like anxiety there are numerous variations of this emotion, and it occurs with varying frequencies and intensities in everyone. The frequency and intensity of this emotion is related to the angered person's internal standards of right and wrong—what other people should and should not do. Blaming and punishment of the outside world for defying or ignoring an individual's rules of conduct are common precipitators of anger and its variations. According to the angry person these injustices should not have occurred and the culprit should be punished for these unpardonable acts.

Depression is an extremely unpleasant emotion characterized by a loss of interest in people and activities that were rewarding in the past. A depressed individual feels low and drained of energy. Even the simplest and easiest daily functions are dreaded and avoided. Although a distinct physiological pattern of responses has not been identified for depression, it is usually associated with a low level of bodily arousal. A depressed person is one whose senses and reactions appear to be dulled and suppressed.

The behavioral component of the Human Response System is the most prominent in depression. Overt behavioral responses are generally inhibited. The individual's activity level is severely diminished. Work, family, and socially related behaviors are often significantly reduced. Depression is a highly individualized emotional state. Some depressed individuals have difficulty sleeping and eating, whereas other sleep and eat excessively. Thinking patterns often include self-critical statements such as: "I'm not worth anything." Statements about the futility of engaging in life's activities are common: "Nothing seems to work out for me."

The depressed individual's self-perception in relation to the outside world is one of helplessness. As Seligman has documented in his laboratories and discussed in his book, *Helplessness,*[17] the depressed person expects that his or her behavior will make no difference in terms of environmental outcomes. Behavior and outcomes are independent of each other as evidenced by the depressed person's attitude: "Why should I do anything? It won't make any difference." Depending on the pervasiveness of this attitude and the intensity of physiological and behavioral inhibition, the depressed feeling may vary from mild sadness and disappointment to severe and debilitating depression.

Anxiety, anger, and depression and their variants are part of every human's life. Along with pleasant emotional states they serve as barometers—positive and negative signals—that provide information and feedback about the Human Response System's coping strategy.

EMOTIONS AND FEEDBACK: WHAT ARE YOUR EMOTIONS TELLING YOU?

Emotions provide bits of information regarding the adequacy of the response system's coping strategy. In this capacity, as givers of critical feedback, they travel through various stages. The first stage includes a set of emotional reactions to the Human Response System's initial coping activities. An encounter takes place. A coping strategy is initiated by the response system. Emotions bob and weave as a reflection of the adequacy of the system's first coping endeavors. Depending on the particular combination of human responses, the predominant emotion may be anxiety, depression, or anger. More commonly, however, the emotional experience will be a peculiar combination of all three emotions. Each one follows the other so instantaneously that they appear to be occurring in unison. In fact, there is a great deal of overlapping of these emotional states and their variants.

Adaptive Coping Reaction

The first stage of emotional reactions can be labeled the Adaptive Coping Reaction. It is a natural consequence of a person's adaptation to the environment. The emotional content of this particular stage of coping can vary from positive to negative emotions, depending upon the adequacy of the response strategy in dealing with the life event. This stage is transient and equilibrium is reestablished quite readily. The feedback you receive from your emotions during this stage is: "You have experienced a significant encounter and have responded adaptively."

Common examples of adaptive coping reactions include responses to a new job, a new relationship, or other situations that demand an adjustment in the Human Response System. A new work situation may present a unique set of circumstances such as a difficult job assignment, a demanding supervisor, and a variety of social relationships. This situation warrants a combination of old and new coping skills. Emotions will vary from one encounter to the next. Apprehension may be experienced because of the new employee's uncertainty about his or her ability to learn the job. Irritation may develop toward the employee's supervisor for not providing sufficient training. Finally, satisfaction may be experienced because the employee accomplishes the work tasks in a reasonable period of time.

The new employee's emotions serve as signals, informing him or her of the demanding nature of the situation. They tell him or her that this new life event warrants an adjustment in coping strategies. This adaptive coping reaction represents a healthy exchange between the individual and the environment.

If the adaptive commerce with the work situation continues in this manner, the individual experiences predominantly positive emotions. Unpleasant emotions are short-lived because they continue to serve as signals that are followed by adaptive changes in human responses. If the adaptive coping reaction continues to lead to constructive, adaptive changes in the response system, the other stages of emotions are never experienced. On the other hand, the second stage of emotional feedback takes place when the system fails to adjust adaptively to new environmental demands.

Maladaptive Coping Reaction

The second stage of emotional experiences represents the initial breakdown in communication between emotions and the Human Response System. An individual is confronted with a demanding situation, and the response system must make the necessary adjustments to cope with this life event. The subsequent emotional reaction informs the system of the adequacy of its coping strategy. At this point there are several problems that can occur. The individual may ignore the feedback and continue to respond as if the event did not occur, that is, deny the existence of an important and demanding situation. Or the response system may overact to the situation and get hyperactively involved in it. Denial and excessive responding are common response strategies, but there are literally hundreds of others. The one thing they have in common is the failure of the response system to change and regulate itself as a result of information about its own behavior.

Old ineffective habits may be used to cope with a new demanding life event. New habits may be attempted but quickly abandoned. Each response strategy proves to be ineffective in dealing with the situation. Each one triggers excessive emotional reactions, negative feeling states that reflect the nature of the maladaptive strategy. These negative emotions are providing warning signals that feed back information to the response system, informing it of its poor adjustment. Unlike the emotions of the adaptive coping reaction, they are intense and long lasting. This stage of emotional disturbance is labeled the Maladaptive Coping Reaction.

The maladaptive coping reaction serves an extremely important function in the Human Response System. It provides information that facilitates adjustments in the system that then precipitate a return to previous states of equilibrium. In this manner the maladaptive coping reaction represents a negative feedback cycle: An appropriate adjustment in the response system can alleviate a negative condition. The discomfort experienced when a person is experiencing intense anxiety, depression, or anger can serve to facilitate response system adjustments. If the system fails to respond to the feedback and the poor response strategy continues, emotional disturbance is experienced.

At this point the person experiences fairly intense emotional pain. These feelings go beyond the experiences of anxiety, anger, and depression. One component of the system may dominate the others, and the emotional experience reflects this dominance. For example, thought processes may be accelerated and the individual feels anxious and worried. Or physiological activity may accelerate to precipitate nausea, a rapid heart beat, or painful tension headaches because of an aroused physiological system. The behavioral component of the response system may dominate and accelerate poor habits such as excessive smoking, overeating, and alcoholism. At this stage the system is not working as a cohesive unit in responding to the environment. The appropriate reactions of anxiety, anger, and depression become muddled with excessive responding from one or more components of the system. The final result is a breakdown in communication between the Human Response System and its feedback mechanism—human emotions. Various levels of disruption in feeling states accumulate to produce intense and debilitating emotional disturbance.

The individual in the previous example experienced an adaptive coping reaction. The new work situation precipitated adequate coping. If the coping skills were inadequate, the individual would have failed to make adjustments in work habits. The work situation would have precipitated a disturbance in his or her emotional state.

The worker may worry excessively and feel apprehensive about work performance. These preoccupations prevent the person from focusing and concentrating on the job tasks. They eventually affect the person's work performance. The emotional disturbance—intense anxiety, excessive worrying, and apprehensions—continue. Work becomes more stressful. It becomes progressively more difficult for the individual to attend to what his or her emotions are communicating. The information is camouflaged in a wealth of disturbing feelings. At this point, the necessary adjustments in the Human Response System become progressively more unlikely.

Feedback Breakdown Reaction

The third stage of emotional reactions is the complete breakdown of communication between various components of the response system. During this stage one experiences the surfacing of severe emotional and psychosomatic problems. The demanding event continues to stress the system. Maladaptive human responses have become habitual and resistant to change. Severe emotional pain is experienced by the individual in the activating situation. The connection between events and emotions fails to provide information and feedback. The system is deafened by its own maladaptive habits.

Numerous problems develop that reflect the poor functioning of one or more components of the response system. These problems no longer serve as warning signals. They are perceived by the stressed individual as unusual and isolated events that are unrelated to the coping strategy. The system becomes compartmentalized at this point. One component works independently of and against the other components of the system. This stage of emotional disturbance is labeled the Feedback Breakdown Reaction.

The Feedback Breakdown Reaction represents a very serious stage of emotional disturbance. The individual suffering from a breakdown in feedback may be experiencing a variety of problems. These are precipitated by the dominance of one or more components of the Human Response System. The thinking component may become severely disrupted, and the person may experience excessive preoccupations and unusual thoughts. Severely disordered thinking may be experienced as delusional ideas.

These problems are accompanied by periodic bouts of anxiety, depression, and other upsets. Physiologically, the breakdown of feedback may precipitate such psychosomatic problems as severe migraine headaches, gastrointestinal ulcers, and hypertension. The stressed person may be engaged excessively in one activity (e.g.,: work) to the exclusion of all others in order to cope with the difficult situation. On the other hand, an avoidance reaction may develop. The person in this case may refuse to confront the life event that precipitated the disturbance. Other habits such as excessive drinking and eating may accompany this reaction.

Oftentimes, one or more of these problems occur simultaneously. At this stage of development it is not uncommon to observe disordered processes in each component of the system. In the Type A individual, for example, the behavior pattern of overwork is combined with an underlying interpersonal hostility and the development of premature coronary artery disease.

The individual in the previous example is now taken through the third stage of emotional development. He or she has failed to attend to the emotional signals that indicate a maladaptive coping strategy. The response system has become compartmentalized. An excessive preoccupation with work is not perceived to be a problem. Hostility toward work associates and family members is rationalized as necessary in order to facilitate performance. Visits to the doctor for chest pains and reports of high blood pressure and cholesterol are seen as isolated events, unrelated to a maladaptive strategy of living. The doctor tells the person to slow down. These instructions precipitate more disordered thinking and behavior, and the individual attempts to reduce the discomfort by working more furiously. The problems eventually become more intense and debilitating. One of the few warning signals that will warrant this individual's attention is a severe breakdown in the response system (e.g., heart attack). He or she will be forced to attend to this feedback and will finally become more receptive to a new strategy of living.

THREE STAGES OF EMOTIONAL REACTIONS: THE CASE OF PAUL

Paul experienced several stages of emotional upset and disturbance before he became profoundly ill. During the early stages of his difficulties he was extremely anxious and tense. These unpleasant emotions were the initial warning signals triggered by the appraisal of a threatening home and work environment. At this time he was continuing to struggle with these problems. The lines of communication with his wife were still open and he was still seeking constructive solutions to his work problems. This was an Adaptive Coping Reaction that resulted from an active interplay with the environment. If Paul had continued with this strategy, he may have arrived at constructive solutions to both difficult situations and the unpleasant emotions would have subsided.

Paul was quite threatened by these events and was confused about dealing with them. He felt overwhelmed and sensed a loss of control. His strategy was to make no response. He ignored the information that he was receiving from his environment and response system. Detachment and social withdrawal became pervasive, and the man who had always been the life of the party began experiencing severe bouts of depression.

Paul began to have difficulty organizing his life on a day-to-day basis. He was described by his friends as depressed an agitated. This withdrawn posture minimized the opportunity for constructive resolutions to domestic and vocational problems. The situations grew more difficult for him, and this withdrawn mode of interaction became habitual (the Maladaptive Coping Reaction).

Anxiety, depression, and withdrawal took a back seat to the emergence of severe neurological problems. Paul lost a significant portion of his memory for past events. He then began forgetting recent events, and everyday activities became obscure and distant to him. Paul no longer interacted with his environment in an organized and cohesive manner. Each part of him appeared to be isolated and disjointed from the remainder of his response system. He was confused by each subsequent interpersonal encounter. Warning signals became more intense and progressively harder to ignore. The end result was the onset of intense seizure activity.

At this point, one part of the system was working against the system as a whole. This best characterizes the Feedback Breakdown Reaction. It is difficult to estimate how long it took Paul to regress to this final stage. The seeds for this maladaptive strategy could have been planted at various stages of his personal development. The stimulus for their growth was a pair of stressful life circumstances. The details of these events and their impact on Paul's breakdown in functioning are now history to you.

THE VARIOUS FACES OF EMOTIONAL UPSET

The general stages of maladaptive coping and the emotional outcomes of these responses have been outlined. Your knowledge of the functioning of the Human Response System has grown considerably, and you have become aware of the potential effects of various coping strategies. Like many first year students in the health professions—medicine, nursing, psychology, and so forth—you may be feeling somewhat apprehensive about this new level of awareness. The initial stages of learning about your response system may be accompanied by an identification with each case and its numerous problems. You may be asking yourself: Am I susceptible to these problems? Perhaps I'm already a victim of them.

The best strategy for dealing with these apprehensions that commonly accompany a new learning experience is to vigorously engage in further learning. In this manner you can become aware of the uniqueness of your own response system. The purpose of this information is not to alarm you but to allow you to utilize this information in your own behalf.

The first stage of this learning process is to observe and assess your emotions and what they are communicating to you. The following discussion, along with Appendix I, provides you with a sample of problems that are generally associated with maladaptive coping strategies. You should approach this material with curiousity but little apprehension. Remember that all serious students of human behavior become alarmed upon their initial exposure to this information. You may find that some of these problems resemble your own. There is a perfectly good reason for this similarity. All of us fluctuate constantly between periods of adaptive and maladaptive coping and, therefore, experience the outcome of these responses at one time or another. The main purpose of this new awareness is to allow you to observe your unique emotional reactions and response system outcomes in order to begin the process of Stress Watching.

The organism cries for help. It cries with anxiety, anger, and depression. When the cry is not heard and it fails to mobilize us into action, the emotions manifest themselves in a variety of ways. Our emotional warning signals do not always provide us with clear readings. Depression, anger, and anxiety are often disguised in a variety of problems. They prevent us from readily using these valuable bits of information for our own behalf. Instead of experiencing a distinct emotional reaction we are preoccupied with worrisome thoughts. We develop severe back pain with no signs of physical injury, and we drink, eat, or smoke incessantly. These problems are not always perceived as signs of emotional disturbance, but each problem contains elements of depression, anger, anxiety, and their variants. It is important to attend more closely to the various faces of emotional upset and the specific manner in which the Human Response System transmits its warning signals.

Appendix I includes a discussion of numerous problems of the Human Response System. No attempt has been made to construct an exhaustive list. The problems represent a small sample of conditions. It will give you a general idea of the variations of Human Response System malfunctioning.

No attempt has been made to categorize these problems in terms of their severity. All of the problems represent a breakdown in response functioning as a result of maladaptive coping.

The emotional disturbance that occurs as a result of this breakdown takes its toll on each individual in a unique manner. Each of us appear to be more easily disturbed at one level of response functioning than another. As a result, one major component of the Human Response System becomes more disrupted and out of balance: Other components tend to hold up in comparison. The one experience that is common to each disturbance, regardless of where it focuses its major assault, is the presence of unpleasant emotional states such as anxiety and depression.

A fairly clear example of a disturbance that affects primarily one part of the response system, the thinking component, is the problem of thought preoccupations. While this problem certainly results from the maladaptive coping of all human response components, the system's malfunctioning is predominantly experienced at the thinking level. Intense anxiety is often observed with this problem, and this unpleasant emotion interacts directly with the individual's thoughts. Physiological reactions and behavior problems seem to take a back seat to the thought component of the response system.

The problems discussed in Appendix I are categorized in Table 4-1

TABLE 4–1. Various Faces of Emotional Upset

Components of The Human Response System	Consequences of Maladaptive Coping

Thoughts	1. Thought preoccupation or obsessions
	  a. Somatic thoughts or hypochondriasis
	  b. Thoughts of jealousy and possessiveness
	  c. Thoughts of suspiciousness
	  d. Other preoccupations
	2. Phobic thoughts

Physiological responses	1. Psychosomatic problems
	  a. Muscle tension
	  b. Type A behavior pattern: premature coronary artery disease

Behavior	1. Maladaptive habits: excessive smoking, obesity, and alcoholism
	2. Relationship problems
	  a. Marital and living-together problems
	  b. Difficulty with intimacy and loneliness
	  c. Interpersonal relationships at work

according to the apparent dominance of one component of the response system over the other; turn to Appendix I for a full description of each problem.

EMOTIONS AND STRESSFUL LIFE EVENTS

The events that activate us and drive us into action vary from one individual to another. A promotion for one person can be exhilarating. For another it can be an anxiety-provoking experience. Marital separation can stimulate a sense of freedom in someone who has felt stiffled by the relationship. For another, it is an unwelcome surprise that throws one into the pits of depression. Despite the enormous range of human vulnerabilities, all of us encounter life events that are capable of pushing our panic button and testing our psychological resources.

In order to appreciate the wide range of potential responses to various life events, you should imagine yourself in the following three situations:

Scene I. You're sitting in the audience listening to an interesting speaker who is discussing a topic that is very important to you. The speaker completes the formal segment of the presentation and then asks for questions from the audience. You're dying to ask the speaker a question. It's been lingering in your mind for the past twenty minutes of the speech. Immediately before raising your hand to be recognized, you experience a significant increase in nervousness: your heart is racing, your palms are perspiring, and disturbing thoughts are racing through your mind. The feelings are overwhelming and you change your mind about asking the question. Immediately after you make this decision your feelings of nervousness and apprehension subside.

Scene II. You're at home alone watching television. You feel restless and can't seem to concentrate on the program. It's impossible to get your mind off the love relationship that ended abruptly without notice. You can't stop thinking about your estranged lover. Your thoughts are preoccupied with trying to understand what happened to the relationship. Food repulses you. You've lost five to ten pounds in the last month alone. The idea of dating turns you off and you've refused numerous social invitations from friends. The only activity that interests you is sitting at home and waiting for a telephone call from your past lover.

Scene III. It's seven o'clock in the evening and you're still working late at the office. You had a quick lunch about seven hours ago and your stomach hasn't yet settled down. You've been working steadily since that time trying to catch up from the previous day's work. Yesterday was even more hectic than today. You never get a chance to relax anymore since the responsibility at work has steadily increased. You feel good about your new promotion and wouldn't give it up for anything. Yet your social life has gone downhill along with your relationship with your spouse. A further insult occured when your physician recently informed you that you are a prime candidate for a heart attack. The doctor found your blood pressure and cholesterol level to be dangerously high. You haven't taken the advice to quit smoking. On the contrary, your smoking along with other undesirable habits appear to be increasing.

IN ALL THREE OF THE PRECEDING SCENES YOU HAVE IMAGINED yourself experiencing various degrees of emotional upset. In each of the scenes the emotional upset was precipitated by an environmental event. Scene I characterizes a common emotional reaction, anxiety, to a very specific situation. You tend to worry about speaking in the presence of others. You are concerned about looking foolish or saying something inappropriate. In this activating situation the emotional response tends to dissipate as soon as the event is terminated.

Scene II represents a much different set of circumstances. The emotional upset is much more intense and serious. The loss of an important love relationship has precipitated a series of behaviors and feelings that are debilitating. You feel lonely and rejected. Your time alone is occupied with more than the usual amount of anxiety and depression. Nagging thoughts are preoccupying you and preventing you from concentrating on other activities. Your behavior is withdrawn and social contacts are minimal. These feelings and thoughts linger in your consciousness during most of your waking moments. The emotional disturbance has plagued you for several months, and there is no sign that things will change in the near future.

Scene III characterizes a relatively chronic, long-lasting disturbance. A style of life or strategy has evolved over many years. The maladaptive strategy is exhibited primarily at work, but it has recently pervaded your family and social life. The responsibilities of work are overwhelming you. Long hours are spent at night and during weekends to assure that you are executing the job in a perfect manner. As the months pass you spend more time on the job but find yourself performing less effectively than before. You have more difficulty relaxing and haven't slept soundly in a long time. The doctor informed you that this style of living is contributing to your bad physical condition.

What can you learn from these three divergent situations about the impact of life events on emotional responses?

1. The events that trigger emotional upset vary from one individual to another. But there are some fairly common examples of events that precipitate upset in many of us. Speaking in the presence of other people, loss of a love relationship, and excessive work responsibility are three common activating, life events.

2. Emotional responses are not isolated events in our lives. They stem from the way we appraise these life circumstances and subsequently react to them.

3. The intensity of emotional upsets is related to the factor of time. Some events precipitate transient upsets. Others produce reactions that are long-lasting. We often fail to handle these events during their early stages. As a result these situations get out of hand and short-term reactions become long-term disturbances.

The Nature of Life Events

Our prehistoric ancestors had very little difficulty identifying activating events in their lives. There was no confusion about the situations they needed to approach and energetically encounter. Early humans had to leave the relative comforts of the cave in order to search for food and other elements of survival. There was little confusion about the situations that they should avoid and skillfully escape. The environment contained an assortment of larger and stronger competitors searching for their own life-sustaining necessities. Steven Yafa, a writer and humorist, discusses this phenomenon in a very entertaining article on stress:

> Nothing similar occurred in the lives of our primitive ancestors. True, they had their own problems; sometimes when they finished their daily domestic cave chores, they would glance up to find a hungry mastodon zeroing in on them for lunch. When that happened, their adrenals instantly secreted substances designed to mobilize strength and energy. They sped to safety, clubbed the beast into submission, or perished. But the adrenal output found release. [23, p. 88]

Thanks to the evolution of a sophisticated response system, particularly the dramatic changes in brain size and capacity, modern individuals have been able to surround themselves with the fruits of technological advancement. These developments make us somewhat immune to the physical dangers that lurk in the environment. While these developments have left us less vulnerable to the direct physical assaults of a dangerous environment, they have contributed to an equally difficult contemporary problem. Modern humans are confronted with a less visible yet equally dangerous state of affairs. Perhaps the best description of this world we modern men and women live in is offered by Albert Ellis in his book *A New Guide to Rational Living.* Ellis is an astute observer of the irrational elements of contemporary living:

> As we have noted throughout this book, you could hardly conceive of a more irrational world than our present society. In spite of the enormous advances in technical knowledge made during the last century, and the theoretical possibility that all of us could live in peace and prosperity, we actually hang on to the brink of local strife, world war, economic insecurity, political skulduggery, organized crime, pollution, ecological bankruptcy, business fraud, sexual violence, racial bigotry, labor and management inefficiency, religious fanaticism, and other manifestations of idiocy and inhumanity.
>
> On a more personal scale, conditions appear equally bad or worse. None of us—no, not a single, solitary one of us—fails to have intimate encounters, almost every day of our lives, with several individuals (bosses or employees, husbands or wives, children or parents, friends or enemies) who behave stupidly, ignorantly, ineffectually, provocatively, frustratingly, viciously, or disturbedly. Modern life, instead of seeming just a bowl of cherries, often more closely resembles a barrel of prune pits.[24, p. 196].

If we were to compare these two environments, the worlds of prehistoric and modern humans, we would see that our early ancestors had to cope primarily with the physical elements of the immediate environment. Unlike their prehistoric ancestors, contemporary humans struggle with the demands forced upon them by fellow men and women. These numerous daily human interactions demand attention. They tax the resources of the Human Response System and set into motion a variety of emotional reactions. These reactions reflect the nature of the system's commerce with its struggling neighbors.

Stressful Life Events

The identification of these activating human interactions is in some cases quite simple. A confrontation with a saber-toothed tiger is not a subtle event. Neither is the breakup of long-term love relationships or the presentation of the annual report to the Board of Directors of a failing business. Each of these situations demand attention and respect. They tend to arouse each human's most remarkable coping strategies. As Yafa eloquently states:

> Now, in a time of more subtle and sinister adversaries, our glands react in those same prehistoric patterns. The intercom buzzes, the secretary announces that Mr. Griffin wishes to see you *immediately* concerning those lost

invoices; her tone conveys anxiety, your hormones surge to help repel the enemy. Wedged behind your desk or shuffling through the office corridors, you flare within, ready for attack; but hand-to-hand combat with Mr. Griffin will not improve your corporate image and, instead, as you sit and suffer the man's abuse, you become the target of your own riotous defense mechanisms.[23, p. 88]

Dr. Thomas Holmes and Dr. Richard Rahe of the University of Washington Medical School have developed a scale for identifying stressful life events.[25] The scale includes both positive and negative events and, according to the investigators, has some value in predicting an individual's chances of developing a future stress-related illness. If an individual completing the scale has experienced a large number of these "life events" in the past twelve months, his or her chance of experiencing a stress-related illness is significantly increased. Each item on the scale is given a point value. Some items, presumably the ones that are more stressful, earn more points than others. For example, if a person has experienced *divorce* in the last twelve months, he or she obtains 73 points for that item. *"Trouble with boss"* earns a value of 23. Ten of the forty-three items are duplicated below to provide you with a sample of the stressful life events identified by these two investigators. The total score is determined by adding the points from each life event experienced by the individual in the last twelve months.

Life Event	Value
Death of a spouse	100
Fired from work	47
Pregnancy	40
Change in financial status	38
Death of a close friend	37
Outstanding personal achievement	28
Spouse begins or stops work	26
Change in residence	20
Change in sleeping habits	26
Change in eating habits	15

As you can observe from this sample of items the focus of this scale is on discrete and separate life events. It does not pinpoint the activating events that people have to cope with on a daily basis. For this reason it is not very useful (and the investigators did not intend to use it) for the process of *Stress Watching.*

Pinpointing Specific Events

Life is not simply a series of direct and obvious confrontations. Many individuals who seek help for emotional difficulties cannot pinpoint the life events that create difficulties for them. More often than not, troubled people are only vaguely aware of the connection between their problems and the activating events in their lives. An important step in the stress management process involves helping people make this difficult connection.

Some people become tremendously upset about work situations. Others handle the daily activity of earning a living in a very calm manner. Social events can precipitate arousal and concern in many people but many others feel that social situations are very innocuous. Love relationships, family activities, and friendships are easily executed by some individuals, whereas these life events precipitate severe disturbance in others. You can certainly remember being confused and puzzled by observing a friend's extreme upset in a situation that was not capable of arousing even the slightest concern in yourself.

Albert Ellis, the originator of Rational Emotive Therapy (RET), has developed a model for understanding the way life events interact with emotional consequences.[24] According to Ellis and other RET advocates, activating events (A) lead to specific emotional consequences (C) because of the repetition of numerous beliefs (B) during these events. This ABC model of emotional upset proposes that event A does not cause emotional consequence C. Rather, it is the belief about event A that causes C. Ellis has identified ten irrational beliefs that people continually repeat to themselves. These irrational beliefs lead them to experience large doses of anxiety, anger, depression, and variations of these three basic emotions.

Ellis' ABC model of emotional disturbance very adequately explains the enormous variability of events that disturb human beings. Event A is distressful to one person and rewarding to another. The first repeats irrational statements in the presence of event A, whereas the other handles event A in a very matter-of-fact manner. A life event becomes an activating and upsetting situation as a result of the way people define it.

There are numerous potential attitudes, expectations, and beliefs that an individual can experience in a day full of life events. Imagine the hundreds and thousands of these internal thinking responses that occur in a week, month, or a year. According to Ellis and other investigators of human thinking responses, an event that precipitates irrational ideas is capable of producing emotional disturbance. Ellis[24] has pinpointed ten irrational ideas. The first three of these ideas are:

1. I must have love or approval from all of the people that I find significant.

2. I must prove thoroughly competent, adequate, and achieving.

3. When people act obnoxiously and unfairly, I should blame and damn them and see them as bad, wicked, or rotten individuals.

Ellis' notions can be incorporated into the Human Response System model in the following manner: An environmental event becomes a demand, a pressure, or a source of potential stress when the thinking component of the system defines the situation as threatening. The response system then triggers irrational thoughts in the presence of the event. Although irrational thoughts vary from one individual to another, there appear to be numerous thinking responses that are common to brain-using human beings. These responses include an excessive concern for the approval of other people, perfectionistic strivings in performance situations (events involving responsibility), and strong tendencies for blaming the environment when it is not meeting our demands and desires.

The adoption of this irrational thinking strategy in coping with life's activities predisposes us to regular episodes of emotional upset and disturbance. An approval-seeking, perfectionistic housewife who tries to meet the demands of raising children and housekeeping can experience as much stress as a corporate executive who seeks continual approval for his or her work performance.

Another cognitively oriented psychologist (one who places a great emphasis on the thinking component of the Human Response System) is Richard Lazarus. He states that the appraisal of life events is important in determining the organism's response to that event.

Four kinds of appraisal are critical to the emotional response, namely that the transaction is damaging, threatening (implying the likelihood of future damage), productive of positive well-being, or challenging (implying the likelihood of overcoming obstacles in the pursuit of something). In lower animals, such as those studied by Tinbergen, the evaluative or appraisal feature of the emotion—eliciting perception—is very concrete, simple, and built into the nervous system. In higher animals, such as man, symbolic thought processes and learning play a predominant role."[3, p. 4. Copyright 1975 by the American Psychological Association. Reprinted by permission.]

The four critical human thinking responses or appraisals of environmental events ("that the transaction is damaging, threatening, productive of positive well-being, or challenging") are more general than Ellis' notion of the determinants of human emotional responses. Yet, there is a great deal of overlap with Ellis' notion of the determinants of human emotional responses.

We are now better prepared to answer a fundamental question: What makes a life event an emotionally upsetting experience? In the situations presented at the beginning of this chapter, one person was reluctant to speak in the presence of others; another was devastated by the break-up of a relationship; and the last person was overwhelmed by work. Each event in the lives of these individuals triggered something very fundamental to them as human beings. If you look closely at the demands made on each person in the three divergent situations, you can see the common human responses of approval-seeking, strivings for perfection, and a chronic sense of responsibility. These events precipitated appraisals of a potentially damaging and threatening environment, one that is capable of blocking highly desirable goals. These events induced fears of failure, criticism, and rejection. Fathom the number of events in your life that can generate these common thinking responses and you have characterized the human potential for upset, disturbance, and misery.

The relationship between thinking and emotions is pursued further in later chapters. Before delving into a detailed discussion of thinking behavior (Chapter 7) and the self-regulation of thoughts (Chapter 8), it is important for you to obtain a basic knowledge of the functioning of the physiological component of the system. Chapter 5 presents a foundation for understanding the system's tendency to become easily aroused and agitated. In Chapter 6 a technique is presented, the Muscular Relaxation Response, that effectively counteracts this tendency. Relaxation is utilized as a basis for each of the subsequent self-regulation techniques, including the self-regulation and management of thoughts and behavior.

5 HUMAN RESPONSE SYSTEM

Physiology

Physiology deals with how a part of the body actually works. The study of body functions has been conducted by specialists in physiology, medicine, and related areas. Very little of the terminology and technology of this vastly interesting field has penetrated the thoughts and vocabulary of other people. It has always been viewed as a science that was relatively esoteric and incomprehensible and, therefore, not the domain of common sense and knowledge. Many of us know more about car engines, mechanics, and electricity than we know about physiology. This state of human affairs is difficult to understand given the intimate connection between body functioning and daily living.

Perhaps this paradoxical gap in our knowledge stems from the common propaganda pervading most classrooms. Math and physics are viewed as too difficult for common consumption, and physiology is lumped into the same category. Any student of physiology can easily dispute that contention. The appropriate level of motivation can take one a long way through the journey into the cells, tissues, and organs that make up the Human Response System. The objective of this chapter is to initiate your studies in this important area and provide this motivation.

Once again I must emphasize the wholistic nature of the system. There is no real distinction between mind and body. Thinking and behavior involve a network of physiological responses similar to the ones that are detailed in the following narrative. Each response of the system at its most basic level represents a physiochemical process. The distinctions between various components of the system have been made in order to help clarify, understand, and modify a system that expresses itself in a complex variety of ways.

The following discussion focuses on two unifying concepts in physiology, homeostasis and feedback, as they are related to stress. Common problems such as muscle tension, hypertension, and Type A Behavior are discussed in relation to a breakdown in the equilibrium of the response system. Research into a relatively new area, the sudden death phenomenon, is introduced. In the final section of this and each remaining chapter, the concept of feedback is used to help integrate a growing number of scientific findings in the area of stress.

THE STRESS RESPONSE

For a long time in the field of psychophysiology, it was difficult to characterize the human component of the Human Response System. Most of the scientific research that investigated organismic responses to environmental demands was conducted with lower animals. As a consequence, we learned a great deal about the manner in which animals coped with their environments. This was valuable information that allowed investigators of human behavior to take the necessary first steps in understanding the Human Response System. The following is a brief review of the work of these early researchers.

One of the early scientists was Dr. Walter B. Cannon of the Harvard Medical School. He studied the manner in which animals responded to dangerous or life-threatening situations. Cannon[16] showed that they respond to events requiring behavioral adjustment by means of a physiological response referred to as the "fight or flight" response. When an animal perceives a threatening situation, its reflexes initiate an integrated physiological response that prepares it for running or fighting. This response is characterized by coordinated changes in metabolism (oxygen consumption), blood pressure, heart rate, rate of breathing, amount of blood pumped by the heart, and amount of blood pumped to the skeletal muscles. Cannon, then, was one of the first investigators to demonstrate the existence of a consistent pattern of physiological responses emitted when an animal copes with its environment.

The next major finding was provided by Dr. Walter R. Hess, a Swiss Nobel laureate.[27] His work further refined Cannon's findings. By stimulating a specific part of a cat's brain, he demonstrated that the controlling center for the fight or flight response was located within a small area of the brain called the hypothalamus. When stimulated, the hypothalamus produces physiological changes in the sympathetic nervous system. The activity of the sympathetic nervous system in turn leads to outpourings of adrenalin. This pattern of physiologic changes initiated by the hypothalamus contributed to Cannon's fight–flight response. Hess showed that the hypothalamus, sympathetic nervous system, and fight-

—flight response were interrelated. Their total effect was to arouse the organism's response system.

The final series of studies summarized here were conducted by Dr. Hans Selye, perhaps the most well-known contemporary researcher in the area of stress. Selye[6] studied the response of animals to a variety of stressors. He injected rats with various impure and toxic gland preparations. Irrespective of the tissue from which they were made or their hormone content, the injections produced a stereotyped syndrome characterized by enlargement and hyperactivity of the adrenal cortex (a part of the adrenal gland that produces hormones called corticoids), shrinkage or atrophy of the thymus gland and lymph nodes (structures involved in immune defense reactions), and the appearance of gastrointestinal ulcers. The same trauma could be precipitated by cold, heat, infections, hemorrhage, and nervous irritation. Selye was one of the first investigators to identify this stereotyped stress response. He showed that there were physically damaging consequences to various structures in the response system due to prolonged exposure to a variety of environmental stressors.

Regarding this nonspecific response of the body to stressors, Selye states:

> . . . in addition to their specific actions, all agents to which we are exposed also produce a nonspecific increase in the need to perform adaptive functions and thereby to re-establish normalcy. This is independent of the specific activity that caused the rise in requirements. The nonspecific demand for activity, as such, is the essence of stress. [6, p. 15]

Other investigators have defined stress in similar terms. For example, Dr. Herbert Benson, in his book, *The Relaxation Response,* defines stressful situations as those which demand continuous behavioral adjustment. He states that:

> Humans, like other animals, react in a predictable way to acute and chronic stressful situations which trigger an inborn response that has been part of our physiologic makeup for perhaps millions of years. This has been popularly labeled the "fight-or-flight" response. When we are faced with situations that require adjustment of our behavior, an involuntary response increases our blood pressure, heart rate, rate of breathing, blood flow to the muscles, and metabolism, preparing us for conflict or escape. [7, pp. 23–24. Copyright © 1975 by William Morrow and Company Inc. By permission of the publisher.]

Each definition of stress includes the notion of an adjustment, a change in the response system's normal flow of behavior in order to meet the demands of an activating event. The concept of homeostasis was introduced in the early part of this book to demonstrate that the response system continually functions to maintain this state of balance of the internal environment. The need for adjustment via a confrontation with a stressful event threatens homeostasis. Stress and homeostasis are intimately related, and a brief discussion of this relationship is warranted at this time.

Stress and Homeostasis

Homeostasis has been defined by physiologists as the maintenance of the body's internal physiological environment in response to stressors that originate within the body or in the external environment. Hormones are chemical regulators of homeostasis. The secretion of these substances are regulated through feedback systems. The following is an example of homeostasis in action: A lower than normal amount of glucose or sugar in the blood (due to a variety of conditions including the initiation of a very strict diet) stimulates a portion of the brain to secrete a chemical substance. This substance, in turn, stimulates an endocrine gland to secrete a hormone that accelerates the rate of the release of stored sugar into the blood. As soon as blood sugar returns to normal, the chemical message from the brain to the gland is shut off and the gland stops secreting the substance that stimulates the release of sugar into the blood. This homeostatic activity is effective in altering a deviant response—low blood sugar. This exchange of information between the blood, the brain, and the endocrine gland is successful in maintaining a uniform chemistry of the internal environment of the body.

Homeostasis is oriented toward counteracting the everyday, ordinary stress of living. The three main structures of the physiological component of the Human Response System that have the major responsibility for maintaining this state of balance are the hypothalamus, the autonomic nervous system, and the endocrine system.

Human Physiological Responses

The hypothalamus and the autonomic nervous system are the same structures that play a major role in understanding the more primitive fight-flight response in animals. The hypothalamus is a tiny structure located in the center of the brain. It has an intimate connection with the cortex; there are tracts of fibers within the nervous system that connect the two structures. Figure 5-1 shows the relationship between the cortex, hypothalamus, and the autonomic nervous system.

Despite its relatively small size, the hypothalamus controls many bodily

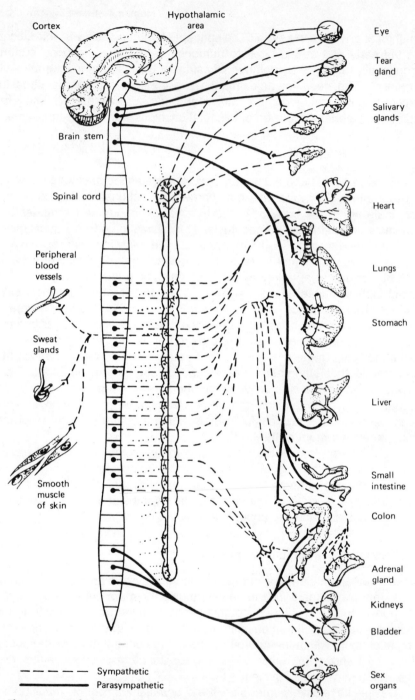

Figure 5-1. Relationship between the cortex, hypothalamus, autonomic nervous system, and the internal organs of the body.

activities that keep the Human Response System in a state of physiological balance. For example certain cells of the hypothalamus serve as a thermostat—a mechanism sensitive to changes in temperature. If blood flowing through these cells is above normal in temperature, the hypothalamus sends impulses over other parts of the nervous system to stimulate activities that promote heat loss. These nervous system responses can relax smooth muscle in the blood vessels and precipitate sweating. Both activities allow heat to be lost. If the temperature of the blood is below normal, the hypothalamus sends out nervous system impulses that promote heat retention by the body. Contraction of cutaneous blood vessels, cessation of sweating, and shivering take place. Heat can be retained in this manner. Through a similar process of feedback between the hypothalamus and other structures of the body, food and water intake are controlled. The hypothalamus also serves as one of the centers that maintains the waking state and sleep patterns.

The autonomic nervous system consists of two principle divisions: the sympathetic and the parasympathetic. Many organs of the body receive nerve impulses from both components of this nervous system (see Figure 5-1): one set of impulses from the sympathetic division and another from the parasympathetic. Impulses transmitted by nerve fibers of one division (sympathetic) stimulate the organ to become active, whereas impulses from the other division (parasympathetic) bring about a decrease or halt in the activity of the organ. The parasympathetic division is primaily concerned with activities that restore and conserve body energy. For example, parasympathetic impulses to the digestive glands and the smooth muscle of the digestive system dominate over impulses from the sympathetic system. This allows energy-supplying foods to be digested and absorbed by the body.

The sympathetic division is primarily concerned with processes that involve the expenditure of energy. Under normal conditions, the sympathetic division counteracts the parasympathetic just enough to generate energy to carry out normal functions. During an extremely stressful situation, however, the sympathetic completely dominates the parasympathetic. When we are confronted with a dangerous situation our bodies become very alert. Feats of unusual strength have even been observed during these times. People in these emergency situations have reportedly lifted extremely heavy objects that would have been impossible to lift from injured victims under ordinary circumstances. These extraordinary reactions are attributed to the excessively high levels of arousal generated by the sympathetic nervous system. Figure 5-1 shows the widespread influence of sympathetic nervous system impulses. Notice that an impulse that starts in one direction and stimulates one organ may subsequently affect many parts of the body.

COMMON EXAMPLES OF PHYSIOLOGICAL AROUSAL IN HUMANS

A number of laboratory experiments on stress have shown that there is a relationship between stress and changes in a variety of physiological functions. One specific response that is effected by stress is the flow of blood to various parts of the body. Stress induces a constriction of the blood vessels in the surface of the body (e.g., the skin), thereby decreasing the amount of blood flowing to this area. On the other hand, the dilation of blood vessels increases blood flow to parts of the body (e.g., the muscles) that are coping with the stressful situation. These physiological responses facilitate the fight-flight response discussed earlier.

One method of measuring the extent of blood flow to the surface of the body is through the use of a device called the photoelectric pulse pick-up.[28] The device is attached to the tip of one finger on either the right or left hand of the subject. It picks up the pulse coming into the finger through tiny blood vessels and measures the volume of blood pulsating through the finger at any one point in time. The results of this response are recorded on a polygraph so that an investigator can observe fluctuations in blood flow (see Figure 5-2). A polygraph, commonly known as the lie detector, is an instrument for recording tracings of several different physiological responses simultaneously.

The amount of blood flow is indicated by the height of the pulse spike. Physiological arousal reduces finger pulse volume. During a stress reaction the height of the pulse spike is small. Dilation of blood vessels has the reverse effect. More blood flows through the vessel, and the pulse spike increases in size. During relaxation or other nonstressful conditions, the pulse spike is generally larger.

Finger pulse volume is a very useful tool for measuring an individual's stress response to a specific life event. A second benefit of using this measure is the ability to obtain another valuable bit of information: pulse rate. Each spike produced by the Photoelectric Pulse Pick-up represents one complete cycle of the alternate expansion and elastic recoil of an artery with each systole of the left ventricle of the heart. Pulse rate corresponds to heart rate. It averages between 70 and 80 beats per minute in the resting state and provides the investigator with another measure that is sensitive to physiological arousal.

The following case examples are used to illustrate one important component of the physiological response to stress. The Photoelectric Pulse Pick-up was used in each case to help people identify events in their lives that produced a stress response and caused them emotional discomfort. The long-term objective of this process was to provide each person with new strategies for dealing with these stressful situations. In addition to providing assistance in the problem identification process, the physiological measures provided the individuals with feedback of success in changing their arousal responses to the stressful events.

Figure 5-2(a) presents the record of an individual who was hospitalized in a private psychiatric hospital for a severe stress reaction. He was the president of a small business, married, and the father of two children. Long-standing difficulties in the marital relationship culminated in a stress reaction that left him emotionally disturbed. He suffered from states of extreme anxiety and panic. His blood pressure was fluctuating dramatically, and he experienced frequent episodes of dizziness. During this stressful period work tended to increase his problems, and he had a great deal of difficulty concentrating on the activities of the business. He was finally hospitalized because of these numerous stress-related problems.

The first portion of Figure 5-2(a) represents the fluctuations in finger pulse volume or digital blood flow during the pretreatment period (a period of time where the client is asked to sit quietly while the measurements are taken). During this time he was instructed to imagine neutral or pleasant scenes. A dramatic change in blood flow takes place when he is asked to imagine himself receiving a phone call from his wife. As you can see from the record, finger pulse volume is reduced and the pulse spikes get smaller. The record indicates that imagining and thinking about a stressful event can precipitate at least one component of the fight-flight response—reduction in blood flow to the surface of the body.

Figure 5-2(b) indicates the same individual's response to another stressful event—talking to his boss. Once again the event was presented in imagery, and a similar response is observed. Blood flow is reduced to the periphery of the body, finger pulse volume is reduced, and the pulse spikes get smaller. The complete details of this case are presented in Chapter 10 (The Case of Richard).

Figure 5-2(c) shows the record of an adolescent girl with school problems. She was an extremely bright individual with a high IQ, but consistently made Ds and Fs on her report card. In addition to the school problem, she had difficulty getting along with her family and displayed anger and hostility toward them.

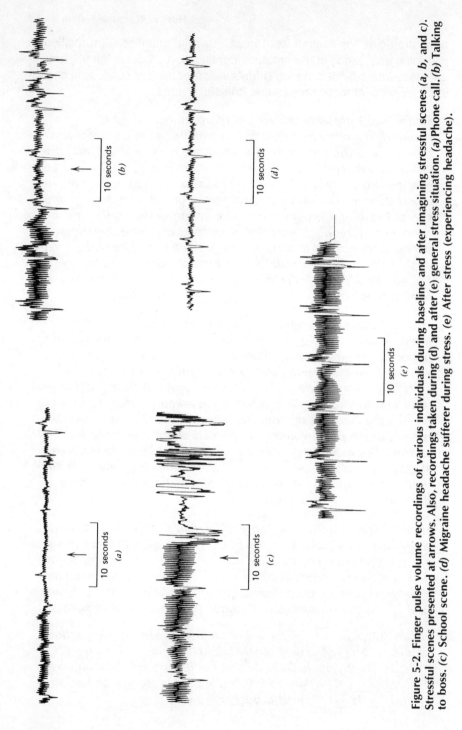

Figure 5-2. Finger pulse volume recordings of various individuals during baseline and after imagining stressful scenes (a, b, and c). Stressful scenes presented at arrows. Also, recordings taken during (d) and after (e) general stress situation. (a) Phone call. (b) Talking to boss. (c) School scene. (d) Migraine headache sufferer during stress. (e) After stress (experiencing headache).

74

She was asked to imagine several school scenes while being monitored by the Pulse Pick-up. The record shows the response to her thoughts and images of a teacher that she intensely disliked. She experienced both anxiety and anger when she was in this particular classroom. Notice the dramatic change in blood flow when this adolescent girl imagines the stressful situation. This arousal response facilitated my understanding and treatment of this adolescent's school problems.

Figure 5-2(d) and (e) were taken from a victim of migraine headaches. The two records show two distinctly different responses taken from the same individual. This person is a professional woman who conducts seminars for managers and executives in a large business. The first record [Figure 5-2(d)] was taken during a period of extreme stress. She was conducting seminars to a group of business executives over a period of several days. During this time she was extremely tense, and her hands and feet were extremely cold. In normal room temperature, excessively cold extremities indicate a constriction of the blood vessels in that part of the body. The reduction in blood flow produces a lowering of body temperature in the hands and feet.

The second record [Figure 5-2(e)] was taken after she completed her work with the executives. She was experiencing an intense migraine headache. Her hands and feet were hot, and finger pulse volume was quite large. The abrupt change from a state of reduced blood flow to a period of enhanced flow to the periphery of the body was related to the onset of her migraine. One component of the treatment in this case was oriented towards teaching her to relax during periods of stress in order to prevent the abrupt changes in blood flow. Further use of these recordings are evident in Chapter 6.

THE PRECEDING DISCUSSION SHOWS THAT HUMANS EMIT A fight-flight response somewhat comparable to the one that arouses an animal's behavior. The Human Response System prepares for emergencies in a way that is similar to the more primitive animal system. The hypothalamus commands the nervous and endocrine systems to charge up the engine for action. When the emergency is over, the first sergeant senses the end of the struggle and withdraws the troops. Internal organs cannot remain charged up for long periods of time without suffering undesirable consequences: tissue damage and deterioration. A segment of the physiological component of the Human Response System is devoted to lowering the high level of arousal precipitated by emergency situations. It's a nice balance of effects: the nervous system is aroused during the appropriate times and relaxes when arousal is no longer necessary. All of this activity is devoted to prolonging the life of the organism.

THE GENERAL STRESS RESPONSE: THE ALARM AND RESISTANCE REACTIONS

When exposure to stress is extreme and long-lasting, the normal ways of maintaining equilibrium may not be adequate. In this situation the response system triggers a wide-ranging set of bodily changes. Selye[6] referred to this stress response as the "General Adaptation Syndrome." It has been labeled by other investigators as the "General Stress Syndrome."[29] This syndrome disrupts homeostasis and creates changes in the internal enviornment that include the fight−flight response (the Alarm Reaction) and the Resistance Reaction, the second stage of the General Stress Syndrome.

The General Stress Syndrome is initiated quite reflexively in animals by the watchdog of the nervous system—the hypothalamus. In humans the syndrome is initiated by the cerebral cortex through its intimate connection with the hypothalamus. The specific role of the cerebral cortex in stress responses is discussed in Chapter 7. At this point it is sufficient to say that the cortex determines which environmental event is interpreted as a stressor and which is not.

In response to the stressor the hypothalamus initiates the General Stress Syndrome through two pathways, the autonomic nervous system and the endocrine system. Each system is activated at different stages of the stress syndrome. The sympathetic nervous system and the adrenal medulla (the gland that secretes adrenalin) produces the immediate fight−flight response or the "alarm reaction." The endocrine system, particularly the anterior pituitary gland and the adrenal cortex, initiate the second pathway—the "resistance reaction." The resistance reaction is slower to start than the alarm reaction, but its effects are longer lasting.

Alarm Reaction

This response is the first reaction of the body to any stressor. It is the "fight-or-flight" response discussed earlier in this chapter. The response mobilizes the body's resources for immediate physical activity by bringing large amounts of glucose and oxygen to the organs that are most active in warding off danger. This includes the heart, which supplies vital organs with nutrients through the circulation of blood through the response system; the brain, which must remain active and alert to continue to survey the environment; and the skeletal muscles, which must prepare to fight or flee from the danger.

Resistance Reaction

The resistance reaction is the long-term, second stage of the General Stress Syndrome, which involves the hypothalamus and the endocrine system. Figure 5-3 shows the relationship between the cortex, hypothalamus, and the endocrine system. The hypothalamus stimulates the pituitary gland, which in turn stimulates the adrenal cortex to release its hormones. The hormones of the adrenal cortex aid in conserving minerals and fluids in the body during its battle with dangerous elements in the environment. One effect of this conservation is an elevation in blood pressure.

Another series of stress reactions that are stimulated by secretions from the adrenal cortex include: the provision of a steady supply of glucose during stress, elevations in blood pressure in order to provide blood (and its nutrients) to organs that continue struggling with the enemy, and the reduction of tissue inflammation that may disrupt other vital functions from taking place. In general, the resistance stage of the General Stress Syndrome allows the body to continue fighting a stressor long after the effects of the alarm reaction have extinguished. Figure 5-4 outlines the two separate stages of the General Stress Response and their specific physiological activities.

The resistance stage of the General Stress Syndrome continues to respond to the stressful event until it is no longer a threat or danger to the response system. The system then returns to normal. If this restoration of homeostasis is not possible the resistance stage continues to function. This long-term activation of the resistance stage can lead to very serious consequences for the response system. The following discussion focuses on a small sample of these problems.

HYPERTENSION, CORONARY ARTERY DISEASE, AND SUDDEN DEATH: POTENTIAL CONSEQUENCES OF A CHRONIC STRESS REACTION

The disruption of homeostasis often takes a dramatic toll on the human organism. People who live under constant stress may experience a chronic stress reaction. Remember that the resistance stage of the Gen-

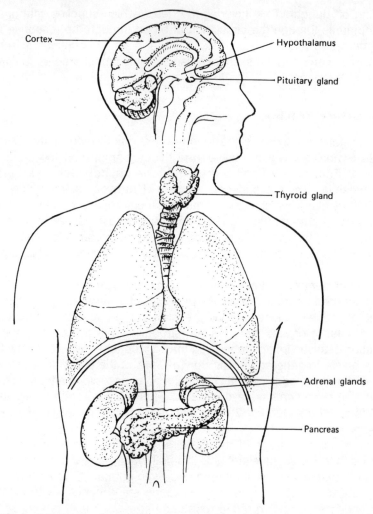

Figure 5-3. Cortex, hypothalamus, and some of the major structures of the endocrine system.

eral Stress Syndrome allows the body to continue fighting a stressor long after the effects of the alarm reaction have expired. During this stage, activities of the physiological component of the response system increase in rate and intensity in order to provide energy for a long-lasting struggle with stressful life events. Three of the numerous potential consequences of this struggle occur within the cardiovascular system—hypertension, coronary artery disease, and, in extreme cases, sudden death.

Hypothalamus

Alarm Reaction	Resistance Reaction
Increases in autonomic nervous system activity including:	Increases in endocrine system activities including:
Heart rate	Discharge of pituitary hormones
Blood to brain and skeletal muscles (decrease blood flow to periphery)	Discharge of hormones of the adrenal cortex
Glucose or blood sugar to vital organs	Blood pressure
Adrenalin	Antiinflamatory responses
	Glucose

Figure 5-4. General stress response.

Hypertension

Hypertension or chronic high blood pressure is one example of an acceleration in physiological activity that has long-term dangerous consequences to the Human Response System. It has been estimated that 15–33 percent of the adult population suffers from varying degrees of hypertension. Statistics indicate that diseases resulting from this problem account for an average of two deaths every minute in the United States. Many leading investigators in the area are convinced that the problem of hypertension stems directly from the stresses of living in a complex and demanding environment.

Dr. Herbert Benson, Director of the Hypertension Section of Boston's Beth Israel Hospital, has conducted an extensive research project on the effects of stress on high blood pressure. Benson believes that environmental stress must be added to the three traditional explanations for hypertension: inappropriate diet, lack of exercise, and family disposition.

Although the relative impact of each factor is still unknown, there is general agreement among investigators about the dangerous consequences of hypertension on the response system. Benson discusses these dangers:

High blood pressure, or hypertension, is very dangerous because it increases the rate of development of what is technically called atherosclerosis, commonly known as hardening of the arteries. The popular name is well chosen. Atherosclerosis is the deposition of blood clots, fats, and calcium within the walls of the arteries, causing the normally soft, elastic, open arteries to become hard, inelastic, and partly or completely blocked.

. . . The risk of developing atherosclerosis or hardening of the arteries is directly related to the level of blood pressure. When you have a higher blood pressure, the risk simply increases. The higher your blood pressure, the greater the risk.

If the arteries to the heart, or coronary arteries, are obstructed, then you experience death of heart cells and what is called a heart attack or a coronary or an infarction.

Strokes may occur in much the same way. If the arteries to the brain become obstructed, there is death of brain tissue because the brain tissue is cut off from sufficient oxygen and other nutrients to continue its normal metabolism and function. Atherosclerosis, by building up in the arteries and ultimately blocking them, thus leads to the major causes of death, heart disease and stroke. [7, pp. 29, 34, 38, and 40. Copyright © 1975 by William Morrow and Company Inc. By permission of the publishers.]

According to Benson, high blood pressure causes other problems that can ultimately lead to heart disease, strokes, and kidney disease. For example, high blood pressure can cause hypertensive heart disease because the heart muscle increases in size when it is forced to pump harder. It then requires more blood and nutrients to meet its larger requirements. When it fails to obtain these essentials, the heart becomes progressively weaker.

Benson believes that the elevated blood pressure and the accompanying problems occur because of the excessive elicitation of the fight–flight response.

By what mechanisms do these situations requiring behavioral adjustment lead to high blood pressure? Man instinctively reacts to such situations by unconsciously activating the fight-or-flight response.

We believe the more often the fight-or-flight response is activated, the more likely it is that you will develop high blood pressure, especially if circumstances do not allow you to actually give battle or flee.[7, pp. 66–67. Copyright © 1975 by William Morrow and Company Inc. By permission of the publishers.]

The chronic arousal of the fight-flight response and its consequence, hypertension, is not strictly a physiological phenomenon. Benson believes that the understanding and effective treatment of hypertension will ultimately be accomplished through the combined efforts of several disciplines including medicine and psychology. Along with many contemporary practicioners, he feels optimistic about a rapidly spreading field of research called "Psychosomatic Medicine." This is the study and treatment of diseases caused or influenced by psychological events. Benson's research on the "Relaxation Response," an effective treatment technique for borderline cases of high blood pressure, is an outgrowth of this psychosomatic orientation. The relaxation response is discussed in detail in Chapter 6.

Type A Behavior Pattern and Coronary Artery Disease

Hypertension is only one consequence of a chronic disruption of homeostasis. Cardiologists Friedman and Rosenman, mentioned earlier in reference to the Type A Behavior Pattern, have pinpointed another potential danger for the cardiovascular system as a result of a long-term stress reaction. The danger results from the system's exposure to an excess discharge of various hormones during the stress response. The Type A individual, according to the two cardiologists, is engaged in a chronic, more-or-less continuous, minute-by-minute struggle with the environment. They discuss the specific consequences of this coping style on the heart's coronary arteries:

> It was no surprise to us to find that most Type A subjects not only discharge more norepinephrine and epinephrine (the nerve hormones or catecholamines), but also "overdrive" their pituitary glands to secrete too much ACTH (a hormone that stimulates the adrenal glands to discharge cortisol and other hormones) and growth hormone. Further most Type A subjects exhibit an excess of the pancreatic hormone insulin in their blood—a sign generally believed to indicate that something is seriously wrong with the disposition of fat and sugar in the body. As a result of these abnormal discharges of catecholamines from the nerve endings and hormones from the pituitary, adrenal, and pancreatic glands, most Type A subjects exhibit 1) an increased blood level of cholesterol and fat, 2) a marked lag in ridding their blood of the cholesterol added to it by the food ingested, 3) a prediabetic state, and 4) an increased tendency for the clotting elements of the blood (the platelets and fibrinogen) to precipitate out. In a sense, Type A subjects too often are exposing their arteries to "high voltage" chemicals even during the "low voltage" periods of their daily living. [8, p. 202. Copyright © Alfred A. Knopf, Inc. By permission.]

When forced to pinpoint the most serious factor in determining the breakdown in functioning of the coronary arteries, Friedman and Rosenman state:

> But if we were forced now to choose . . . the worst chemical insult, the guess is that it is the chronic excess discharge and circulation of the catecholamines. This may be the chief factor in the total process of arterial decay and thrombosis. We have seen coronary heart disease erupt in many subjects whose blood insulin level and metabolism of cholesterol, fat, and sugar were

quite normal. But rarely have we ever witnessed the onset of this disease in a person whose rate of manufacture and secretion of catecholamines we did not know or suspect to have been increased. [8, pp. 205–206. Copyright © Alfred A. Knopf, Inc. By permission.]

Like Benson, Friedman and Rosenman focus on the vital connection between psychological and physiological events. It is the Type A individual's strategy of handling life events, particularly work-related activities, that precipitates a series of dangerous activities in the response system.

Sudden Death: The Complete Breakdown of Equilibrium in the Human Response System

The complete breakdown of the balance and equilibrium of the Human Response System leads to death. A long-term or intense stress reaction puts heavy demands on the physiological component of the response system, particularly on the heart and blood vessels. They may suddenly fail under the strain as evidenced by the phenomenon of "Sudden Death." Investigators such as Dr. George Engel have analyzed the life circumstances surrounding the death of a large number of individuals who died suddenly and unexpectedly. Four main categories of life events emerged. Engel elaborates on these activating events:

The most common (135 deaths) was an exceptionally traumatic disruption of a close human relationship or the anniversary of the loss of a loved one. The second category (103 deaths) involved situations of danger, struggle, or attack. Loss of status, self-esteem, or valued possessions, as well as disappointment, failure, defeat, or humiliation, accounted for the third group of deaths (21 in all). And the fourth category (16 deaths) consisted of people who died suddenly at moments of triumph, public recognition, reunion, or "happy ending." Fifty-seven deaths in the first category were immediately preceded by the collapse or death—often abrupt—of a loved one. Some survivors were reported to have cried out that they could not go on without the deceased. Many were in the midst of some frantic activity—attempting to revive the loved one, get help, or rush the person to the hospital—when they, too, collapsed and died.

One common denominator emerges from the medical literature and the 275 press reports on sudden death. For the most part, the victims are confronted with events which are impossible to ignore, either because of their abrupt, unexpected, or dramatic quality or because of their intensity, irreversibility, or persistence. The individual experiences or is threatened with overwhelming excitation.

Implicit, also, is the idea that he no longer has, or no longer believes that he has, mastery or control over the situation or himself, or fears that he may lose what control he has. [30, pp. 118 and 153–154]

Dr. Engel proceeds to explain this phenomenon from a psychosomatic standpoint, stating that the disruption of the critical balance between the two basic emergency systems of the body—sympathetic and parasympathetic components of the Autonomic Nervous System—during coping activities may provide the underlying explanation for sudden death.

> Each system is mediated by its own neural organizations. The two are usually finely balanced in a reciprocal relationship, but sometimes, when one system is overactivated, the other may be totally inhibited. Reciprocity may break down under extreme or conflicting stimulation—for example, whenever overriding psychological uncertainty exists.
>
> Many animal studies have shown that even minor uncertainty may be associated with momentary cessation of motor activity and cardiac deceleration. A frightened animal's physiological reaction may begin with arousal and anticipation, but enough psychic conflict and uncertainty may invoke the inhibitory conservation-withdrawal response as well. We postulate that rapid shifts from one response to the other may have serious consequences for maintenance of effective functioning of the heart and circulation.
>
> Laboratory animals die suddenly under psychological circumstances that are very similar to those that often accompany such deaths in humans. Further, the immediate cause of death is frequently derangement of cardiac rhythm—which considerable evidence suggests is the most frequent cause in humans. For humans and other animals, certain hormonal substances secreted in excess quantities during stress are known to predispose the heart to just such lethal arrhythmias. In the laboratory, animals can be saved from heart attacks with drugs that block nerve pathways to the heart and stabilize heart rhythm. [30, p. 154]

The phenomenon of sudden death is a dramatic example of the response system's loss of homeostatic balance. The system suffers from severe and abrupt exhaustion and collapse. The incidence of this severe reaction is still relatively small in the general population, although future investigators may refine their assessment tools and someday may include other deaths in this category.

THE STRESS RESPONSE: SUMMARY

Physiological reactions that are normal and necessary for survival can pose a threat to you when they occur too frequently and for chronically long periods of time. A variety of common life situations can precipitate these reactions, depending upon your appraisal of these events. Whereas animals and prehistoric humans responded primarily to life and death encounters, you are stuck with stress responses to interpersonal events that represent no comparable threat to physical survival.

The Human Response System seems to be easily aroused and emotionally upset by the daily encounters of life. In addition to the regular and large doses of anxiety and depression, the alarm and resistance reactions take their toll on the delicate balance of the internal environment. Ultimately, excessive pressure in the system begins to wear and tear on its own life-sustaining pump—the heart.

Yafa humorously summarizes man's modern plight and offers us some comic relief:

> The stress hormones begin to behave like friends who stay too long and wear out the furniture. These corticoids have a nasty habit of inhibiting cell regeneration, so that holes that normally heal themselves in the lining of the stomach and intestines are no longer readily repaired with new cell growth, and peptic or duodenal ulcers form. Excessive corticoids also throw women's menstrual cycles out of phase, disturb biorhythms, and cause insomnia, not to mention their encouraging attacks of colitis, asthma, diabetes, and migraine. Meanwhile, they combine with catecholamines, stimulated by aggressiveness, to raise the content of cholesterol and fat in our blood and congest our arteries. [23, p. 122]

Hypertension, coronary artery disease, and sudden death are dramatic examples of a disruption in homeostasis. They represent the end results of a long process of maladaptive physiological reactions to stressful life events. The fight–flight (alarm) reaction and resistance stage of the stress response are adaptive functions of the system that become maladaptive when they occur at a chronic level.

Are the stages of this destructive process amenable to analysis? Can you pinpoint these maladaptive responses in the early stages of their development? The following section focuses on this analysis for a common problem—muscle tension. Although muscle tension is not as debilitating and destructive as the problems discussed earlier, the analysis of its development can provide a model for understanding and pinpointing the critical stages involved in the disruption of homeostasis at a physiological level.

MUSCLE TENSION: A COMMON EXAMPLE OF A DISRUPTION IN HOMEOSTASIS

The electromyograph is an instrument which records the level of muscular activity from a group of muscles in a specific part of the response system. If electrodes from this instrument were placed directly on the frontalis muscle in the region of the forehead, the amount of muscular activity in this area of the body would be accurately measured. For example, contraction of the frontalis muscle occurs when you draw your scalp forward, raise your eyebrows, and wrinkle your forehead. The electromyograph is sensitive to this increase in muscular activity. An investigator can observe this change in muscular responding by recording the responses on a polygraph. This record of muscular activity is called an Electromyogram (EMG). Generally speaking, increases in muscular contractions produce an increase in the number and intensity of EMG responses that are observed within a given period of time.

Figure 5-5 shows several recordings from a client who suffered from severe tension headaches on a daily basis. This individual also periodically experienced migraine headaches. She was thirty-one years old at the time of treatment, divorced, and working in a high-pressured job. She had been experiencing extreme tension headaches since she was eighteen years of age. The frequency and intensity of the headaches had increased dramatically in the last year and a half. She used medication on a regular basis in order to alleviate the pain of these headaches. When she developed a migraine, she would simply take a strong dose of medication and sleep until the pain expired.

Figure 5-5(a) shows the EMG recordings from her forehead during a tension headache. At the same time that this recording was obtained, she was asked to rate her level of pain on the following scale: 0 to 9 represented mild pain, 10 to 15 represented moderate pain, and 16 to 25 was severe pain. The rating which coincided with this EMG record was 16. Figure 5-6 shows her ratings of headache pain at different times during the day for eleven days. Notice that her ratings varied from mild to severe levels.

Figure 5-5(b) shows the EMG recordings from the forehead region immediately after practicing a special relaxation technique (presented in the next chapter) during one of the treatment sessions. Her rating that coincided with this record was 6—mild headache pain. As you can see by comparing one record with the other, the headache pain varied directly with the amount of muscle activity taking place in the forehead region. Higher levels of muscular activity were associated with more intense headache pain. The low level of muscular activity produced by relaxation reduced the pain significantly.

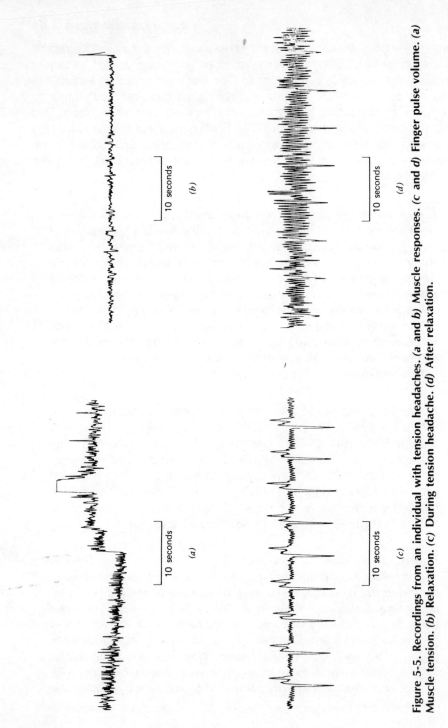

Figure 5-5. Recordings from an individual with tension headaches. (*a* and *b*) Muscle responses. (*c* and *d*) Finger pulse volume. (*a*) Muscle tension. (*b*) Relaxation. (*c*) During tension headache. (*d*) After relaxation.

86

Figures 5-5(c) and (d) show the measures of blood flow taken by the Photoelectric Pulse Pick-Up. Figure 5-5(c) was recorded during an extreme headache, whereas Figure 5-5(d) was recorded immediately after relaxation, when her headache pain was less intense. Notice the change in blood flow after relaxation. This individual reported that her hands were frequently cold but were always warmer after relaxation. This woman's headache activity was associated with a chronic level of muscular tension in the head region and perhaps even a reduction of blood flow to the extremities of the body. The complete details of this case are presented in Chapter 6 (The Case of Joy).

Muscle Activity and Feedback

Under normal circumstances the muscles of the body contract in response to specific messages sent to them by the brain. The brain initiates a series of contractions of the muscles in different parts of the body in order to carry out activities such as speech, facial gestures, and movement of the arms and legs. Hundreds and thousands of these messages are sent to various parts of the body throughout the day. Once the contraction of the muscle has taken place and the designated movement is completed, this information is fed back to the brain in order to terminate the contraction. The complete feedback cycle is carried out continously with very little conscious awareness and effort on the part of the individual.

One way of understanding muscular tension is to look at it as a breakdown in the feedback system between the brain and the muscles. Muscles are instructed by the brain to contract in order to carry out the functions of daily living—talking, walking, eating, and other complex activities. The muscles used for these activities are activated many times during an ordinary day. During stressful encounters, they are continuously activated. When the brain becomes inundated with excessive stimulation it may loose some of its ability to regulate human responses. The stage is set for a breakdown in communication.

The build-up of tension in these muscles may stem from the failure of the brain to complete the feedback cycle; that is, to deactivate the muscles once they are no longer in use. The brain fails to obtain the information: "This muscle no longer needs to be contracted." Without this knowledge of results of muscular activity, it cannot alter its own functioning.

Imagine the potential build-up of muscular contractions in the head region. These muscles are called on frequently during daily human interactions. Given an excessively stressful day involving thousands of facial expressions, gestures, and verbalizations, it seems quite feasible that a

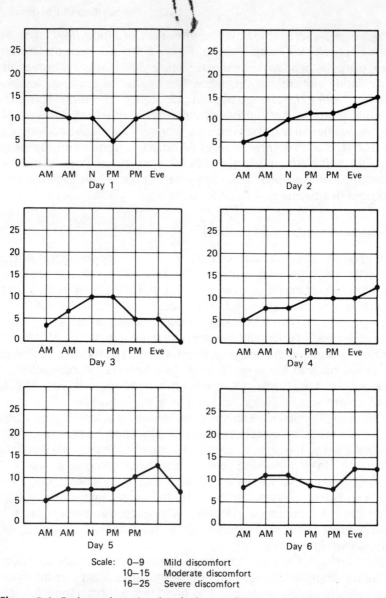

Scale: 0–9   Mild discomfort
       10–15 Moderate discomfort
       16–25 Severe discomfort

Figure 5-6. Ratings of tension headaches at different times during the day (morning, noon, afternoon and evening).

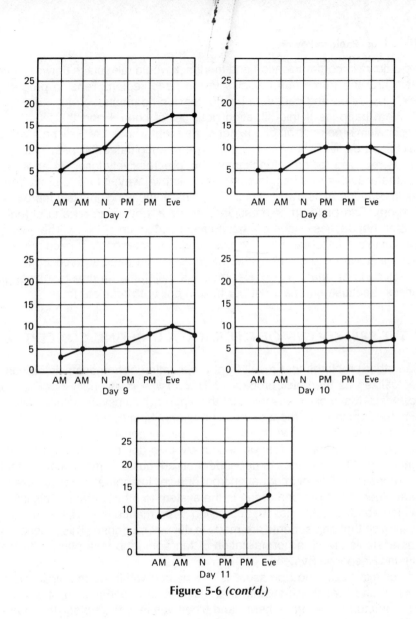

Figure 5-6 *(cont'd.)*

breakdown in communication and feedback would take place between the brain and the numerous muscles in the head region. Tension progressively builds up and causes a painful tension headache.

What happens if this situation gets out of control and the feedback mechanism breaks down altogether? The client whose EMG records were discussed earlier is a case in point. The brain initiates the muscular activities required for daily functioning, but progressively loses its ability to call the activities to a halt. In some yet unknown way, it fails to profit from the knowledge of its own actions. Technically speaking, this is a feedback problem. The build-up of muscular activity is not reversed and chronic tension headaches become a habitual consequence of living. The young woman in this case experienced one headache after another because she lost the ability to profit from the information that she received from the muscles in her head region. Her muscles maintained a constant level of tension because she had lost her built-in ability to regulate them.

THE BREAKDOWN OF FEEDBACK: A UNIFYING CONCEPT

Can other problems that result from a disruption of homeostasis be conceptualized as feedback problems? The answer is still hotly pursued by scientists. Many clinicians feel that this approach to psychosomatic disorders helps in the treatment of these problems. Many psychosomatic problems involve a breakdown in the ability of the response system to maintain the steady equilibrium that is necessary in order to maintain adaptive functioning. This balance is dependent on adequate communication: that is, a consistent flow of information from one cell to another, from one tissue to another, and from one organ in the system to other organs. This information about cellular, tissue, and organ performance is fed back into the system so that adjustments are made in deviant response. This process of homeostasis allows a normalization of functioning to take place with the Human Response System.

For example, blood pressure is maintained within normal limits by a sophisticated feedback system that includes the coordination of several vital structures: the brain, heart, and blood vessels. Physiologists Tortora and Anagnostakos, in their book *Principles of Anatomy and Physiology,* discuss feedback in the maintenance of normal blood pressure:

> Blood pressure is the force exerted by blood against the walls of the blood vessels, especially the arteries. It is determined primarily by three factors: the rate and strength of the heartbeat, the amount of blood, and the resistance offered by the arteries as blood passes through them. The resistance of the arteries results from the chemical properties of the blood and the size of the arteries at any given time.

If some stress, either internal or external, causes the heartbeat to speed up, the following sequence occurs: As the heart pumps faster, it pushes more blood into the arteries per minute—a situation that raises pressure in the arteries. The higher pressure is detected by pressure-sensitive cells in the walls of certain arteries, which send nerve impulses to the brain. The brain interprets the message and sends impulses to the heart to slow the heart rate.

. . . You will see that a second feedback control is also involved in maintaining a normal blood pressure. Small arteries, called arterioles, have muscular walls that normally "squeeze" the hollow tubes which the blood flows through. When the blood pressure increases, sensors in the arterioles send messages to the brain, and the brain signals the muscular walls to relax so that the diameter of the small tubes increases. As a consequence, the blood flowing through the arterioles is offered less resistance, and blood pressure drops back to normal. In sum, then, a suddenly increased blood pressure is brought back to normal by mechanisms that slow the heartbeat and widen the diameter of the arterioles. Conversely, a fall in blood pressure would be counteracted by increased heart activity and a decrease in the diameter of the arterioles. The net result, in either case, is a change in blood pressure back to normal. [29, pp. 11−12]

IN THE CASE OF BLOOD PRESSURE, IT IS OBVIOUS THAT THE SYStem must coordinate a tremendous amount of information in a short period of time. There are numerous points in the information exchange where messages can potentially fail to reach their destination. If they reach their point of exchange the messages may not be received by the critical organ—the brain.

One of the foremost experts in the field of hypertension, Herbert Benson, puts forth a theory about the possible cause of high blood pressure:

When a single situation requiring behavioral adjustments occurs again and again, the fight-or-flight response is repeatedly activated. Ultimately, this repetition may lead to higher blood pressure on a permanent basis. It is our underlying theory that this is what happens in man in the development of permanent hypertension. The chronic arousal of the fight−flight response goes from the just transient elevation in blood pressure to permanent high blood pressure. [7, p. 70. Copyright © 1975 by William Morrow and Company Inc. By permission of the publishers.]

How does chronic arousal produce a state of hypertension? One possible answer originates from a feedback explanation of maladaptive responses. The deviant response is repeated under so many different circumstances that the brain fails to regulate its functioning. Signals are sent out to decrease blood pressure, but the results of these actions are no longer perceived.

The hypertensive response becomes a habitual response similar to other maladaptive habits. For example, a cigarette smoker engages in a chain of responses that become highly automatic. The system adapts to highly painful events—burning sensations, respiratory irritation, and the noxious effects of nicotine—because of the constant habitual repetition of the smoking response. In a sense the brain nods off on the job of perceiving the physically aversive effects of smoking. This feedback has no effect on the smoker's behavior.

High blood pressure and other psychosomatic problems may stem from similar deficits of feedback. The brain, as the primary sensor of ongoing physiological activity, loses awareness of the activity of its own response system. After repeated exposure to the fight-or-flight messages from the cardiovascular system, the brain fails to discriminate this situation (hypertension) from a normal state of affairs. It loses the ability to profit from this information and neglects to send messages that counteract the disruption in cardiovascular balance. A new baseline of responding is established, and high blood pressure becomes an acceptable deviancy in a system that has lost the ability to regulate itself for homeostatic purposes.

The human situation may seem alarming and somewhat grim in view of the information presented in this chapter. In reality, the opposite is true and there is room for optimism. In addition to providing us with the grim realities of the human system, researchers such as Benson, Friedman, Rosenman, and Engel have provided a reservoir of knowledge for the effective modification of the system and its vulnerabilities. In fact, a major portion of their respective books are devoted to scientifically derived, effective therapeutic techniques. Chapter 6 focuses on these techniques and their effect on the self-regulation of the physiological component of the response system. Also, the feedback model presented here and additional techniques derived from this model are utilized throughout the book to assist a nodding-off brain in coming back to its senses.

6 SELF-REGULATION

Physiology

THE CASE OF JOY

Joy was the type of person who took life very seriously. She would thrust herself totally into work, recreational, and social activities. Joy was well liked and respected by her friends and associates and was particularly effective at her work. In spite of this success Joy tended to avoid these situations. She preferred to spend time reading, listening to music, and watching television. Joy was characterized by her work associates and friends as a loner.

Joy suffered from extreme headaches. They occurred during periods in her life when she regularly held a job or had an active social life. Joy was an attractive, intelligent, and witty individual who easily developed friendships. Yet the onset of a period of painful headaches predictably occurred when she forced herself to become interpersonally active. As a consequence Joy would fluctuate between periods of extreme productivity and solitude.

When I first met Joy I was struck by the intense look on her face. She reached out to shake my hand in a very aggressive, rigid manner. I noticed a clammy coldness as her hand touched mine and was aware of the quickness with which she withdrew it once the greeting was over. Joy's eyes were large and piercing. She stretched them open to their fullest width when she began speaking. Each word she spoke was emphasized and punctuated in a firm manner. Her facial muscles vigorously moved in unison to express a thought. Her forehead remained wrinkled throughout our conversation. I remember wondering whether it would ever smooth out to its normal state.

When our visit was over and she left my office, I felt exhausted and drained. Every word she spoke demanded an enormous amount of energy. I realized after several encounters with Joy that this was her normal way of relating. She was always on and very intense. She seldom let up from her rigid emotional and physical posture.

I asked Joy about the onset and frequency of her headaches. According to Joy, they would begin at any point during the day when she made her first contact with people. The first daily encounter would precipitate feelings of tightness at the back of her neck and head. After a busy morning at work and several conversations later, her head would be extremely tense. By lunchtime she was drained of energy. At the end of an active day Joy would be experiencing a severe headache. This sequence of events took place each day of the week. Under these circumstances it was easy to see why Joy had developed an unusual life style, one that fluctuated abruptly from periods of intense activity to complete withdrawal.

People easily aroused Joy's anxiety. She sought the approval of significant people in her life and wanted desperately for them to think she was intelligent, friendly, and attractive. Each interpersonal encounter was a challenge to Joy. Every event in her life was an activating experience. She literally charged herself up for each social interaction and activated the entire musculature of her body in meeting the demands of the day's activities. Every event involved talking, smiling, and other responses that automatically involve numerous muscles in the head, neck and facial region. These muscles ordinarily relax after the social responses are completed. With Joy they remained in a state of contraction for long periods of time during the day and well into the evening.

Joy was aware that she exerted an immense amount of energy in social interactions. She was somewhat less knowledgeable about the relationship between these responses and the onset of her muscle tension headaches. It was critically important for her to make this connection between her style of coping with people and the onset of excessive muscular activity. One alternative strategy for preventing the onset of a severe headache was to develop an awareness of the tension very early in its development. The muscles could be more easily relaxed at this time.

Once the pain was intense it would be difficult to regulate and control the headache.

Joy is the woman with tension headaches whose EMG recordings and headache ratings are discussed in Chapter 5. The recordings were taken at various points in her treatment. A major component of the treatment process was the use of muscular relaxation training. Joy learned how to relax. She practiced this response daily in the privacy of her home. It was important for her to learn to use this response during interpersonal encounters: to initiate social contact without the vigorous contraction of the major muscle groups in her body, particularly the ones in her face, forehead, and the back of the head. She accomplished this objective by learning to repeat the relaxation instructions to herself while she was interacting with other people. This private, relaxing self-dialogue facilitated Joy's control of the muscle tension headaches.

Relaxation training became the core of a treatment program that also involved the monitoring of the intensity of each headache. Joy learned to identify the signals that occurred at the beginning stages of tension. She would practice relaxing whenever the slightest feelings of tightness occurred in the region of her head. In this way she could prevent the build-up of excessive muscular contractions and, subsequently, the onset of a severe headache. As soon as a conversation started and she felt the tension creeping into her head, she would silently relax her forehead, eyes, mouth, and entire facial region. Soon her headaches became less and less frequent, and the intensity of each one diminished. The ratings in Figure 6-1 indicate the reduction in her tension headaches over a period of ten days as a result of this early detection of tension and the relaxation training.

Relaxation training was not a panacea for Joy. She continued to exhibit problems in her work and social life related to her excessive strivings for approval from friends and associates. However, the reduction in the frequency of tension headaches allowed her to remain interpersonally active for longer periods of time. Her tendency to withdraw into the solitude of her own dwelling was significantly decreased. The reduction in headaches and subsequent increase in interpersonal encounters allowed us to work further on her general strategy of living.

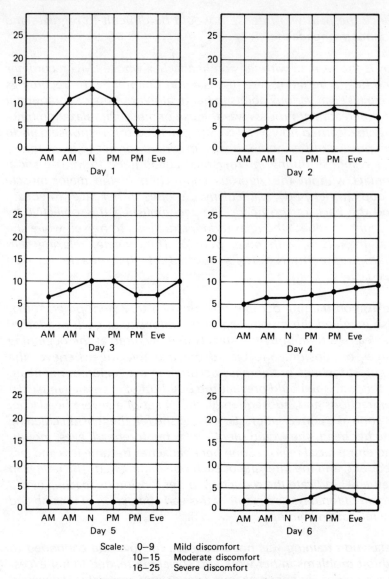

Scale: 0–9   Mild discomfort
         10–15   Moderate discomfort
         16–25   Severe discomfort

Figure 6-1. Ratings of tension headaches.

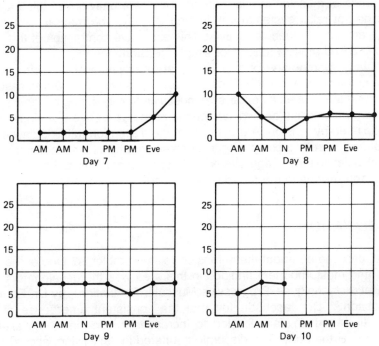

Figure 6-1 *(cont'd.)*

MUSCLE TENSION

Most of us use the word tension to cover a variety of uncomfortable feelings such as anxiety, stress, and irritability. Although these emotional states are related to and sometimes precipitated by tension, the term usually refers specifically to muscular tension. This state involves the excessive contraction of various muscles in the body leading to psychophysical discomfort and a general feeling of tightness.

We use our muscles throughout the day to walk, make gestures, and talk. This is a very natural use of muscular activity to help us function and to communicate to other people. In the course of using these muscles we tend to muscularly overreact in situations where excessive muscular activity is unnecessary. For example, talking to other people should involve only those muscles of the face and throat that are necessary for speech. Yet if you observe yourself talking you are often wrinkling your forehead, tightening the muscles at the back of your neck, and clenching your fists. During a particularly busy or stressful day you may contract and use hundreds of muscles in this manner. If you are unaware of this process and do not relax systematically during the day, you may accumulate a large amount of muscular activity. This excessive contraction of the muscles is called muscle tension or simply "tension."

A large percentage of headaches are precipitated by tension in the area of the head and neck. These are tension headaches. Some cases of insomnia are caused by excessive muscular activity during bedtime. More subtle problems like general nervousness and excessive worrying can be precipitated by tension. A great deal of the discomfort in life is caused by emotional upset—anxiety, anger, depression, and other emotions. Emotional upset, in turn, is aggravated by tension. In part, this tension accumulates and resides in the muscles of the body.

RELAXATION

What can one do about these tension-related problems? One of the earliest and most important findings in this area was the development of a relaxation technique—Progressive Muscular Relaxation—by Dr. Edmond Jacobson.[31] Dr. Jacobson felt that the consistent emergence of the arousal pattern in daily life led to increases in tension in the skeletal muscles of the body. The discomfort suffered in daily living, according to Jacobson, was partly a function of excessive muscular tension.

The body is perfectly capable of producing a state of relaxation. There is built within the body's nervous system a network of responses that can elevate and lower the body's level of physiological arousal the way a starter in a car arouses the engine and then, in turn, shuts it off. The problem in contemporary society is that we remain aroused most of our waking hours and fail to elicit our natural, biological capacity to relax. Jacobson's muscular relaxation technique elicits this relaxation response.

The technique works by vigorously tensing a muscle for a short period of time and then slowly letting the tension go. Through this method a muscle that is tense is allowed to return to its previously normal, relaxed state. This process is repeated for all of the major muscle groups of the body from the toes to the large muscles in the trunk of the body and then to the head region. By contracting and relaxing the muscles in this way the body's regularly high level of physiological arousal is reduced to a low and relaxed state. A modified version of Jacobson's technique has been used by a variety of investigators to help alleviate problems such as tension and migraine headaches, insomnia, and other problems that are precipitated by excessive muscular tension.

In order to illustrate the technique and the principle behind it you can practice this simple exercise. Sit upright in your chair, place your arms on the sides of the chair and make a fist with your right hand. Tense your right hand vigorously by clenching your fist very tightly. Concentrate on the tension and the feelings coming from your fist and forearm. Notice the pain beginning to set in as your muscles contract tighter and tighter.

Hold that state of tension for ten seconds. Now let that tension go slowly and concentrate on the feeling in your fist and forearm once again. Notice that the feelings change from tightness and pain to a tingling sensation and relaxation. Compare these feelings with ones coming from your left arm that has not been contracted and relaxed. Your left forearm and hand do not feel the same as your right forearm and right hand. It feels less heavy and relaxed.

This is an important discrimination for you to make. You can learn to tell the difference between a relaxed muscle and a tense one. A relaxed muscle feels somewhat heavier and more flexible than a tense one. A tense muscle is tight and more rigid than a relaxed one. This discrimination will be useful to you when you learn the complete relaxation technique. You will be able to tell when each part of your body is tense and relaxed. This discrimination is the first step in learning to cope with tension.

The Muscular Relaxation Response

I developed the Muscular Relaxation Response after years of teaching individuals how to relax through a variety of other techniques. I urged these people to practice relaxing, but often found that they would simply not take the time to do it. The prospect of having to relax for one hour or more was punishing. By reducing the time required to relax to fifteen minutes I dramatically increased the regular use of the relaxation technique. I added five minutes of concentration exercises at the end of the muscular component of the technique in order to enhance the deep state of relaxation produced by the muscle contractions. Deep breathing and concentration have been used effectively by another investigator (discussed below) to produce the relaxation response. The Muscular Relaxation Response combines the muscular response characteristic of progressive muscular relaxation with deep breathing and concentration exercises and takes 20 minutes to complete.

There are several steps involved in learning the Muscular Relaxation Response:

- First get in a comfortable sitting position. Lying down is not a good idea because it tends to put you to sleep. An important distinction is usually made here between relaxation and sleep. One can fall asleep and still be extremely tense. You can awaken in the morning and sometimes be as tense as you were before the night's sleep. So you are to relax, not sleep.

• Second, you will be instructed to focus on one particular part of the body—the toes, for example. The toes are tensed tightly and the tension is held for 5−10 seconds. This vigorously contracts the muscles in the body part that you are focusing on. The tension is then slowly released and the muscles in the toes are relaxed. You are asked to focus on the change in sensations that occur from contraction to relaxation. There is a distinct change that takes place—usually a heavy, tingly sensation that marks the beginning of a deep state of relaxation.

• Third, you will complete the contraction and relaxation of the one body part before progressing to another part of the body. A slight pause for rest between body parts is suggested. Each major muscle group is progressively relaxed in this fashion, starting with the toes through the calves and thighs, up to the stomach, chest, shoulders and arms, and finally through the neck, face, and head regions.

• The fourth step is to coordinate a breathing technique with the contraction and relaxation of the muscles. You close your eyes, contract the muscles for 5−10 seconds, take a deep breath, and relax the muscle, all in a smooth, coordinated manner. The word "relax" is repeated covertly, to yourself, when the breath is expired. The breathing and repetition of the word "relax" is done with each contraction and relaxation of all muscle groups.

• During the final stage of the technique, the word "relax" is repeated rhythmically as you focus on each body part that was muscularly relaxed in steps one through four.

In summary, you are taught to (1) tense a muscle for 5−10 seconds, (2) take a deep breath, (3) let go of the tension, (4) let the breath out and say "relax" to yourself, and (5) repeat the word "relax" to yourself as you focus on each body part.

Before going on to the next section you can complete the instructions for the relaxation technique in Appendix II.

APPLICATIONS OF RELAXATION: GENERAL USE AND HIGH BLOOD PRESSURE

Chapter 8 focuses on the use of relaxation as an adjunct to the self-regulation of thinking responses. Relaxation training facilitates the clear straight thinking that is necessary for counteracting the disordered thoughts that make up the foundation of many irrational fears, ideas, and attitudes. Along with the technology specifically oriented towards counteracting disordered thoughts, relaxation sets the stage for many other positive human responses to take place.

The remainder of this discussion focuses on the specific applications of relaxation training when it is used independently of other self-regulation techniques. The first and perhaps the most frequent use of relaxation is to counteract the tendency of the response system to become easily aroused and to remain in that state for long periods of time. In a general way, relaxation can be used to counteract the consequences of this chronic arousal response. These unpleasant effects of arousal include general tension, tension headaches, some cases of insomnia, excessive worrying, irritability, and other tension related problems.

The second and third applications of relaxation focus on two more specific problems: hypertension and seizures. In the case of hypertension Dr. Herbert Benson's research on the use of relaxation with victims of high blood pressure will be reviewed. The use of relaxation in counteracting seizure activity in the case of Paul follows the discussion of Benson's work. This provides you with a sample of the variety of uses of the naturally occurring response state called relaxation. There are many other applications of this response, and research is currently being conducted to discover additional ones.

The final discussion in this chapter deals with the effect of relaxation on the homeostatic or balancing mechanisms of the response system and attempts to show the intimate relationship between relaxation and feedback. You will be left with the notion that relaxation is very basic to functioning of the human response system.

Given our modern style of living with its tendency to generate chronic levels of arousal, it is important to learn to elicit this relaxation response on a regular basis. Like many other skills, a training effect takes place. The more you practice it, the better results you obtain. Highly trained individuals can elicit the response very quickly and use it almost reflexively in a variety of difficult daily encounters.

The General Use of Relaxation

One of the simplest uses of relaxation training is perhaps the most valuable of its numerous applications. That is its use as a means of calming a response system that is easily aroused during daily coping activities. This arousal tends to accumulate during the span of a day. Anxiety and tension are experienced at various points in the day, depending on this cumulative effect. Relaxation training can be used to counteract this effect and thereby prevent the unpleasant feelings associated with high levels of arousal.

The increases in respiration rate, heart rate, and muscular tension associated with a hectic schedule at work, during social engagements, or at home can be counteracted. They can be replaced by slower and more regular respiration, decreased heart rate, and muscular tension by eliciting the relaxation response. Relaxation training is simple and executed in a short period of time. Taking a relaxation break is feasible even within the busiest of schedules. Fifteen minutes in the morning after an action-packed board meeting can relax a response system that is beginning to rapidly pace itself into Type A behavior. The same amount of time spent after car pooling, community functions, and housework can prevent the irritable feelings that result from an accumulation of tension during the day.

I often tell my clients and the participants of my stress management seminars not to underestimate the value of this brief and simple training. If I was limited to a brief period of time to teach people how to cope with life more effectively, I would use the opportunity to teach them the relaxation response. A pleasant side effect of relaxation when practiced regularly each day is the ability to elicit the response without going through the entire training sequence. The system becomes conditioned to the point that relaxation can be elicited even during conversations and other activating events. Simply repeating the word "relax" to oneself activates a calming effect on the entire response system. This is a valuable tool for preventing the chronic arousal response which is commonplace in numerous life events.

Hypertension

Dr. Herbert Benson has studied the effects of relaxation on a problem that has traditionally been the private domain of the medical profession: hypertension or high blood pressure. Essential hypertension is high blood pressure that is not associated with a specific medical disease or problem. As stated in Chapter 5, Benson feels that hypertension and the arousal of the fight–flight response are closely related. He states that the excessive elicitation of the arousal pattern in daily living leads to an elevation in blood pressure which becomes chronic and dangerous. The focus of his research has been on the development of a relaxation technique—The Relaxation Response—that helps prevent excessive arousal from becoming chronic and leading to elevations in blood pressure levels. In addition, the Relaxation Response helps borderline hypertensive individuals to reduce their blood pressure. Dr. Benson explains the effects of the relaxation response on hypertension in the following manner:

> We have pointed out that the regular inappropriate activation of the fight-or-flight response may lead to such diseases as hypertension with its often

deadly consequences of heart attacks and strokes. We have also shown that a response opposite to the flight-or-flight response resides within all of us. Because the Relaxation Response counteracts the arousal of the fight-or-flight response, it is not unreasonable to expect that the regular evocation of the Relaxation Response might lead to lower blood pressure in patients *who already have high blood pressure.* We are aware, of course, that nondrug approaches to the treatment of high blood pressure, such as rest, are not original. But the Relaxation Response as such had not been previously used in therapy. To consider the Relaxation Response as an adjuctive therapeutic tool to those which already exist is a new concept. [7, p. 141, Copyright © 1975 by William Morrow and Company, Inc. By permission of the publishers.]

Benson's first experiments[7] were with individuals who produced the relaxation response through meditation. The initial results of his studies on meditators indicated a marked decrease in the body's oxygen consumption during meditation (see Figure 6-2). Metabolism is the utilization of

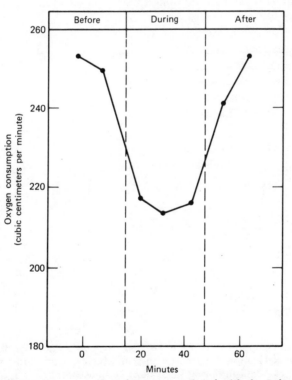

Figure 6-2. Oxygen-consumption changes associated with the Relaxation Response. Note the marked decrease in the rate of metabolism. (From H. Benson, *The Relaxation Response,* 1975, William Morrow, by permission.)

oxygen by the cells of the body in order to make use of the energy in food. The cells use the oxygen that is brought to it by the blood by slowly burning the nutrients. According to Benson's research, the major physiologic change associated with meditation is a decrease in the rate of metabolism, which he calls "hypometabolism." Meditation causes energy resources of the body to be taxed less than when the body is in a nonmeditative state.

Benson's later experiments showed that meditation was a restful state like sleep. However, the physiological changes associated with meditation and the relaxation response showed very little resemblance to sleep. As shown in Figure 6-3, there are marked differences in the decreased rate of oxygen consumption during sleep and relaxation. Sleep was characterized by a progressive decrease in oxygen consumption to a maximum of 8 percent lower than wakefulness. Relaxation showed a 10–20 percent decrease a few minutes after the initiation of the response.

Benson concluded from his experiments that there were no significant physiological differences between meditation and the relaxation response. Regarding this conclusion, he states:

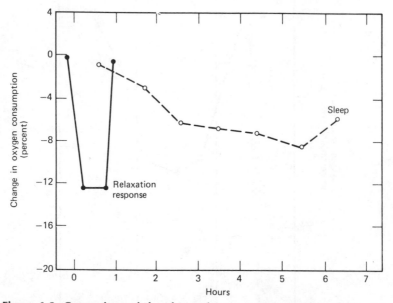

Figure 6-3. Comparison of the change in oxygen consumption that occurs during the Relaxation Response with that which occurs during sleep. The decreased metabolism during Relaxation Response continues as long as the response is being elicited. (From H. Benson, *The Relaxation Response*, 1975, William Morrow, by permission.)

As the experiments progressed over several years, the concept developed that various physiologic changes that accompanied Transcendental Meditation were part of an integrated response opposite to the fight-or-flight response and that they were in no way unique to Transcendental Meditation. Indeed, lowered oxygen consumption, heart rate, respiration and blood lactate are indicative of decreased activity of the sympathetic nervous system and represent a hypometabolic, or restful, state. [7, pp. 95–96. Copyright © 1975 by William Morrow and Company, Inc. By permission of the publishers.]

Regular Relaxation Breaks and Blood Pressure

Dr. Benson and a colleague, Ruanne K. Peters, recently completed a study that tested the effects of relaxation response breaks on blood pressure in a work setting.[32] This was a tightly controlled study comparing four groups of subjects which obtained different sets of relaxation instructions. Group A was taught the relaxation response. Group B was instructed to sit quietly and relax. Group C received no instructions concerning relaxation. Group D were subjects who did not volunteer for the study but later agreed to be tested before and after the study was completed. Groups A and B were asked to take two fifteen-minute relaxation breaks every day for eight weeks.

Significant decreases in blood pressure occurred only in Group A, the group that was taught the relaxation response. There was an average decrease of 12 millimeters of mercury (mm Hg) in systolic blood pressure (the pressure of the blood on the walls of the arteries when the heart muscle contracts). Diastolic blood pressure (the pressure of the blood on the walls of the arteries when the heart muscle relaxes) decreased 7.9 mm Hg in Group A. Benson summarized the benefits of this relaxation-induced reduction by stating:

Such a decrease is desirable even in an individual whose blood pressure falls within the normal range, for the risk of developing heart attacks and strokes (the cause of over 50% of the deaths in the United States today) is directly proportional to the level of blood pressure. As blood pressure goes down, the risk diminishes. [32, p. 123. Copyright © 1975 by William Morrow and Company Inc. By permission of the publishers.]

The self-management procedure of relaxation training provides an adjunct to the traditional medical treatment of the problem of hypertension. The use of medication in cases of high blood pressure facilitates the system's return to homeostasis from previously levels of high arousal. Relaxation apparently affects the system in a similar manner. Benson explains this mechanism in the following way:

> Standard medical therapy means taking antihypertensive drugs which often act by interrupting the activity of the sympathetic nervous system, thus lowering blood pressure. The pharmacologic method of lowering blood pressure is very effective and extremely important since, to again emphasize, lowered blood pressure leads to a lower risk of developing atherosclerosis and its related diseases such as heart attacks and strokes. The regular practice of the Relaxation Response is yet another way to lower blood pressure. Indications are that this response affects the same mechanism and lowers blood pressure by the same means as some antihypertensive drugs. Both counteract the activity of the sympathetic nervous system. It is unlikely that the regular elicitation of the Relaxation Response by itself will prove to be adequate therapy for severe or moderate high blood pressure. Probably it would act to enhance the lowering of blood pressure along with antihypertensive drugs, and thus lead to the use of fewer drugs or a lesser dosage. In the case of mild hypertension, the regular evocation of the Relaxation Response may be of great value, since it has none of the pharmacologic side effects often present with drugs and might possibly supplant their use. *But no matter how encouraging these initial results, no person should treat himself for high blood pressure by regularly eliciting the Relaxation Response. You should always do so under the care of your physician, who will routinely monitor your blood pressure to make sure it is adequately controlled.* [pp. 146–147. Copyright © 1975 by William Morrow and Company, Inc. By permission of the publisher.]

Benson's summary statement and warning are well taken. Relaxation has not replaced traditional medical treatment for high blood pressure, but can be used as an adjunct to this treatment. The technique is often used in conjunction with medication.

Benson's relaxation technique is very simple and the instructions are included in Appendix II. It differs from the Muscular Relaxation Response in terms of its strict use of concentration and the absence of the use of muscular contractions. Like meditation, the Relaxation Response elicits the state of relaxation through the subject's concentration on a word that is repeated to oneself in a rhymical fashion. The Muscular Relaxation Response, on the other hand, elicits the state of relaxation first through the use of isometric contractions and secondly through the rhymical breathing and repetition of the word relax.

The Muscular Relaxation Response is helpful to individuals who have difficulty concentrating during the early stages of training. The isometric contractions produce a preliminary level of relaxation that facilitates the ability to concentrate. You should try both techniques in order to arrive at the approach to relaxation training that suits you the best.

Seizures and Relaxation

Seizures are brought about by abnormal and irregular discharges of electricity by millions of neurons in the brain. These abnormal discharges can stimulate a variety of involuntary responses depending on the area of the brain which is stimulated. If the stimulation occurs over the portion of the brain that is responsible for muscle contraction, involuntary contraction of the skeletal muscles occurs and precipitates the following responses: muscular spasms passing up or down one side of the body, smacking of the lips, clapping of the hands, or movement of the hands and legs simultaneously in a dance-like motion. These are categorized as motor seizures because they effect the area of the brain that is primarily responsible for movement of muscles.

Grand mal seizures are produced by abnormal electrical discharges that spread throughout several parts of the brain. Since the motor areas and the areas of consciousness in the hypothalamus are involved in the discharge, the seizure-victim experiences spasms of the voluntary muscles and in addition, loses consciousness. If the discharge spreads further to intellectual areas and portions of the brain that control sensations, the individual sees flashing lights and experiences peculiar tastes. After several minutes of unconsciousness and uncontrollable motor activity the muscles relax. The individual then awakes somewhat confused and tired.

The electrical activity generated by the brain cells are called brain waves. These brain waves indicate the general activity of the cerebral cortex. A record of such waves obtained by attaching electrodes to the surface of the skull is an electroencephalogram or EEG. Distinct EEG patterns appear in certain abnormalities such as seizure disorders. Grand mal seizures are characterized by rapid brain waves when compared with the normal pre-seizure wave frequency. In contrast to the grand mal seizure, petit mal seizures show an abnormally slow brain wave pattern, loss of consciousness for 5−30 seconds, but no loss of muscular control. The victim merely seems to be out of contact for a short period of time.

The general disorder characterized by these various seizures is epilepsy. There are different types of epilepsy, which are diagnosed on the basis of the nature of the seizure activity observed. In many cases, the seizures are alleviated by drugs (e.g., Dilantin) that reduce the discharge of periodic bursts of electrical activity by making neurons more difficult to stimulate. Regarding the varied causes of epilepsy physiologists Tortora and Anagnostakos state that:

> Many conditions can cause nerve cells to produce periodic bursts of impulses. Head injuries, tumors and abcesses of the brain, and childhood infections such as mumps, whooping cough and measles, are some of the causes. [29, p. 275]

At this point in our study of the response system, several questions can be posed. Can the same set of deviant neurological responses occur in the absence of a discrete assault to the brain? Can an abnormal discharge of electricity in the neurons of the brain arise from a breakdown in the homeostatic mechanisms of the human response system that ordinarily maintain a balance in neurological functioning? Finally, can emotional stimuli precipitate seizures? The definite answers to these questions are still awaiting advances in scientific research. There is sufficient evidence to postulate that stress reactions can precipitate a breakdown in a variety of human responses including neurological functioning. This appears to be the most valid explanation for the problems incurred in the case of Paul.

Paul's most observable problem was the high frequency of seizures occurring throughout the day. In addition to the seizure activity it was apparent that he was extremely muscularly tense. Paul's posture changed during the early days of his illness. His body seemed to shrink with tension as he slumped his shoulders and stared at the ground. He became progressively more withdrawn from reality. The relaxed man who had confidently entertained thousands on television became tense, self-conscious, and shy.

The exact relationship between extreme tension, behavioral withdrawal, and the breakdown in neurological responding is not yet clear. One component of the problem may have been the chronic elicitation of the fight–flight response, as explained by Benson in the case of hypertension. The abundance of nervous system reactions under constant fight–flight arousal interfered with the smooth functioning of activity in the neurons of the brain, thereby precipitating periodic abnormal bursts of electricity. Equilibrium was disrupted. The abnormal response then became habitual and was repeated when stimulus conditions elicited the chronic stress reaction.

Regardless of the specific changes that took place in the nervous system, one factor that contributed significantly to the restoration of homeostasis was Paul's relaxation training. The initiation of training in relaxation had an immediate and profound effect on his memory for past and current events and his state of mental confusion. Perhaps the most profound effect of this training was the dramatic drop in the frequency and intensity of seizure activity. In some yet unknown manner the low level of physiological arousal and restoration of equilibrium provided by relaxation training reduced the tendency of cells in Paul's brain to emit abnormal bursts of electrical activity. This, in turn, facilitated a smooth flow of electrochemical responses from one neuron to another. As a consequence the seizures were reduced to a low level in only several months of treatment. Although the relaxation response was only one component of the treatment process, Paul gave it a major portion of the credit in his recovery. He often stated that he could anticipate the onset of a seizure, take a deep breath, tell himself to relax, and prevent its occurrence.

Seizures and Other Behavioral Treatment Approaches

When I was treating Paul in the winter and spring of 1970, the behavioral treatment of seizures was uncommon. The fact that he improved was even more unusual. Other interested professionals were quick to deny the findings and postulate other mechanisms to account for his improvement. Today, however, we can observe a variety of successful behavioral treatment approaches to seizure disorders.

Zlutnick, Mayvill, and Moffat[33] have developed a technique to reduce the frequency of minor motor seizures in children. The strategy involves interrupting the chain of responses that occur prior to the occurrence of the seizure. In certain children the seizure response is preceded by an overt motor response. The investigators showed that the seizures could be aborted by stopping the motor activity prior to the seizure. Also, reinforcing the children with tangible reinforcement (e.g., money or candy) for not having a seizure has also been effective.

Another successful behavioral procedure for controlling epileptic disorders has been developed by Sterman.[34] It is a biofeedback strategy that involves the feedback of brain wave activity to seizure victims. The brain waves are displayed to them through the use of an electroencephalograph. Sterman observed an increase in a specific type of brain wave activity in a particular part of the brain (cortex) during periods when epileptics could prevent their seizures. He attempted to increase this brain wave response by feedback and reinforcement. Epileptics were reinforced when they could consistently produce the desired brain wave. They became progressively more successful at producing the desired response.

The brain wave activity that Sterman has hypothesized to be related to the inhibition of seizures is called the Sensorimotor Rhythm (SMR). Feedback for SMR has been provided to patients representing a cross-section of several different types of epilepsy by Lubar and Bahler.[35] Both auditory and visual feedback were provided whenever SMR activity was detected by the electroencephalograph. During this treatment period most of the patients showed varying degrees of improvement. Two of the patients who had been severely epileptic, having multiple seizures per week, have been seizure free for periods of up to one month. Other patients have developed the ability to block many of their seizures. Seizure data for one of the eight patients treated with SMR training are provided in Figure 6–4. The data before treatment indicated 12–15 seizures in five days. During the first

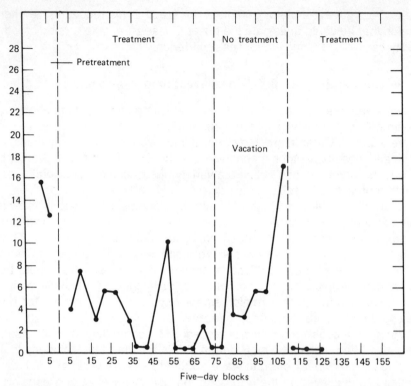

Figure 6-4. Seizure data over the course of treatment. (from J. L. Lubar and W. W. Bahler, *Behavioral Management of Epileptic Seizures Following EEG Biofeedback Training of Sensorimotor Rhythm*, 1976, Plenum, pp. 1, 77–104, by permission.)

treatment phase the seizures were reduced to zero only to return again during the no treatment (vacation) period. The second (final) treatment phase of SMR training indicates a dramatic reduction in the frequency of seizures once again.

Sterman has recently developed a home trainer that provides measurements of brain waves to prevent the return of seizures when treatment is withdrawn. His results along with the results of other labs have demonstrated decreases in seizure activity even during nonfeedback conditions.

The work on the control of seizure activity through biofeedback training is still in the preliminary stages of development. The future will hopefully see the acceleration of the merger between medical means of treatment (anti-seizure medication) and self-management procedures. It is particularly impressive to observe that the effects of SMR training transfer to the home environment where equipment and biofeedback are not available. Some subjects have apparently learned to control the seizures through self-management and personal feedback techniques. The effectiveness of relaxation training on seizure activity, memory, and general disorientation in the case of Paul may ultimately be explained in terms of the positive effect of relaxation training on SMR activity.

FEEDBACK AND RELAXATION

Relaxation training had a pronounced effect on Joy's rigidity and excessive muscular contractions, thereby short-circuiting the onset of severe tension headaches. It helped Paul control seizures that were occurring at a disturbingly high frequency. The relaxation response is rapidly becoming an important part of the treatment regime for individuals who suffer from hypertension. It enables a human response system to return from a state of arousal and imbalance to a restful and recuperative level of equilibrium. New practical applications for the relaxation response to problems of the Human Response System are being discovered on a regular basis through systematic research.

The response can be easily elicited by techniques that quiet the system, minimize internal and external distractions, and increase concentration. Is there something fundamental about this response that allows a system-gone-astray to return to a state of functioning that is basically healthy? When we left the brain in the previous chapter, it was nodding off on the job of regulating excessive muscular contractions, high blood pressure, and other maladaptive responses. It seemed to be overwhelmed by an extraordinary input of stimulation. It failed to regulate the functioning of the response system because it could not utilize the results of its own actions.

Signals were sent from the brain to increase certain activities (such as muscular activity and blood pressure), but the results of those signals failed to be used in subsequently lowering these functions. The increased activities became habitual and chronic and disrupted the balance of the whole system. The brain then failed to profit from feedback: the knowledge of the results of its own actions.

Does relaxation help a brain that is nodding off on the job of effectively controlling the response system? One basic fact about relaxation training that continues to arise as an explanation for its success is its effect on personal feedback. The focusing of attention away from stimuli from the world outside and towards a constant, rhythmical, and internal stimulus allows the system to regulate itself in a desirable direction. The system appears to naturally move towards this balance when given the chance. Relaxation training of various kinds provides this opportunity.

The switch from high to low levels of arousal provided by relaxation training is a perfect medium for the exchange of information from one part of the system to another; the focus of the system's attention away from the environment and towards itself. The sensor of the system, the brain, is thus better prepared to receive information about its own functioning.

During the first stages of relaxation, arousal from numerous encounters with the environment still prevails. There are thoughts about one's moment-to-moment performances during the day. Images of things gone well and some that did not impinge upon consciousness. The general feeling-state fluctuates from tension to calm. A perception of physical arousal and alertness is prominent. There are numerous other responses and emotional states that characterize the nature of the system's previous interplay with the environment.

In the solitude of one's own response system, the brain can perceive the action occurring down under. It's the only real chance that it's had in a long time to do this. The outside world has demanded all of its attention. It has been busy conducting the business of survival in a far broader and more complex sense than our prehistoric ancestors ever imagined. Now it knows for its own good and the good of the system as a whole that it must return to a more basic and restful level of functioning. Through the knowledge that it is beginning to obtain about the result of its own functioning, the system through its chief regulator, the brain, begins to self-regulate.

Self-regulation begins with the elimination of extraneous responses— those thoughts, images, and memories that reflect only the functioning of the past and contribute nothing to the hoped-for new level. Ideas and memories of the recent and distant past are reduced. Even preoccupations and worries, resistant as they are to regulation, faulter in their ability to penetrate the brain's current focus of attention. The knowledge of success at reducing these extraneous responses, that is, the awareness of the system's inherent power to exhibit control, is fed back to the brain. Knowing success at this level the brain is allowed to direct the system to the next stage of equilibrium.

The feedback obtained in this manner reinforces further self-regulatory action until structured thinking activity is reduced to a minimum. It is replaced by a pleasant, free-floating thought process. At the same time the physical sensations that were so prominent before relaxation, when the system was still vibrating from the day's interaction, drift away. Sensations from muscles and joints, skin and hair, and from the internal organs of the body lose their individuality. In their place an integrated sense of wholeness takes hold and a general feeling of calm is prominent. This information also finds its way to the "regulator" and is used to further modify functioning in the desirable direction.

Under these circumstances each component in the whole system grabs at the chance to do its own bit for regulation and control. Organ communication increases, and responses gone-astray from the general goal of homeostasis get a chance to do their thing, right their wrongs, and contribute to the whole. Again the sensor senses this activity and absorbs this knowledge for furthering the system's attempts at recuperation.

And the plight toward equilibrium continues in this manner: focused attention, response alteration, knowledge of results, and further action—feedback, self-regulation, and control. There is a temporary but valuable return to a state of balance.

7 HUMAN RESPONSE SYSTEM

Thinking

Thinking is a complex activity that is generated by the brain, particularly the part of the brain called the cerebral cortex. Although specific structures in the cortex have been identified for the reception and processing of sensory information from the environment (stimuli that produce vision, hearing, and the sensations of touch, smell, and taste) and motor output (muscular responses associated with speech, movement, and so on), no single cortical structure has been indentified for the function of thinking. Thinking appears to be a general function of the brain with numerous cortical structures playing their part in producing coordinated thought patterns.

For a long time in the study of scientific psychology, thinking was ignored as a respectable response to observe and investigate. It is a private event that is only observable to the thinker and, therefore, very difficult to submit to the scrutiny of science. Recently, however, the thinking component of the Human Response System has been subject to wide-scale interest and investigation. Behavior modifiers who are interested in studying the things people say to themselves have defined an area for themselves called Cognitive Behavior Modification. Their main tenet is that people talk to themselves on a regular basis. The things they say, their internal dialogues, are extremely important in determining the way they behave and feel. Cognitive Behavior Modifiers are particularly interested in faulty cognitions: disordered thoughts, images, beliefs, and attitudes. These disordered habits of the thinking component of the response system are partially responsible, according to these investigators, for our emotional upsets and disturbances.

Thinking habits are formed very early in life and continue to develop and influence the remainder of the response system until it ceases to respond. Many of these internal statements, beliefs, and attitudes are repeated so frequently throughout a person's life that they become over-learned and automatic. Some of these thoughts flash into consciousness in the form of images. Most people are unaware of the numerous thoughts and images that they emit during daily life encounters. Thus faulty thinking responses in pictorial or verbal form frequently determine an individual's reaction to a situation without the person's direct awareness of this influence.

These internal, private responses occur quite rapidly and spontaneously. An elaborate idea can be generated by the brain in a fraction of a second. A combination of ideas in the form of an attitude can be expressed in a few moments. These rapid pictorial and verbal cognitions are the main subject of interest of these behaviorists who wish to understand and modify the things people say to themselves.

In order to understand the relationship between this extremely important brain function—thinking—and the remainder of the response system, it is important to take a brief and simplified look at the functioning of the human brain.

THE BRAIN

The adult brain is one of the largest organs in the human body. It weighs approximately three pounds and contains about 100 billion cells. Ten billion of these cells are nerve cells or "neurons," while the remaining 90 billion are a special kind of connective tissue that binds nervous tissue together but does not itself transmit impulses. It is the neuron that is of utmost importance in the thinking component of the Human Response System. These 10 billion cells are the givers of consciousness. Each neuron is capable of linking up across special pathways with between 60,000 and 300,000 other cells, producing a phenomenal number of cellular combinations. It is this intricate network of computer-like connections that allows us to speak intelligently in a number of different languages, to create the sounds of a great musical masterpiece, and to place a man on the moon.

The brain can be divided into three sections. At the base of the brain, closest to the spinal cord, is the brainstem ("old brain"). Attached to the brain stem and behind it is the cerebellum. Above the brain stem and cerebellum bulges the pair of cerebral hemispheres of the cerebrum, the third section of the brain. At the very top of the cerebrum lies the heavily convoluted cerebral cortex. The cortex covers the two cerebral hemispheres of the brain and dominates their appearance.

The brainstem is referred to as the "old brain" because it goes back in evolution some 200 million years. It seems to have the same functions in all higher animals: it controls gut reactions, ritualistic behavior, courting and mating behavior, and crucial reflexes such as swallowing, coughing, and blinking. It also governs saliva secretions, monitors respiration and heart rate, and controls other major organs and glands. The hypothalamus, discussed in Chapter 5, is a major structure of the brain stem. In view of the many vital activities controlled by this part of the brain, it is not surprising that a hard blow to the base of the skull can be fatal.

The cerebrum is divided into right and left hemispheres, and each hemisphere is specialized for a different function. According to David Galin, a leading investigator of the cerebral hemispheres of the brain:

> It is important to emphasize that what most characterizes the hemispheres is not that they are specialized to work with different types of material (the left with words and the right with spatial forms); rather, each hemisphere is specialized for a different cognitive style; the left for an analytic, logical mode for which words are an excellent tool, and the right for a holistic, Gestalt mode, which happens to be particularly suitable for spatial relations. [36, p. 28]

Research on the "hemispheric disconnection syndrome," where the two hemispheres have been surgically separated for the treatment of certain rare cases of epilepsy (the so-called "split brain"), has shown that the cerebral hemispheres are specialized for different kinds of thinking. The left hemisphere is "analytical." It is good at taking things apart and dealing with the separate parts at one time. For example, scientific achievement is dependent on this ability because it relies heavily on analytical methods.

The right hemisphere is specialized for a "holistic" style. It easily grasps patterns of relations. A craftsman, sculptor, or a dancer must consider the holistic patterns or Gestalt. During their respective activities they use a different style of information processing in comparison to the analytical scientist. In spite of this hemispheric specialization, the two sides of the brain are constantly communicating to one another and in many situations work together to produce coordinated thought processes.

Each cerebral hemisphere is divided into four lobes: frontal, temporal, parietal, and occipital. The frontal lobe is located behind the eye and forehead, the temporal lobe is just above the ears, the parietal is situated at the top of the brain behind the frontal lobe, and the occipital lobe is located at the back of the head. You can see these sections of the cerebrum in Figure 7-1.

Because of the positioning of the lobes in relation to the brain stem, the brain resembles a rather large, stocky mushroom. The large structure to the left of the brainstem is the cerebellum. This structure is

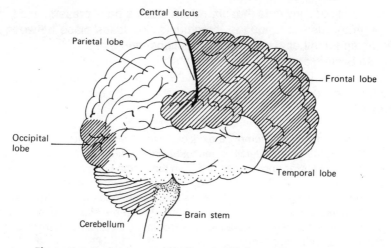

Figure 7-1. Brain stem, cerebellum, and lobes of the cerebrum.

responsible for producing unconscious movements in the skeletal muscles. These movements are required for coordination, posture, and balance of the body. The cortex is continually sending signals to this structure in order to produce smooth, coordinated movements.

The cerebral lobes of the cortex are somewhat specialized for particular functions. Each one handles a particular type of information from the environment; it processes that information and then transmits it to the appropriate site in another part of the brain. The frontal lobe transmits voluntary nervous impulses to skeletal muscles to produce simple and complex movements; the temporal lobe receives impulses from the ears for hearing and is also concerned with the sense of smell; the parietal lobe helps detect the position of the body in space; and the occipital lobe processes visual information. Sensory input and awareness, motor output and the control of the body's muscles are centered on either side of a fissure between the frontal and parietal lobes. Regions in the frontal, temporal and parietal lobes are concerned with speaking and writing. Through a combined effort, the major lobes of the brain coordinate the major functions of sensation, motor output and speech.

In addition to their highly specialized functions, each lobe also contains large tracts of "associative" or "interpretive" nerve cells that are assumed to be responsible for thought processes, the ability to reason abstractly, and consciousness. The association area of the cortex occupies the greater portion of the lateral surfaces of each lobe. An extremely important component of its functioning is the ability to use language in its broadest sense—to transmit, store, and communicate complex information. This information contains data that are relevant to the past, present, and future. Through the use of language, communication takes place between one person and another. The problems, actions, and plans of the Human Response System are transmitted through this complex activity.

Dr. John C. Lilly, in a short article, "Brain Size and Language," discusses the notion of a critical, absolute brain size below which language is impossible.

> In the case of the adult human, the critical brain size seems to be of the order of 900 to 1,000 grams. Detailed, microscopic examination of other mammalian brains of lesser and greater size than that of the human have shown the cerebral cortices of all to be remarkably alike. However, there are definite differences among brains of different sizes. Some areas are not involved in the immediate input–output computations. These are silent areas, the so-called associational or interpretive or 'uncommitted' cortex, present in larger brains and not in smaller ones.
>
> The silent areas are those that add computational abilities to the brain in such a way that language, as we know it, can be generated. Children born without these areas of cortex (microcephalics) are incapable of learning language as we know it.
>
> In the primate series, the macaque monkey, whose brain weighs 100 grams, has no silent areas; all of his cortex is sensory-motor, that is, engaged in the business of seeing, moving, eating, and regulating body functions. In the chimpanzee, who is able to use his hands for a very rapid sign language, the silent areas are small. In the human, the silent areas have expanded; of the 1,500 grams of brain weight, most of the expansion over that of the macaque and of the chimpanzee is in the silent areas and their related nuclei. [37, p. 10]

The cerebral cortex is viewed as the commander of the Human Response System. It senses and assimilates information from the environment, stores and restores it for present and future use, and communicates inwardly to itself and outwardly to the environment in the systems initial stages of coping. This internal communication process—the silent dialogue—must be understood in order to effectively deal with uniquely human problems.

THINKING AND THE ENVIRONMENT: THE SILENT DIALOGUE

Richard Lazarus, a psychologist who has conducted research on the thinking component of the Human Response System, views a human being as an organism that is constantly evaluating and appraising its environment.

According to Lazarus, various kinds of appraisals take place to apprehend and interpret the environmental situation. These internalized responses are important for understanding human emotions and stress reactions. Every emotion, according to Lazarus, must be understood in terms of a particular type of appraisal.

> . . . we have a great need for an adequate transactional language to describe individual differences in the way a person relates psychologically to the environment. I have constructed a simple hypothetical example. Consider two different persons who perceive that they are facing a demand, or the juxtaposition of several demands, which seems to them to be at the border-line or beyond their capacity to master—too much is expected of them. As a result of their individual histories and particular personalities, Person A feels that failure of mastery reflects his own inadequacy, while Person B, by contrast, feels the same inadequacy but interprets the situation as one in which people are constantly trying to use or abuse him. Both experience similar degrees of anticipatory stress and are mobilized to cope with the problem. Prior to the confrontation that will reveal the success or failure of mastery, both experience anxiety, an anticipatory emotion in the context of appraised threat. In Person A, the anxiety is mixed, perhaps with anticipatory depression, while in Person B, the anxiety is mixed with external blaming and anger. Following confrontation in which, let us say, both perform badly, Person A experiences mainly loss and depression, while Person B experiences mainly anger and resentment. A similar set of overwhelming demands have been construed or appraised quite differently because of different personality dispositions. If these persons do well in the confrontation, both may experience elation because they have overcome the difficulty, depending on whether the explanation of the success is luck or their own perseverance and skill . . . [3, p. 6. Copyright © 1975 by the American Psychological Association. Reprinted by permission.]

Variations among individuals in their emotional reactions depend, in part, upon these subtle differences in the way they appraise a stressful commerce with the environment.

According to Martin Seligman,[17] the most critical appraisal that a human being can make in relation to environmental events is the perception of control. Seligman has found from his research that a sense of unpredictability regarding environmental consequences can precipitate helplessness in lower organisms and man. If an organism learns that its responses make no difference in terms of obtaining predictable outcomes from the environment, it experiences a loss of control. Motivation to behave drops dramatically, and severe depression is the emotional outcome. According to Seligman a sense of control over the environment is critical for humans if they are to develop normally, function with an adequate degree of motivation, and avoid emotional disturbance. This sense of predictability and control begins developing in infancy and continues throughout life.

Seligman's findings indicate that one of the causes of depression is the belief that action is futile. The depression-prone individual is one who reacts to a variety of life events by generating a series of thoughts that accumulate to form the appraisal: "My behavior really makes no difference in these situations. I am not in control of my environment." Seligman gives several brief examples of these life events and the perceptions that they precipitate in people who subsequently become depressed.

> . . . the depressed patient believes or has learned that he cannot control those elements of his life that relieve suffering, bring gratification, or provide nurture—in short, he believes that he is helpless. Consider a few of the precipitating events: What is the meaning of job failure or incompetence at school? Often it means that all of a person's efforts have been in vain, that his responses have failed to achieve his desires. When an individual is rejected by someone he loves, he can no longer control this significant source of gratification and support. When a parent or lover dies, the bereaved is powerless to elicit love from the dead person. Physical disease and growing old are helpless conditions par excellence; the person finds his own responses ineffective and is thrown upon the care of others. [17, p. 94 From *Helplessness: On Depression, Development, and Death,* by Martin E. P. Seligman. W. H. Freeman and Company. Copyright © 1975. Reprinted by permission.]

The type of emotional outcome that you experience in relation to one or more life events is intimately related to your thoughts, beliefs and overall appraisal of these situations. The following overly simplified life event will provide you with an example of the intimate connection between your thoughts and emotions. Imagine yourself in this situation:

You are standing in the middle of a crowded elevator waiting for it to take its long ride to the eleventh floor. The elevator stops at that floor and the people behind you begin to move towards the exit. The door hesitates for a moment and the person behind you nudges, bumps, and then literally jabs you from behind. What is your immediate emotion? Chances are good that you are feeling mildly irritated, angry, or very volatile. Think of what you might have said to yourself immediately before experiencing the emotion. "What the hell is going on? Can't that person see that the elevator door is not open yet. How stupid and inconsiderate! He or she should not be doing that." One or more of these statements probably instantaneously popped into your consciousness and provoked the feeling of mild or intense anger.

You turn around to say something to this rude person and are surprised by what you see. The individual is wearing dark glasses and is carrying a cane. It was the cane that provided the jabs that ultimately aroused your emotions. You notice now that there is an abrupt change in your emotions. You feel sympathetic and sorry for the person behind you. You may even feel guilty for getting angry. Think of the thoughts that you may have experienced as you realized that the individual was blind. "This person is blind. No wonder he or she hit me from behind. How stupid of me to get angry." The change in your emotions from anger to compassion resulted from a change in your appraisal of the event. The content of your silent self-dialogue helped determine the nature of the emotion that you experienced.

Positive and negative emotional experiences can be connected directly to these fluctuating thoughts, beliefs, and appraisals. The following example describes a man's transaction with his environment that leads to a consistently positive emotional outcome.

THE CASE OF DR. T

Dr. T is a college professor. He performs a variety of functions in this position. He is most intensively involved in teaching various courses to undergraduate students. Dr. T's preparation for teaching his freshman class of students is conducted in a calm and organized fashion. He observes that the freshman students are energetic and eager to learn. Dr. T perceives this event in his life as a challenge and a potentially positive experience. He knows that he can do well because he has executed these teaching skills numerous times in the past. He is always well prepared. When he confronts the class, Dr. T is relaxed and ready to lecture with spontaneity, humor, and verbal eloquence. He effectively executes the behaviors that are necessary for transmitting knowledge to his students and feels exhilarated when the task is completed. The experiences of teaching to freshman students are very positive life events for Dr. T.

Dr. T achieves a positive outcome in these situations because he: (1) accurately perceives the environment and what it represents—a threat, challenge, positive or neutral experience, (2) accurately appraises his skills for coping with the environmental demand, and (3) maintains a sense of control over the environment. Dr. T knows that his actions count or pay off in terms of a predictable outcome.

Later in this chapter, we revisit Dr. T and observe that he does not always appraise life events in an adaptive manner. In fact, Dr. T spends a large portion of his life in a state of intense emotional upset. The following discussion will prepare you for an understanding of the kinds of thinking responses that consistently lead to negative emotional outcomes.

DISORDERED THINKING

Given the sophisticated nature of the human brain and the pervasive evidence of its complex functioning, one might prematurely assume that since humans possess such a refined piece of biological equipment, life is simply one blissful moment after another. Quite to the contrary each of us have directly experienced sad doses of reality in this respect. We have personally experienced and closely observed in others the marriage of rational and sane behavior on the one hand and irrational behavior on the other. In the same brain-using person, we see common sense and senselessness. The two live side by side like neighbors with divergent working schedules who only pass each other in the night.

The architect who creatively contributes to the building of mammoth skyscrapers during the day tears the house apart at night during fits of uncontrollable anger. The tennis pro markets his skill during lessons at a plush country club. Later in the day he exhibits himself to children returning home from elementary school. Examples of this curious mixture of human sanity and insanity are easy to come by. Every mental health clinician's repertoire of cases is more than adequate in this respect.

Disordered thinking contributes heavily to this marriage of the rational and irrational components of human behavior. Each one of us can testify to the fact that at times we spend a large percentage of our waking hours engaged in counterproductive thinking. Threatening thoughts can sometimes leap into consciousness and spoil an ongoing pleasant activity. Distracting thoughts and images can creep into awareness and interrupt an important event that demands attention and intense concentration. These internal, disruptive responses seem to arrive involuntarily, abruptly sabotaging a pleasant experience and altering a positive emotional state into a negative one. People are not only vulnerable to what appear to be involuntary thinking responses. Under the best of circumstances, we are capable of voluntarily generating a set of irrational ideas and beliefs that subsequently contribute to negative feelings and general misery.

Psychological investigators have recently become extremely interested in pinpointing and categorizing these habits of disordered thinking. One of the first psychologists to write about the tendency for humans to engage in maladaptive thinking is Dr. Albert Ellis, originator of Rational-Emotive Therapy (RET). Ellis' main thesis can be summarized by the following statement: People are not disturbed by life's events, but by the irrational beliefs they tell themselves about these events. He has spent a major portion of his professional life identifying, categorizing, modifying, and writing about humans' irrational thinking tendencies.

Ellis has pinpointed ten irrational ideas that seem to consistently accompany emotional upset and disturbance. Each of these ideas is dealt with separately in his famous book, *The New Guide to Rational Living.*[24] As you recall from a previous discussion, irrational idea number one is: I must have love or approval from all of the people I find significant. Irrational idea number two is: I must prove thoroughly competent, adequate, and achieving. According to Ellis, people generate these thoughts quite frequently during the waking, functioning moments in their lives. Since we cannot, as fallible humans, achieve these unreasonable and unreachable objectives of total approval and perfectionism, and since life often dispenses regular doses of frustration and failure, the frequent repetition of these and other similar beliefs produces emotional upsets, frustrations, and disturbances.

Ellis maintains that humans are capable of high-powered thinking of a reasonable nature. They also have a knack, a biosocial tendency, to generate negative, counterproductive thoughts and beliefs.

Let's face it, humans have trouble thinking straight and emoting well. No matter how bright and well educated they may seem, they find it easy, horribly easy, to act like dunces. And not merely once or twice in a lifetime. Continually, rather! Yes, almost continually.

Can we, then, call humans truly rational animals? Yes, we can. And no, we can't. They have the most incredibly mixed-up 'combination' of common sense and uncommon senselessness you ever did see. They of course have done and will continue to do wonders with their mental processes, and remain so far removed from their closest animal neighbors (the higher apes) in this respect that human morons have distinctly more intelligence than the brightest of subhumans.

Yes, people grow up as highly reasonable, brain-using creatures. But they also have strong prejudiced, amazingly assinine ways. They incline quite normally and naturally toward childish, suggestible, superstitious, bigoted, and downright idiotic behavior, particularly in their relations with other members of their own species. And even when they 'know' they behave in a self-defeating, perfectly senseless manner, and 'know' they would feel far happier and healthier if they acted otherwise, they have such difficulty achieving and sustaining a level of sound and sane behavior that they rarely do so for any length of time, but keep falling back to puerile ways. [24, p. 60]

According to Ellis, disordered thinking comes very easy to most people. It's not something we have to try to do. Rather, due to biological tendencies and social learning experiences, humans tend quite naturally to generate self-defeating and counterproductive beliefs. This is readily reflected in the way people talk to themselves. The self-dialogues, in turn, affect the way that they behave and subsequently the way they feel.

For example, the belief that you must obtain approval from all of the significant people in your life can generate rigid habits oriented towards consistently obtaining this approval. You may become a reassurance-seeker. In each important interpersonal encounter with family and friends, you find yourself demanding excessive attention, approval, and reassurance of their love for you. Inevitably you will encounter a life event where you simply cannot obtain these results no matter how hard you try. If you hold on tenaciously to the belief that you must obtain them, you are in store for heavy doses of anxiety and depression.

Aaron Beck[38] is another investigator who has studied the role of faulty thinking patterns and their contribution to negative emotional states. Beck feels that disordered thinking styles lead to maladaptive behaviors and severe emotional consequences. He states that emotionally disturbed individuals tend to regularly engage in the following thought patterns:

- *Dichotomous reasoning:* to think in terms of extremes or opposites. Internalized statements that indicate a tendency to think in absolutes are: "Everyone is against me." "Nobody seems to like me."

- *Overgeneralization:* to generate a series of thoughts and beliefs on the basis of a small amount of data. An individual who overgeneralizes allows one incident of failure and criticism to influence thoughts and attitudes about other, similar incidences. "I'll never confide in my boss again. He'll always criticize me and see me as a failure."

- *Magnification:* to view events as much more threatening and dangerous than they are in reality. Hypochondriacs, for example, tend to assume that each ache and pain in their body represents the beginning of a dreaded disease.

- *Arbitrary inference:* to base beliefs and conclusions on evidence that is totally unrelated to the context of the present situation. This tendency reflects a failure in discrimination. For example, the boss's bad mood is taken very personally. "I don't know why he or she's mad at me. I didn't do anything to warrant that reaction."

Beck has concluded, on the basis of his research with emotionally disturbed individuals, that disordered thinking is a major contributor to emotions such as depression. The four types of faulty thinking habits identified by Beck further document the human's tendency to misperceive the information provided to the response system by the environment.

Further Identification of Disordered Thinking Habits

Can these habits of disordered thinking be clearly identified and summarized in one cohesive system? The following discussion focuses on categorizing disordered thinking responses as they occur when an individual is facing a stressful situation. The responses reflect an adjustment made on the part of the system to cope with the event(s). They are obviously not all of the thinking responses that occur under these circumstances. Research into this component of the Human Response System is still in its infancy, and further thinking habits will be identified in the future.

The Dangerous Environment Hypothesis

Humans readily appraise and evaluate their environment as threatening and dangerous. Some investigators feel that humans are biologically programmed to respond to the dangerous elements in the environment because of the efficacy of this response in facilitating survival. Early humans had to size up their environments quite rapidly in order to appraise the danger that was constantly lurking there. This ability to size up dangerous and threatening situations paid off in terms of survival. In the same manner, thinking patterns that were slow and insensitive to threats were readily extinguished.

Other investigators emphasize the importance of early social learning in programming humans to respond in a highly threatened fashion to life events. Adults are constantly coping in a high-pressured and irrational world and easily transmit their thoughts and internalized strategies to the younger, more vulnerable members of society. Perhaps the most adequate explanation that accounts for the human tendency to be easily threatened by the environment is a biosocial one; that is, biological tendencies and social learning contribute equally to our tendency to appraise life events as threatening and dangerous.

Once a threatening appraisal or evaluation of the environment is made by the thinking component of the response system, other accompanying internalized responses are emitted. This initial assessment influences the system's subsequent thoughts and images. The individuals self-dialogue becomes programmed for danger. Each subsequent internal event aggravates an already alerted and frightened response system.

The system, after this initial assessment of danger, tends to sense a loss of control in its attempts to cope with the threat. At the same time it is disrupted by its own maneuvers to defend against the dangerous situation. At this point the ability to concentrate is reduced, and irrational thinking is increased. The disordered thinking responses are listed below in succession for the sake of convenience. In reality they do not occur successively but more or less simultaneously, all at once, in an attempt to cope with a situation that has been defined as dangerous.

- *Loss of Control.* Thoughts of losing control become prominent when the environment has been defined as dangerous. The situation appears to be overwhelming to the appraiser. Statements and images of falling apart (cracking up) are common during this stage of responding. "I can't handle this situation. It's too overwhelming for me. I feel like I'm going to fall apart." The threatened individual thinks about the worst possible things that can happen. Ellis refers to this tendency as "catastrophizing" and "awfulizing." The threatened person's self-dialogue states that: "It's terrible, horrible, and awful. It's a catastrophe."

- *Thought Distractions and Loss of Concentration.* Concentration is displaced from the demands of the situation at hand and focused on the fantasized, catastrophic consequences. These thoughts distract the system from adequately coping with the event. The distracting thoughts sometimes take the system so far away from the threatening event itself that the thoughts appear to be unrelated to that event. Preoccupations that don't have anything to do with the threatening situation pervade the system. The threatening appraisal triggers excessive worrying that distracts the system from arriving at constructive solutions to problems. The worries become cyclical and simply lead to more worries.

- *Irrational Thinking.* Irrational ideas become quite prominent. These ideas and beliefs have been discussed and may include internalized statements such as: "I'll lose love and approval in this situation. I can't stand it. Why didn't I perform more adequately?" There appears to be a general overconcern for approval and perfectionism.

The sense of helplessness, along with the thought distractions and irrational worries reinforce the initial evaluation of the environment as dangerous. At this point, the system is so preoccupied with the anticipated catastrophic consequences of a confrontation with the environment that it fails to process new, potentially counteractive ideas and information. The thought processes become cyclical and unresponsive to change.

Let's return to Dr. T for another, less adaptive, environmental transaction that predictably leads to a negative emotional state. This case illustrates the disordered habits we have discussed.

Case of Dr. T revisited

Dr. T teaches another class of students. They are seniors who are several years older and considerably more mature and knowledgeable than his freshman students. He is threatened by them. These older, more experienced students represent a potential danger. Dr. T does not look forward to teaching his senior class. He reluctantly agrees to do so because he must. Dr. T is equally skilled and prepared to teach seniors as he is to teach freshmen. Yet, he underestimates his ability to cope with this situation.

Dr. T's thoughts before, during, and after class are disordered. He senses a loss of control and helplessness. He worries about cracking up before the class starts and never being able to arrive at the classroom. While he is teaching the class, he imagines himself being embarrassed by his own behavior. Images of childish acts such as defecating and urinating in his clothes intrude into his consciousness and distract him from conducting the lecture. He doesn't understand these thoughts. They are absurd and silly to him. These things have never happened, yet he is constantly preoccupied with them.

Dr. T is afraid that his students will be critical of his mediocre lectures and feels that he will fail miserably as a professor of upper level students. He worries constantly about this class and cancels it whenever the opportunity to do so arises. Dr. T is extremely upright about this situation. His heart races when he merely thinks about teaching the class. He is stiff, overly serious, and humorless when speaking to senior students.

Preoccupying thoughts about these regular events in Dr. T's life prevent him from acting and feeling the way he wants to at school. He is getting progressively more upset and disturbed because of his inability to cope with this situation.

Dr. T has defined this situation as threatening and dangerous. He underestimates his ability to cope with it and feels helpless. Distractions and preoccupations prevade his consciousness and pre-

vent him from developing an effective coping strategy for dealing with this regularly occurring life event. His overall belief about senior students is irrational. These disordered thoughts inevitably pervade his entire life.

DISORDERED THINKING AND THE BREAKDOWN OF FEEDBACK

Feedback has been defined as the knowledge of results of response functioning and has been discussed as a critical variable in understanding the functioning of the physiological component of the Human Response System. In order for homeostasis to take place, information from one organ of the body must communicate to other organs in an intricate network of ongoing feedback systems. The breakdown of this communication process leads to a breakdown in functioning.

The same model helps us understand disordered thinking responses. One predictable response that occurs when a human being has defined a situation as threatening is a breakdown in feedback. New information fails to be assimilated by the organ that generates thoughts—the brain. In its attempt to deal with the threatening stimulus, the brain is cluttered by its own disordered activity. Knowledge of response functioning becomes impossible under these conditions.

Dr. T's problem and the disordered thought patterns of other individuals stem, in part, from this breakdown of feedback. Information from an activating, environmental event is misperceived. Once the event is sensed by the cortical processes of the brain as potentially dangerous, thoughts and images alert the remainder of the system for an emergency. Subsequent thinking responses are emitted that accompany the emergency status of the system: loss of control, thought distractions, and irrational thinking. Counteracting thoughts of a rational nature cannot be emitted.

The system is distracted by its own defensive maneuvers, and further information from the environment is lost in a wealth of worries and preoccupations. There are numerous examples from other areas of the response system of the damaging effects of stimulating an inopportune and harmful fight against an event that is innocuous. For example, inflammation is a basic physiological defense mechanism. Its main purpose is to localize irritants by putting a barricade of inflammatory tissue around them. This process prevents blood poisoning by inhibiting the spread of microbes into the blood. This adaptive response in one situation (in response to a serious cut) can be maladaptive in another. Hans Selye, in his book

Stress Without Distress, discusses the harmful effects on the system of this defense mechanism.

> Here, inflammation itself is what we experience as a disease. Thus in many patients who suffer from hay fever or extreme swelling after an insect sting, suppression of defensive inflammation is essentially a cure. This is because the invading stressor agent is not in itself dangerous or likely to spread and kill. In the case of grafts, it may even be lifesaving. [6, p. 39]

In the thinking component of the response system, the defensive reaction to an imagined threat, whether it be stimulated by the loss of approval or the fear of rejection, prevents the system from adjusting in an adaptive fashion.

These responses perpetuate themselves, and the Human Response System loses its ability to adjust itself in relation to its environment. Equilibrium is distorted, and the thinking component dominates the remainder of the system in a maladaptive manner. This breakdown of feedback from one component of the system to the other results in emotional upset and disturbance. Further breakdown is imminent if the system cannot return to homeostasis.

The case of Paul illustrates the dire consequences of a coping strategy that severely reduces the ongoing exchange of information between the brain and the external environment. Paul perceived his environment as dangerous and quickly detached himself from it. During the initial stages of the treatment process, I was desperately searching for information that would enlighten me about the life events that surrounded his illness. I was surprised to find that there were very little data available from Paul, his family, and friends. No one had access to it. There was no dialogue about his problems with significant people in his life. There was little self-dialogue. The detachment had been accomplished swiftly and completely.

The chain of thinking responses subsequent to Paul's appraisal of danger in his life is a matter of speculation. Even to this day, he has great difficulty in remembering the specific series of events. My in-depth knowledge of his general strategy of coping leads me to believe that he felt an acute sense of helplessness. His thoughts were distracted from the threatening marital and work-related events, and he became preoccupied with a variety of unrelated, distracting thoughts. His pace became hurried and his thoughts more disordered. Paul become exceptionally sensitive to the approval of others and criticism from colleagues. This style of thinking was conducive to further detachment and denial.

Paul left the arena of psychological threat and conflicts that characterized his life. This defensive maneuver precipitated a severe state of deprivation from potentially constructive information and feedback. Disordered thinking became cyclical, and his thoughts were isolated from the remainder of his response system, as well as from the world outside. The stage was set for a progressive deterioration in the ability of his system to profit from the knowledge of its own activities. Paul was not to benefit from the wisdom of his response system until he returned to the arena of conflict during the process of therapy.

SUMMARY

Several disruptive responses are emitted by the thinking component of the Human Response System when an event is handled in a maladaptive manner. The following is a summary of these responses.

a. The situation is misperceived as dangerous and threatening. A challenge may be seen as too overwhelming. A potentially positive experience is distorted into a negative one. And, a mild threat may be blown up into a catastrophe.

b. The evaluation of one's coping skills in the situation is underestimated and an inability to cope is sensed by the system. Thoughts of being overwhelmed by the event increase and a loss of control is perceived. The system is easily distracted at this point and loses its ability to concentrate on the task at hand. Irrational concerns about loss of approval, poor performance, failure and criticism increase dramatically and the system becomes preoccupied with itself.

c. The ability to transmit accurate information to the remainder of the system is effected by these internal responses. The Human Response System is prepared for an emergency. High levels of arousal are precipitated and overt behavior is disrupted.

d. The overall strategy of the system is effected and the exchange of information from one component of the system to another breaks down. Thinking responses become isolated from potentially helpful environmental information, and they function independently of the remainder of the response system. Emotional arousal and disturbance increases in intensity.

Psychological investigators in the newly defined area of Cognitive Behavior Modification are interested in understanding and, subsequently, changing the thinking component of the Human Response System. They have found that the human brain, along with its unique ability to generate brilliant and creative thoughts, images, and fantasies, is capable of producing an uncomfortably high frequency of disordered and faulty responses. According to these cognitive behavior modifiers, this component of the response system is a primary contributor to emotional upset and disturbance. In turn, they feel that a better understanding of these private events will facilitate self-control and regulation of one's own internal dialogue. Chapter 8 focuses on the intricate details of this self-management process.

8 SELF-REGULATION

Thinking

THE CASE OF DR. T

If you asked Dr. T's students about their impressions of him as a professor, they would overwhelmingly respond with admiration and praise. A few might casually mention that he wasn't easy to get close to. Some students might say that he was detached, aloof, and sometimes arrogant. None of them would question his intellectual power or his teaching ability. The students would certainly not attribute Dr. T's interpersonal detachment to irrational fears of criticism and failure. They would most likely justify Dr. T's detached attitude and aloofness by stating: "He wants to keep a professional distance from those of us that he must teach and evaluate."

Fellow faculty members would not deviate significantly from the college students in their impressions of Dr. T. They might possibly add other superlatives to the description: "He is a fantastic participant for a panel discussion. Very articulate! His wealth of knowledge in a variety of fields is intimidating." Few of them would attribute his failure to participate in campus-wide academic and social functions to severe interpersonal anxiety. None of the faculty would suspect that he had an extreme fear of speaking in their presence. According to their impressions, Dr. T was eccentric and somewhat different from the rest of them. They felt that he was unwilling to go along with the crowd because of intense philosophical differences from other faculty members.

Other people in Dr. T's life who knew him away from campus would describe him as strong, silent, and extremely independent. Only a few people who knew him intimately had access to the intense emotional and physical pain that he suffered. This very

small, select group of relatives and friends were aware that Dr. T
was frightened, and that his independent and detached posture in
academic and social circles was often an outgrowth of fear and
insecurity.

Dr. T wanted desperately to be comfortable with students at all
levels of academic development. He hoped for relief from his fear
of being negatively evaluated by fellow colleagues. The same attitude that made him feel threatened in an academic setting per-
sisted in his relationships with friends, relatives, and even family
members.

Such divergent perceptions between the way people talk to themselves and the manner in which others talk about them is not
uncommon. All of us have received feedback from other people
that failed miserably to jive with the information we had about
ourselves. This discrepancy was particularly pronounced in Dr. T.
He tended to be easily threatened by students and colleagues
who were in sincere awe of him.

Dr. T's appraisal of his environment was generally distorted. He
underestimated his ability to cope with academic and social situations and, as a consequence, sensed a chronic loss of control.
Disordered thinking of one type or another—catastrophic fantasies, obsessions, and irrational beliefs and attitudes—
continually distracted him from potentially important encounters
with students, colleagues, family, and friends. Deprived of important sources of information to help him dispute his irrational perceptions, Dr. T wallowed in a vicious cycle of disordered thinking,
detachment, and emotional disturbance.

How was Dr. T going to bridge the gap between fantasy and reality? How was he going to counteract his disordered thinking and
experience a rational exchange with his environment? The solution depended on the development of alternative thinking responses that would compete with the disordered ones currently in
residence. Disordered thinking habits had to be eliminated and
rational thoughts had to be strengthened and firmly entrenched in
his response system.

The first step was to reevaluate the environment regarding its
capacity for danger. At the same time a strengthening of his cop-

ing skills was necessary. The relaxation response was elicited, and the stage was set for low levels of arousal and clear thinking. Dr. T encountered the "dangerous" environment in the safe environment of my office. He vividly imagined, in detail, each threatening life event. This experience with academic and interpersonal events provided a painful but important exposure to an environment that had previously been a stimulus for detachment and escape.

Through a series of important imagined confrontations, both in my office and at home, Dr. T began reevaluating his fundamental hypotheses about life. He generated new ideas and beliefs about himself and began challenging his approval-seeking and perfectionistic tendencies. Dr. T started feeling a sense of self-control as his new self-dialogue helped him to regulate his negative emotions and to strengthen his positive ones.

The new insights obtained by a systematic exposure to threatening life events through imagery training transferred to real life situations. He learned to challenge old beliefs and supplement them with new, more rational ones. Each change in his internal dialogue facilitated new emotional consequences. The knowledge of this success provided him with additional feedback that ultimately led to new heights of self-regulation and control.

The following discussion focuses on the details of the technology used with Dr. T and others in the self-regulation of thinking.

COUNTERACTING THE "DANGEROUS ENVIRONMENT" HYPOTHESIS

People are prone to perceive their surroundings as dangerous and threatening. The disordered and faulty thinking that follows the "dangerous environment" hypothesis removes them from the situation that is defined as threatening. Under these circumstances there is little opportunity for invalidating the distorted perception. This escape precludes the acquisition of any new information about the "threatening" event. Deprived of this valuable information that is obtained by an ongoing interplay with the environment, the human response system suffers from a loss of ability to control and regulate its own responses. Maladaptive thinking habits prevail, and they affect the functioning of the system as a whole.

The first step in altering this pattern of disordered thinking is to counteract the tendency to readily generate the "dangerous environment" hypothesis. The environment can only be reappraised if the threatened individual is willing to take another look at it. A new exposure to the situation is critical. It sets the stage for new, more adaptive human responses.

Desensitization and Imagery Training

Dr. Joseph Wolpe[39] was one of the first investigators to recognize the benefits of repeated exposure to life events for individuals who were afraid of encountering specific situations. His original work with phobics (people who are afraid of discrete situations) showed that fearful individuals reduced their anxiety in these situations as a result of repeated exposure. This experience also increased the chances that they would enter the situation again in the future.

People who are afraid of closed spaces (claustrophobics), open spaces (agoraphobics), and other specific events develop strong avoidance responses and are reluctant to encounter these situations. Wolpe developed a technique that prepared these phobic people for their fearful encounter by creating the possibility of a safe confrontation between them and their feared stimuli. The technique is called "desensitization." It involves the use of imagery and a deep state of relaxation.

In desensitization the phobic individual imagines a gradual confrontation with the feared situation while in a deep state of relaxation. The desensitization trainer closely monitors the phobic's emotional reactions and never allows the individual to experience high levels of anxiety while he or she is imagining the scene. The fearful stimulus is presented in stages. For example, a person who is afraid of heights may first imagine climbing one step of a ten-step ladder. Each stage is taken gradually, and the least threatening step in chain of responses toward the feared object is accomplished before the next step is taken. When all of the steps are completed in imagery, the individual is then ready to confront the fearful situation in reality.

According to Wolpe, the most important component of this fear reduction process is the association between low levels of bodily arousal and the feared stimulus. As long as a state of relaxation is present during each exposure the stimulus cannot elicit the fear response. In this manner repeated exposure deconditions the fear response. According to Wolpe[40] all of the following steps in the desensitization process are necessary:

1. A deep state of relaxation achieved through progressive muscular relaxation.

2. Identification of the anxiety-provoking stimulus or situation.

3. Breaking down the final goal to be accomplished (confronting the feared event) into small steps.

4. A presentation of the steps to the client, one at a time, in imagery. The subject never progresses to a higher step toward the goal until the previous step can be imagined with little discomfort.

5. Instructions to the client to encounter the anxiety-provoking situation in reality.

Other investigators of the fear reduction process feel that positive results can occur without the use of all of the steps in desensitization.[41] Many of them feel that relaxation and the use of gradual exposure are desirable but not necessary conditions for success. To these individuals the important factors are the subjects' repeated exposure to the feared stimulus and the modification of the thoughts that accompany the fear. The individual must take another look and redefine an environment that has been defined as dangerous and threatening.

I have found several simple steps extremely valuable for counteracting the fears people have in specific situations. These steps helped these individuals to "take another look" and, in turn, assisted them in counteracting the "dangerous environment" hypothesis. You can utilize this technique for your own benefit.

1. Choose an activating life event, one that precipitates disordered thinking, fear and anxiety.

2. Elicit the relaxation response by the muscular relaxation technique outlined in Appendix II. It is desirable to relax during imagery, but you can proceed with the following steps even if you are not completely relaxed.

3. Imagine the anxiety-provoking situation as vividly as possible. Continue to imagine the situation until you feel that you are deeply involved in it. It helps to imagine it vividly enough to get mildly emotionally aroused by what you are imagining.

4. Alternate between imagining the scene and relaxing until you get more and more comfortable with the imagined event.

5. Plan a time to confront yourself with the situation and do it. If you aren't as comfortable in the situation as you would like to be, repeat the steps outlined above and try it once again.

This approach to fear reduction has been helpful with a variety of problems. The following case study outlines the steps in imagery training with an actual problem and shows the potential results of this technique.

Case Study: Imagery Training and the Fear of Public Speaking

The fear of public speaking is a fairly common problem. Most of you can surely remember being terrified by your school teachers when you were required to answer a question or give a recitation in class. You can probably recall the elaborate manuevers you performed in order to avoid being called on by your teacher: Your head tilted downward to avoid eye contact and your body slumped down in your seat. The student sitting in front of you provided you with a convenient cover from the teacher's roaming glances. In this manner you successfully avoided the fantasized embarrassment of looking bad in the presence of your equally fearful friends. For the majority of you this fear and accompanying avoidance response rarely affects your functioning as adults. Unless your job and financial well-being depends on public speaking you can successfully avoid the results of this common fear.

Peter came to see me because of an extreme fear of public speaking. As a child and adolescent, he had the normal experiences with this problem. Like most of us he was apprehensive about "looking stupid" in the presence of others. As an adult he became involved in an occupation (psychology) that demanded regular presentations to psychology students, groups of patients, other health workers, and professional colleagues. He was required at least once a week to give a presentation to these groups. Peter's reaction to this environmental demand was quite disturbing to him. He would imagine the dreadful consequences of participating in such an activity: "There's no way I can handle this. I'll fall apart. I'll make an ass out of myself. Even if I can stick with it, I'll stammer and stutter all the way through it."

His first impulse was to avoid the confrontation altogether. Practically speaking, there was no way to escape this responsibility apart from resigning from his position. He frequently considered this alternative on occasions when the fear would overwhelm him. I instructed Peter to practice the relaxation response regularly. When he learned to relax, I began pairing the state of relaxation with several anxiety-provoking stimuli. We worked together with the following events:

1. Requests by his supervisor for Peter to make a public presentation.
2. Leading a group therapy session.
3. Conducting a training session for mental health professionals.
4. Speaking to a group of psychologists.

After the procedure was clear to him and he learned how to relax, each event became the topic of several self-imagery sessions in the privacy of his home. During his sessions at home, I instructed Peter to vividly imagine the details of the anxiety-provoking situation while his eyes were closed and his body was relaxed. Event number four, speaking to a group of psychologists, was identified by Peter as the most anxiety-provoking activating event. What follows is a brief analysis of the self-imagery procedure with this fearful situation.

Peter imagined several scenes and engaged in a dialogue with himself during the imagery process.

Scene 1: Introduction of the speaker (Peter) to a group of ten psychologists. "I am sitting among the psychologists to whom I will be speaking. I know several of them personally. The remainder of them are acquaintances. They are listening to the introductory statements being made about me by one of my colleagues. I can see myself somewhat anxious as I sit among them. However, I can imagine myself getting progressively more relaxed."

This scene was repeated several times before it was visualized with an almost complete state of relaxation.

Scene 2: Peter is beginning to speak to the group. "I am standing in front of the group ready to make my introductory statements. I look at the group and notice that their eyes are on me. I feel nervous as the first few words are uttered. My nervousness declines as I make the first statements. I'm getting progressively more relaxed as I look out at the group and speak."

This scene was less difficult than the previous one, and only two or three visualizations were necessary for a complete state of relaxation.

Peter prepared in this manner for every presentation, diligently pairing the state of relaxation with these specific anxiety-provoking events. He found that his anxiety diminished significantly after each imagery session. He no longer became terrified when his supervisor asked him to speak in public. Peter began to feel comfortable in training sessions with other mental health staff members and groups of patients. The event that he feared the most was the presentation to members of his own profession. In his fantasies, they were the most likely to criticize him and negatively evaluate his performance. He soon overcame this fear and found that his colleagues were quite receptive to his professional knowledge and skills in public speaking.

COUNTERACTING THOUGHT DISTRACTIONS
AND INCREASING CONCENTRATION

Investigators who are interested in altering the thinking component of the human response system maintain that repeated exposure to stressful situations through desensitization modifies only one level of the fearful individual's responses. Desensitization, according to these cognitive behavior modifiers, deconditions an individual to one specific event but leaves the person vulnerable to new stressful encounters with the environment. What is necessary, they say, is a total change in the thinking strategy, one that prepares the fearful individual for all difficult encounters. They propose to do this by altering the fearful person's self-dialogue. Cognitive behavior modifiers focus on changing the things people say to themselves about stressful life events.

The following discussion focuses on giving you a comprehensive approach to the problem of altering human thinking responses: Cognitive Behavior Modification and Imagery Training are combined with relaxation to provide you with an alternative style of thinking.

Now that you are more relaxed and have learned to use the relaxation response in a variety of situations that previously made you uncomfortable, you have counteracted the brain's tendency to generate the "dangerous environment" hypothesis. You no longer get violently upset when things get difficult for you at work, home, or in social settings. The ability to relax has become an alternative way of responding to situations that you often avoided in the past. Activating events are not quite as arousing as they used to be, and you are not as easily threatened by criticism, excessive responsibility, loss of approval, or other difficult life encounters.

Things are definitely better for you, but you still have trouble with your ability to concentrate during stressful encounters. Even though your system has calmed down you still tend to think crookedly in these situations, and you often distract yourself from the task at hand. If an important meeting, social encounter, or recreational event is somewhat threatening to you, you tend to generate distracting, anxiety-provoking thoughts such as: "What if I don't do this right. I'll look terrible." "What if I miss this tennis shot. I'll look like a fool." "I can't do this right. If I can't do it to perfection, I might as well quit."

How can you stop these unproductive and distracting thoughts? How can you replace them with thoughts which facilitate concentration and, subsequently, performance? You talk to yourself in almost all situations, particularly events that involve performance, responsibility, and a possible evaluation of your own abilities. You can use this natural ability to generate internal statements to help yourself effectively concentrate on performance tasks.

If you can think yourself into trouble, you can think yourself out of it. When an event causes you to be upset and you tend to loose your concentration in this situation, you can counteract this tendency by privately repeating specific instructions to yourself about the task at hand. This technique, along with the consistent repetition of relaxation-inducing thoughts, creates an overall strategy for counteracting distractions and minimizing emotional upset.

Stress Innoculation

The research on the approach outlined above has been spearheaded by several investigators. Dr. Donald Meichenbaum is one of the most active investigators in the area of Cognitive Behavior Modification. Meichenbaum's[42] approach is to teach people to talk to themselves in a constructive manner. New thinking styles are taught by means of small steps and successive approximations of the final desirable self-dialogue. Cognitive self-guidance is used to alter thinking responses that contribute to a number of problems including hyperactivity and impulsiveness in school children, inappropriate verbal behavior in institutionalized adult schizophrenics, high test anxiety in college students, and low creativity in adults. A related cognitive behavioral procedure for dealing with fear and anxiety is called *stress innoculation.* Meichenbaum outlines the steps for this procedure as follows:

1. Preparing for a stressor.
2. Confronting and handling a stressor.
3. Coping with the feeling of being overwhelmed.
4. Reinforcing self-statements.

Each step includes the repetition of thoughts that reduce distractions, increase concentration, and eliminate anxiety. Some of the steps can be practiced in imagery before the confrontation with the stressor. Others are repeated directly in the stressful situation itself. The idea is to teach the participant a learning set, a general way of talking to one's self in order to cope more effectively with the stressful situation. Table 8-1 includes examples of self-statements that are rehearsed during each step of Meichenbaum's Stress Innoculation Training.

As you can see from the self-dialogue practiced in stress innoculation, the procedure minimizes the tendency to be distracted by unpleasant thoughts when you are confronting the stressor. Stress innoculation guides you through an environmental encounter in a way that reduces

TABLE 8–1. Examples of Coping Self-Statements Rehearsed in Stress Innoculation Training

Step 1: Preparing for a Stressor

- What is it you have to do?
- You can develop a plan to deal with it.
- Just think about what you can do about it. That's better than getting anxious.
- No negative self-statements; just think rationally.
- Don't worry; worry won't help anything.
- Maybe what you think is anxiety is eagerness to confront it.

Step 2: Confronting and Handling a Stressor

- Just "psych" yourself up—you can meet this challenge.
- One step at a time; you can handle the situation.
- Don't think about fear; just think about what you have to do. Stay relevant.
- This anxiety is what the doctor said you would feel. It's a reminder to use your coping exercises.
- This tenseness can be an ally, a cue to cope.
- Relax, you are in control. Take a slow, deep breath. Ah, good.

Step 3: Coping with the Feeling of Being Overwhelmed

- When fear comes, just pause.
- Keep the focus on the present; what is it you have to do?
- Label your fear from "0" to "10" and watch it change.
- You should expect your fear to rise.
- Don't try to eliminate fear totally; just keep it manageable.
- You can convince yourself to do it. You can reason your fear away.
- It will be over shortly.
- It's not the worst thing that can happen.
- Do something to prevent you from thinking about fear.
- Describe what is around you. That way you won't think about worrying.

Step 4: Reinforcing Self-Statements

- It worked, you did it.
- Wait until you tell your therapist about this.
- It wasn't as bad as you expected.
- You made more out of the fear than it was worth.
- Your damn ideas—that's the problem. When you control them, you control your fear.
- It's getting better each time you use the procedures.
- You can be pleased with the progress you're making.
- You did it!

Source: Donald Meichenbaum, *Cognitive Behavior Modification*. © 1974 General Learning Corporation (Morristown, N. J.: General Learning Press). Reprinted by permission of Silver Burdett Company.

distractions, increases self-control, and strengthens concentration on the stressful situation. It adds an important component to the fear-reduction process. Not only does it increase exposure to the fearful situation, but it guarantees a style of thinking that keeps you in constant touch with the environment. In this manner, the "dangerous environment" hypothesis is counteracted and the probability of a successful encounter is maximized.

The steps involved in "stress innoculation" can be incorporated into the ones previously outlined for imagery training. Relaxation and imagery training provide a good basis for executing the stress innoculation technique.

Steps 1, 2, 3, and 5 of the imagery training process remain the same. An additional component is added to Step 4. Using the case of Peter and the speech anxiety problem as an example, the stress innoculation component is added to the imagery in the following way:

Step 4a. Talk to yourself about the emotional arousal that you are experiencing: "My anxiety is increasing somewhat. I understand that this is a natural consequence of my fear of public speaking. It's not debilitating. I can relax. Even if it doesn't go away altogether, it won't get that bad. I can handle it."

Step 4b. Talk to yourself about the task to be completed and the need for intensive concentration: "What are the steps involved in completing this task? I need to speak slowly and clearly. I'd better have good eye contact with my audience. Don't let those thoughts distract you. I don't have to listen to them. Concentrate on your audience and slow down your conversation.

Step 4c. Self-Reinforcement. "I'm doing great. Very good!"

Step 4d. Alternate between imagining the scene, talking to yourself and relaxing until you get more and more comfortable with the imagined event.

Step 4e. Repeat steps 4a, b, and c before and during your confrontation with the stressful life event.

Case Study: Relaxation, Imagery Training, and Stress Innoculation

Al was in his early forties, married, and the father of four children. Al and his wife Joan came to see me because of marital difficulties. One of the primary complaints that Joan voiced about their relationship was Al's detachment from the remainder of the family.

Joan was very outgoing and received a great deal of reinforcement from attending social activities with the entire family. Al refused to participate. He complained of nervousness and agitation during family outings. Al experienced very little reinforcement from these activities, and he vigorously avoided them.

I was very interested in Al's strategy for coping with family-related events. He was experiencing high levels of emotional upset during these situations. My hypothesis was that Al was coping with family interactions in a maladaptive fashion.

Al and Joan both confirmed my expectations. Al could see the benefits of more frequent family interactions, but he would habitually conjure up excuses in order to avoid these events. "I get too nervous when I'm around all of the kids." "I don't enjoy myself, and I tend to ruin it for everyone else." When Al was forced to attend an activity because of intense family pressure, he would approach the event in a highly nervous state. He would procrastinate and leave all of the preparations until the very last minute. During the drive to the family's destination, Al would nervously listen to everyone's conversation. He had difficulty concentrating on the task of driving. He would often become agitated, turn off to the side of the road, and relinquish the responsibility of driving to Joan. At other times, Al would simply turn around and drive home.

The single most disturbing event for Al was the car trip to and from the family's destination. He conveyed to me the thoughts and images that made up his thinking strategy during these trips. Al was preoccupied with a strong sense of responsibility for the family. He believed that the family's safety was his total responsibility and that he must execute this task in a near-perfect manner. Thoughts and images of wrecking the station wagon raced through his consciousness before and during family trips. He would imagine terrible injuries to his wife and children. The thoughts of facing this overwhelming responsibility caused him to be too cautious and easily distracted. They ultimately effected his ability to concentrate on the task of driving. As a consequence, he was highly tense during these events and failed to obtain any enjoyment from them.

I taught Al the relaxation response and worked with him on the use of imagery and stress innoculation. We rehearsed a new *strategy for coping with family related, activating events. One particular series of scenes focused on the apprehension and fear surrounding the family's trips in the station wagon. I felt that a new strategy for dealing with this responsibility would be a good starting point for an increase in the enjoyment of family activities. The long-term goal was an overall increase in family interactions and an improvement in the marital relationship.*

Al was instructed to practice the following steps as part of the imagery and stress-innoculation training:

Step 1. *Pinpointing the Activating Event:* Driving the station wagon to and from a family activity with all family members present.

Step 2. *The Relaxation Response:* Al learned the response and practiced it regularly.

Step 3. *Vividly Imagining the Scene:* The following scene was practiced in imagery and paired with the state of relaxation: "The station wagon is in the driveway. Everyone is preparing to leave on the trip. The kids are piled into the back seats, and your wife is sitting in the front. You open the door to climb into the driver's seat. You are somewhat apprehensive." Al was instructed to continue imagining the scene until his level of discomfort was significantly reduced.

Step 4a. *Self-Dialogue about Emotional Arousal:* Al was instructed to repeat several statements to himself about his anxiety. "My anxiety is increasing somewhat. It's not that bad. I know why its there. It's natural because I'm trying a new strategy. I can handle it. I can relax."

b. *Self-Dialogue about the Steps to be Completed and the Ability to Concentrate on the Task:* "What are the steps involved in completing this task? I must not be distracted by the kids. I can concentrate on starting the car and the steps involved in getting to our destination. I'll keep my eyes on the road and listen to the music on the radio. I don't need to do this perfectly. Everyone will understand if I make a mistake."

c. *Self-Reinforcement:* "Good! I am relaxed. It feels good to be in control."

d. *Repeating the Scene:* Al repeated the scene numerous times until he felt relaxed and confident about his ability to duplicate this self-dialogue in the driving situation itself.

Step 5. *Live Confrontation:* Al planned a time to take part in a family activity. He relaxed immediately before the event and rehearsed the scenes several times. While he was driving, he continually engaged in a constructive self-dialogue and used cognitive self-guidance in addition to the other steps discussed above.

This one success was a small one for Al, but it set a precedent for subsequent family-related activities. The new thinking style and self-dialogue generalized to other life events. He always had difficulty accepting any kind of responsibility. Once he was effectively prepared for taking on additional tasks and made some decisions on his own, he approached the situation in a much less apprehensive and cautious manner. This one victory went a long way in altering his general style of coping with situations that involved firm decision-making and responsibility. Al succeeded in becoming comfortable about his portion of the responsibility for the family. The success he experienced had the added benefit of facilitating his relationship with Joan.

COUNTERACTING IRRATIONAL THINKING

Up to this point the technology for counteracting disordered thinking has been utilized primarily for coping with specific life events that were defined as threatening by the response system. The discussion has shown that repeated exposure to these events in imagery facilitates new, more adaptive perceptions of the environment. Furthermore, constructive self-dialogues were shown to counteract the brain's tendency to be easily distracted. This alternative thinking strategy was proposed for coping with any stressful life event.

Does this new strategy guarantee a set of thinking responses that minimizes emotional upset and disturbance? Is the change in thinking responses comprehensive enough to increase emotional well-being and happiness? According to some investigators, the job is not complete until an individual's basic irrational ideas, beliefs, and attitudes about life are uprooted. These, in turn, must be replaced with a more rational style of thinking. In order to create a truly rational thinking strategy, people must counteract their general and pervasive irrational thinking tendencies. This is accomplished through a total reprogramming of the response system for a rational self-dialogue.

As indicated in Chapter 7, thoughts are generated instantaneously. In a fraction of a second you can think several thoughts. In a minute you can say a hundred things to yourself. You don't have to energetically work at it or voluntarily command yourself to think. On the contrary! Thoughts keep popping into your consciousness with little work or provocation. On the other hand, it takes a great deal of energy to stop a chain of negative thoughts from occurring. It is even more difficult to generate thoughts that are facilitative, comfort-producing, and productive.

The human response system is perfectly capable of stopping negative anxiety-provoking thoughts and replacing them with more rational, positive statements. Why not use this inherent ability to produce internal self-dialogues for your own behalf? Albert Ellis has been teaching people how to acquire this skill for numerous years. He has developed a valuable technique—disputation—that helps people counteract irrational thinking.

Disputation and the Alteration of Thinking Styles

Irrational, nonproductive thinking that occurs spontaneously throughout the waking moments of our lives can be stopped. The disputation technique teaches people to pinpoint and uproot the irrational ideas that accompany irrational thoughts. Once these ideas are uprooted, they can be eliminated by engaging oneself in a vigorous self-dialogue. The focus of this dialogue is to dispute the relevance and truthfulness of the irrational thoughts and ideas.

Albert Ellis suggests numerous steps for executing the disputation technique. The following example represents one sample of the disputation exercises advocated by Ellis.

"Disputing Irrational Beliefs (DIBS). At the Institute for Advanced Study in Rational Psycho-therapy in New York City, we have found that one of the exercises that people get best results with in helping themselves change their self-defeating ideas consists of Disputing Irrational Beliefs (DIBS). You can practice this as follows:

"Take any irrational Belief (iB) that you want to give up and stop acting upon, such as the irrational Belief, 'I must succeed in helping my neurotic mate act much less neurotically,' and write it down on a sheet of paper or record it on a cassette tape recorder and then Dispute it with these questions, all of which you force yourself to think through very carefully and to which you can write down or record the answers:

"**1.**   What Irrational Belief Do I Want to Dispute and Surrender?
Illustrative Answer: I must succeed in helping my neurotic mate act less neurotically.

"**2.**   Can I Prove this Belief True?
Illustrative Answer: No, I don't think that I can.

"**3.**   What Evidence Exists of the Falseness of this Belief?
Illustrative Answer: No law of the universe exists that says that any 'neurotic' that I care for *has* to improve and behave less neurotically—although I would find it highly desirable if that person did!

"**4.**   Does any Evidence Exist of the Truth of this Belief?
Illustrative Answer: No, not that I can see. Considerable evidence

exists that if I did help my neurotic mate act less neurotically, we both would get better results and lead a more enjoyable life. But that still doesn't prove that either or both of us *have* to improve and receive favorable results. No matter how much anything *would prove better* that never means that *it must occur.* The main proposition that I can really substantiate about my mate's neurosis and my helping him or her change amount to: 'How desirable!' and not 'How necessary!' I do not *need* what I *want*. Unless I foolishly *think* I do!

"**5.** What Worse Things Could Actually Happen if I Don't Get What I Think I Must (or Do Get What I Think I Mustn't)?
Illustrative Answer: If my mate never acts less neurotically and I fail completely to help him or her do so, I would fail to get all the satisfactions I would like to get from living with him or her.

"**6.** What Good Things Could I Make Happen if I Don't Get What I Think I Must (or Do Get What I Think I Mustn't)?
Illustrative Answer: I can think of at least a few good things that might occur or I could make occur. If I find it impossible to help this mate with his or her disturbance, I could devote more time and energy, and receive a good deal of enjoyment, trying to help other people who may feel more receptive to my helping efforts—such as my children, my friends, my other relatives." [26, pp. 137–140.]

In the language of the Human Response System, Ellis' Disputing Irrational Beliefs technique pumps information into the system that it previously failed to utilize in its own behalf. A system that is easily threatened and aroused tends to generate faulty information about itself. It misperceives the environment, thinks in a disordered fashion, and negatively evaluates itself.

The DIBS approach facilitates the effects of repeated exposure and cognitive self-guidance by providing the system with alternative thoughts that compete with irrational thoughts and ideas. The frequency of rational thinking increases with practice. The desired goal is to generate a thinking style that accurately appraises life events, even negative life events. The new thinking style also counteracts irrational thoughts that occur in the face of these inevitable, negative life circumstances.

I have used the technique successfully with individuals by following some fairly simple steps. The steps can be executed along with imagery techniques and stress innoculation in order to effectively prepare for activating life events. They can also be used on a regular basis throughout the day to counteract spontaneously occurring irrational thoughts and to increase the frequency of rational self-dialogues. The steps outlined below can be used with imagery training and stress innoculation by integrating them into the five steps that were discussed earlier in the chapter. They can also be utilized as an independent strategy for altering your style of thinking.

Step 1.   The first step in counteracting your irrational thoughts is to pinpoint the chain of events that occur when you find yourself emotionally upset and disturbed. For example, if you are continually anxious when you speak to your supervisor at work, you are probably generating one or more irrational thoughts about this person. In addition to repeated exposure to this individual in relaxed imagery and in the real-life situation of the office, it is important for you to pinpoint your irrational ideas. They may include one or more of the following statements: "I must have his or her approval. I want him/her to like me so desperately. What if he or she doesn't find my work performance satisfactory. I can't stand his or her criticism."

Step 2.   Once the idea(s) have been pinpointed, you can challenge them by: (a) Questioning the truthfulness of these internal thoughts by asking yourself, "Where is the evidence?" (b) Providing yourself with new information about the life event that you had not previously considered. "Where is the evidence that I need his or her approval so desperately? Who says that I have to be perfect? What makes me think that I can't stand criticism? I can live without his or her approval although all of the evidence indicates that he or she really does like me. People will probably care about me even though I'm not perfect. Nobody is perfect. I can handle criticism if I have to. It won't kill me."

Step 3.   Once the irrational ideas have been identified and challenged, and new information is being pumped into the response system, self-instructions can be utilized to encourage yourself to engage in an active interplay with the environment. "Now, relax and concentrate on him or her as you talk to him or her. Try to keep looking at this person. Get to know this individual as he or she really is and not what you have made up in your head about him or her. Good! Hang in there."

The new self-dialogue combines exposure, self-guidance, and disputation (challenging old information and pumping in new data): "Relax! Concentrate! Where is the evidence? And, internal statements such as "I don't have to be perfect;" "I don't need everyone's approval;" assist the thinking component of the response system in its encounters with difficult life events.

Case Study: Changing a Maladaptive Thinking Style by Counteracting Irrational Thoughts

Motherhood has become a very stressful occupation in our culture. The act of mothering can be as high pressured as managing a large business organization. Mothers have the major responsibility for one or more relatively helpless and dependent members of our society. In addition, they are usually involved in numerous other activities such as the PTA, special school projects, fund raisers, and neighborhood functions. Unfortunately the standards for qualifying as a "good" mother are very high. They include perserverance, courage, and above all the ability to forego one's own pleasures for the benefit of one's children. The list of musts and shoulds, what mothers can and cannot do, is endless. Some of the more common ones include: I should not do anything that causes my child emotional distress; I should consider my child's desires above my own: and I should follow the rules and regulations set up by other mothers. Thus it is not surprising that mothers as a group have their share of emotional upsets and disturbances.

Pat asked me for help with a problem that I have encountered many times in my professional work. She was recently divorced and the mother of a young girl. Pat's primary concern when she separated from her husband was the potential impact of this event on her child's emotional well-being. Would the child suffer emotionally from the divorce? Would she blame her mother for it? Could the child continue to relate at the same level with her friends? These were a few of the concerns that plagued Pat for months after the separation.

Pat was preoccupied with these thoughts when she was alone. When she and the child were at home together, Pat was extremely sensitive about the child's behavior. Every deviation from the child's normal behavior was perceived as a consequence of the separation. During these times Pat would feel apprehensive, jittery, and depressed about her current style of living. She was ambivalent about establishing new relationships and placed numerous restrictions on herself in order to minimize any further emotional assault to her child. Pat was miserable with this lonely and tense style of living.

My approach to Pat's problem was to help her identify the maladaptive thinking responses that made up her coping strategy.

I assisted her in identifying her irrational beliefs about the effects of the divorce on the child's emotional well-being. She learned to vigorously dispute these ideas and trained herself to significantly reduce the frequency of negative self-judgments. She engaged in the following process of identifying and disputing irrational beliefs.

Identifying irrational beliefs (six irrational beliefs were identified):

1. The divorce will inevitably scar my child emotionally.
2. I am responsible for anything that happens to her because I initiated the divorce.
3. My child will blame me for what has happened and see me as a bad mother.
4. This current family situation will hinder her ability to get along with her friends and their families.
5. I must not be seen as a bad mother by my child or anyone else.
6. I must not lose approval from my child or anyone else.

Disputing irrational beliefs (each belief was counteracted individually):

1. There is no concrete evidence indicating that divorce always has negative effects. In many cases, given a bad relationship between husband and wife, the break-up can be actually beneficial.
2. Although I am currently responsible for the welfare of my child, the responsibility for the break-up was not one-sided.
3. My child may, in fact, blame me for what happened, but the blaming is not terrible, and it won't kill me. Besides, it will probably be a temporary response on her part, particularly if I refuse to be upset by it.
4. Some of her friends' families may look at the divorce in a negative way and may criticize me for initiating it. That's unfortunate. I probably can't change their beliefs about it anyway so why am I allowing myself to get upset about them. Besides, do I really care about their beliefs if they are going to react to me in such a close-minded and narrow manner.
5. I probably won't be seen as a bad mother by anyone. But I surely can tolerate not being seen as perfect by some people.
6. The chances are very slim indeed that my child or anyone else would refuse to give me their approval because of the break-up of a relationship that will probably be beneficial in the long run to all of us. However, I can stand a loss of approval if I have to. My child is not fully capable of understanding the situation because of her age and may temporarily withdraw her love and approval. Others will never understand totally because they did not experience the situation as I did.

Pat learned to talk to herself in this way when activating events (being around her child's friends, her child acting "unlike herself," and so on.) triggered irrational thoughts. Her new style of thinking about the divorce and the subsequent positive effect on her child allowed Pat to behave more freely and spontaneously toward other people. In addition, it helped her alleviate the effects of anxiety, guilt, and depression.

Once Pat was trained in readily identifying and disputing irrational beliefs, she could use this response with her previously learned skills of relaxation, imagery training, and stress innoculation. On one particular occasion, Pat was abruptly confronted with a direct criticism from the mother of her daughter's friend. This lady very abruptly informed Pat that her daughter was no longer welcome in her home because of the negative influence a fatherless child might have on her own child. Pat took a deep breath and engaged in the following self-dialogue. "Relax! You know that you have prepared for this before. Concentrate on this lady and tell her what you really think. You don't need her approval and your daughter can live without her little friend." Pat looked at this lady straight in the eyes and stated: "I feel sorry for you and your daughter. Your narrow-mindedness will certainly effect your daughter much more seriously than her exposure to several fatherless children ever will."

COUNTERACTING DISORDERED THINKING: SUMMARY

Through the sophisticated organ of our brain, we have an inherent capacity to generate thoughts, beliefs, and images. These responses accumulate to produce a private self-dialogue. We can talk to ourselves in a way that facilitates pleasant emotions, personal effectiveness, and happiness. Yet, this constructive thinking style often yields to the forces of our disordered thinking habits. We tend to spend a large portion of our conscious brain-using time worrying about present and future events, distracting ourselves from meaningful daily activities, and thinking irrationally about the difficult world in which we live. These preoccupations leave less time and energy for adaptive self-dialogues.

The most important strategy for increasing the frequency of adaptive self-statements and images is to develop skills that counteract these disordered thinking habits. Each habit can be counteracted separately by the use and practice of an alternative thinking response. Together these skills for counteracting disordered thinking facilitate the development of a constructive general style of thinking. In order to summarize the process of developing this new style of thinking it will be helpful to consider an example from the sports world.

Coaches, professional athletes, and sports enthusiasts readily expound the virtues of athletic skills. Most of them feel that the phenomenon of mind over matter is an important factor in athletic endeavors. It is fairly common to attribute one athlete's success over another, given equal physical abilities, to some undefined mental capacity. According to many armchair psychologists, it is this capacity that distinguishes the superior performer from the mediocre one.

Tim Gallway has attempted to systematize this idea, at least for the game of tennis, in his book *The Inner Game of Tennis.* Gallway states the basic thesis of his book in the introduction.

It is the thesis of this book that neither mastery nor satisfaction can be found in the playing of any game without giving some attention to the relatively neglected skills of the inner game. This is the game that takes place in the mind of the player, and it is played against such obstacles as lapses in concentration, nervousness, self-doubt, and self-condemnation. In short, it is played to overcome all habits of mind which inhibit excellence in performance. [43, p. 13]

In the previous discussion, the "habits of the mind" have been outlined in terms of disruptive thinking responses of the Human Response System. Take a look at these responses as they take place on the tennis court. It will help for you to imagine the following scene.

You are warming up for a set of tennis with a friend. You've played with this individual several times before and feel that your respective abilities to play the game are equal. Your strokes feel good today; you are keeping your eye on the ball and following through on your forehand and backhand. It looks like it might be a good day for you. The ball has remained in play for several minutes, and you are impressed with your performance up to this point.

The warm-up period is complete, and it is time to play; time to get serious and keep score. Your friend won the right to serve, and you are waiting to receive it. The first serve arrives briskly at the net; the second one makes it over. You approach it very cautiously, take a jerky half-swing, and contact the ball at the top portion of the racket. The ball trickles over the net, much to your amazement. During the remainder of the set, you are confused about the abrupt transition in your game that took place between warm-up and play. The smooth and effective pre-game strategy has been replaced with a cautious, uptight approach to the tennis match.

If you were the tennis player in the scene presented above, you were the victim of a maladaptive inner strategy. You noticed that during the non-threatening conditions of the warm-up period, your responses were executed in a satisfactory manner. The activating event was the initiation of play. The onset of competition and subsequent pressure of performance were defined as threatening. Under these competitive conditions, you were more likely to emit the following disordered thinking responses:

Loss of Control: You lost the ability to coordinate all of your responses—thoughts, physiological reactions, and behavior—for your own behalf. Instead, the game seems to be out of your hands and in the hands of some mysterious force that you have very little control over. You may have said to yourself: "What is going wrong? I don't understand this."

Thought Distractions: You took your eye off the ball and focused on the movements of the player on the other side of the court. You may have been distracted by the activity on the next court. Your concentration was diverted from the major focus of the game—to watch the course of the ball and return it to the other side of the tennis court. You may have said to yourself: "I can't seem to concentrate on the game. There are so many distractions."

Irrational Thinking: As the set proceeds you tend to evaluate your performance. "I'll never learn how to play this game. Why do I stick with it." Self-blaming takes place: "I wouldn't be in this mess if I would practice more often. And, finally, self-criticism: "I've never been good at sports anyway. Why do I keep trying? I can't stand to lose. What if I don't win. What will my opponent think of me?"

The behavioral outcome of this strategy is a cautious, uptight, and inadequate performance. You may leave the court mildly anxious and angry. If the inner strategy proceeds into the remainder of the day's activities, you may experience depression and further emotional disturbance. All of this for a game that was supposed to be fun!

The development of a new thinking strategy in this activating situation, the harmless competition of a game of tennis, will provide you with a good model for counteracting negative thinking responses in the other games of life. As Gallway states:

> Victories in the inner game may provide no additions to the trophy case, but they bring valuable rewards which are permanent and which contribute significantly to one's success thereafter, off the court, as well as on. [43, p. 13]

The player who has his or her head together about the game of tennis can execute a new inner strategy when confronted with the activating event—

the onset of play and competition. There is virtually no change in thinking style from the warm-up period to the period of play. Play is not defined as dangerous. The player counteracts disruptive thinking responses by relaxing and minimizing the tendency to sense a loss of control, by maintaining concentration on the focus of the game and refusing to be distracted by extraneous stimuli, and by disputing and putting a stop to irrational thinking.

In the terminology of the Human Response System, the specific steps may be executed in the following manner: *You relax and take another, more adaptive, look at the situation that you have defined as threatening and then:*

Step 1. *Counteract the Tendency to Sense A Loss of Control:* "I can be relaxed. I can quiet my mind. My nervousness will subside as soon as I hit the first few balls."

Step 2. *Reduce Thought Distractions and Increase Concentration:* "I can pay attention to this game and forget about everything else. Keep your eye on the ball. Watch it flow across the net. Watch the way it meets the racket."

Step 3. *Counteract Irrational Thinking:* "I don't have to win. My life doesn't depend on this game. It's fun to win, but it won't be terrible if I lose. Just less fun."

The same rules for the self-regulation of thinking in the game of tennis can be used to play the game of life.

SELF-REGULATION OF THINKING AND FEEDBACK

The techniques discussed in the previous section for altering the thinking component of the Human Response System in a very systematic way provide the system with information and feedback that it previously, under the conditions of disordered thinking, did not have access to. The repeated exposure to stressful situations provided by relaxation and imagery training allows the system to take another clear, unbiased look at events that it has defined as threatening and dangerous. Several looks later, the system finds that the environment has been partially or even totally misperceived. This is new datum and information for the system to use in its own behalf.

The self-instructions provided by stress innoculation help guide the system through the steps involved in confronting any life event. It confronts the system with the specific details of an activating situation that it may have overlooked. Self-instructions facilitate concentration and minimize distractions. This detailed analysis of the environment leaves no room for faulty thinking. It leaves no doubt about what is expected from the environment and facilitates the continual accumulation of old and new data about life events. It provides an ongoing exchange of information between the environment and the Human Response System.

The continual challenge levied on existing ideas, beliefs, and attitudes; the constant exchange of old ideas for new ones; and the pumping-in of sentences and images that characterizes the disputation technique feeds the system with regular doses of empirically derived information. Combined with repeated exposure and self-instructions, the rational self-dialogue always questions appraisals and corrects misappraisals of the environment. It provides the response system with alternative thinking responses when old habits fail to jive with existing environmental conditions. The continual flow of information provided by these new "habits of the mind" allows the system to accurately size up the environment.

The system's adaptive response to stressful life events (as a result of this new thinking style) is fed back to the system for the sake of maintaining equilibrium. When the system remains open to an exchange with the environment, opportunities for response regulation and control abound. These new thinking habits guarantee the continual exchange of information. The information gathering response, knowledge of response impact, and response adjustment guaranteed by a system that is constantly pumping in new data about life events provides many opportunities for self-regulation and self-control.

Overt behavior acts on the environment and receives a response in return. We talk to people and they talk back to us. The feedback is usually immediate and continuous. We can choose to ignore the results of our actions or we can use these results to change our behavior. Thinking, on the other hand, does not profit from such an immediate return. It tends to perpetuate itself with no consistent feedback from its actions. Thus you can see the importance of creating a constructive self-dialogue. These new internal responses can observe and evaluate the results of outdated thoughts and beliefs, and then utilize this feedback for thought regulation and change. Without the benefit of this feedback, habitual disordered thoughts tend to usurp the system.

The positive effect of feedback-induced thought regulation and a new self-dialogue was profound in the case of Paul. Relaxation training had set the stage for a return to the arena of psychological threat and conflict. Under the conditions of a low level of physiological arousal, Paul was better prepared to confront his stressors. The tendency of the system to leap into a detached and disordered strategy was reduced and there was a significant increase in ordered and clear thinking. Under these conditions, information about life events that was previously unpalatable became progressively more acceptable to his response system.

Through desensitization and imagery training, Paul was exposed to information about past and present life events. In a safe and non-threatening environment, he began to absorb bits and pieces of his life that were previously unavailable. New thoughts about threatening life events were generated. Old ones were discarded. A series of ordered thinking responses developed into a new belief about himself and several of these beliefs facilitated a sense of response control. Paul's general attitude changed and knowledge of this change reinforced further adaptive thinking responses.

Paul began to confront events in his life with a new coping strategy. He developed a sense of control about life events at the hospital and in his newly acquired position at the television station. The ability to concentrate during stressful work and interpersonal encounters increased dramatically and his memory for past and current events improved. Rational thoughts systematically replaced irrational ones and he learned to challenge and counteract his excessive concern for approval and perfectionism. His pace slowed down considerably and he approached life in a more easy-going manner.

By taking another look at an environment that was appraised as overwhelming and dangerous, Paul opened his response system to information and feedback that was critical to self-regulation and control. His strategy has faltered at times when a series of stressors have taken a cumulative toll on his system. Yet his newly acquired coping strategy is always open to constructive solutions to the problems of living.

Dr. T, Pat, and Paul, along with those who play the inner game of tennis, have constructed personal feedback systems that check and balance disordered thinking. This personal feedback and the systematic use of it is an important component of the adaptive functioning and positive well-being created by modifying what people say to themselves.

9 HUMAN RESPONSE SYSTEM

Behavior

THE CASE OF FRED

Fred is an executive for a large company that is located in a city in the southeastern part of the United States. He is responsible for the supervision and management of several department managers. These individuals are responsible for departments that consists of 50–60 employees. This means that Fred is ultimately responsible for the work and performance of several hundred people.

Fred is fairly young to be in this position. Because of his twenty-five pounds of excess weight and a receding hair line, he appears to be older than thirty-seven. In the last ten years with the company, he hasn't taken the time to adequately care for himself. His six and seven twelve-hour working days leave him very little time to spend with his family and friends. Fred has even less time to exercise regularly and has virtually no interest in changing his eating habits.

In terms of behavioral style, Fred would be categorized as a Type A individual. He is constantly struggling with his environment to reach greater heights of achievement. Fred has accelerated to an executive position in the company quite rapidly. He accomplished this self-imposed goal by being hard-driving, persistent, and, of course, working more than the required number of hours.

Fred is described by his co-workers as hyperactive. He never wastes any time and is rarely seen socializing with fellow col-

leagues or subordinates. He walks and talks very rapidly, and it is difficult to get Fred's attention for even a short period of time. During scheduled appointments with co-workers, he does most of the talking for both parties. If you are speaking to Fred and fail to complete a sentence or express an idea rapidly enough, he will finish it for you. Fred is proud of the fact that, in comparison with his co-workers, he gets the most work done in the least amount of time.

Fred has reaped the financial benefits of his executive status. He is fond of displaying his real estate investments—a condominium at the beach, several pieces of choice acreage outside of town, and a $100,000 home in a plush suburban community. Two cars, one boat, and a small airplane are also among his most highly prized possessions. Although Fred does not spend a great deal of time away from work engaging in domestic and recreational activities, he feels good about these tangible possessions. Fred is rewarded by the fact that he has accumulated wealth and a large number of valuable assets in a short period of time.

Myra is Fred's wife. She spends a large portion of her time with two children and two pets in their large suburban home. Myra is happy about her financial security, but she has difficulty understanding Fred's incessant drive. She is equally puzzled by his hyperactive behavior. Her frequent question to him is: "Why obtain all these potentially satisfying objects when we don't have enough time together to share and enjoy them?" Fred gets very hostile about Myra's attitude. He feels that she simply lacks the ability to understand him. Their relationship has deteriorated progressively in the last ten years. Fred's relationship with the children is virtually nonexistent.

If we look inside Fred's head for a moment, we will see a number of private responses that are not readily surmised from observing his behavior. Fred is a very frightened individual. He is easily threatened by authority figures, co-workers, and even subordinates. Their evaluations of him are exceedingly important. He fears their criticism and is apprehensive about the potential withdrawal of their support and approval. You would never expect it, but Fred is in a constant struggle to perform in a perfectionistic manner in order to avoid imagined, negative consequences from his work associates. Criticism is to be escaped at all costs. Fred has avoided feedback from people throughout his life by moving fast, talking incessantly, and trying to be perfect. The feedback, however, finally caught up with him.

Fred was recently ordered by his boss to attend an encounter group. The goal of this group, as spelled out to Fred by his boss, was to loosen him up, to encourage honesty and openness, and to change his compulsive behavior pattern. Fred reluctantly attended the group. An important component of the group learning experience was to give each group member a chance to provide other participants with positive and negative feedback. Although Fred received a substantial amount of positive feedback, he could not tolerate even the smallest amount of criticism. He withdrew from the sessions prematurely and began experiencing episodes of panic and severe anxiety. When he returned to work, he was quite aggravated with his co-workers. He became extremely sensitive about their casual comments and was suspicious of their motives. He eventually became so agitated and irrational that he had to be hospitalized for short-term psychiatric treatment. Treatment. was oriented towards stabilizing his acute agitation. Fred was discharged from inpatient status after three weeks. Intensive outpatient therapy was recommended in order to modify his coping strategy.

THE CASE OF JAMES: A PHOBIC BEHAVIOR PATTERN

James is in his late twenties and has requested therapy for a very long-standing and debilitating problem. His life has become extremely confined because of his strong fear of being contaminated by objects and people from Arizona and California. The problem sounds humorous and almost unbelievable. Yet, James described the following life events that led to this unusual fear: While he was serving in the Armed Services, he was first stationed in Arizona and then in California. After he was discharged from the service and moved to another part of the country, he found that exposure to anything or anyone from these two states precipitated uncomfortable feelings. He felt contaminated by germs and dirty when he was around these objects and people. Immediately after the contact he felt compelled to vigorously wash and shower in order to decontaminate himself. James would wash his hands four or five times, shower several times in succession, completely wash his clothes, and then clean his apartment thoroughly.

A very important component of James' fear is his desire to avoid social contacts. He avoids anyone who might have been in physical contact with the two states. He has not visited his parents in another state (nor have they visited him) in several years because they were contaminated during their first visit to the Arizona base. Social dates are also out of the question. There is always the possibility that a companion may have previously known and perhaps even touched someone from Arizona or California. If there is even the slightest chance of contamination, James avoids the situation.

James uses gloves to handle letters from friends and relatives because of the possibility of further contamination. Dirt and germs have been an overwhelming preoccupation with James for the last ten years of his life.

As you would suspect from an individual who is afraid of dirt and germs, most of James' time away from work is oriented around anxiety-reducing activities: washing, showering, and avoiding social contacts. He is highly anxious most of the time. The anxiety is significantly reduced, however, after all of his cleansing rituals are performed.

James exhibits many signs of anxiety when he is exposed to the contaminating object or person. The anxiety continues for hours after the exposure. When first contaminated by something or someone from Arizona and/or California, he becomes extremely tense, his pulse rate increases, he perspires profusely, his mind races with thoughts of escaping the situation, and his physical movements become stiff and jerky. Other physiological responses to the threatening stimulus are undoubtedly occurring, but they are difficult to observe without monitoring his physiological responses with special equipment. Hours after the initial exposure, James continues to exhibit these physiological reactions. James does not relax until he is free to perform his ritualistic behaviors.

Behaviorally, James will do everything in his power to avoid a contaminating situation. He avoids spending holidays with his parents, he won't touch mail from friends and relatives who have previously visited him in the two states, and he refuses to buy products from either state. He carefully checks to see if any materials at work have been received from Arizona or California. If forced to confront any of these situations out of necessity or by accident (e.g., buying a product that he later discovered was from California), he engages in complusive, ritualistic washing, cleaning, and showering until he feels somewhat less contaminated and anxious. James never succeeds in feeling totally decontaminated and relaxed. Consequently, the compulsive behaviors continue throughout the day depending on his freedom to perform them.

When I ask James about the situations that threaten him and cause him severe discomfort he replys: "I'm anxious all the time, every moment of the day." This is a typical response from a phobic individual, one who is irrationally afraid of a discrete and harmless object in his or her environment. Pinpointing specific activating situations in an individual who is chronically and pervasively anxious is a real challenge.

Observations of James' past and present interpersonal relationships reveal some interesting facts. As you would suspect from the description of the case, heterosexual relations are difficult for him. James has virtually detached himself from this area of human relations. He does not date or engage in sexual relations and has very few friends. Family relationships are also very difficult for James. In spite of the fact that he comes from a very close-knit family that regularly exerts pressure on him for a home visit, he has not been to their home in years. He does, however, have regular contact with them through telephone calls and letters. Through these periodic contacts, they still exert a tremendous influence on him. In a sense, James is still extremely dependent on them for love, approval, and emotional support.

The only area of James' life that makes him even mildly comfortable is his work. He works regularly and dilligently with very little avoidance or passive behaviors. Even though he is not a high achiever and does not strive for great heights of productivity, when James is at work he does not exhibit the intense anxiety and stress that he displays in family and social situations.

It is quite difficult to totally understand the development of a phobia. Yet, in James' case, there is some clear-cut motivation to his behavior: James is a very frightened individual. He is threatened by his family and their incessant demands upon him to *be productive and to be a "good" son. Despite the fact that he has not seen them in years, he is extremely dependent upon them for recognition and approval. His current passive, phobic strategy allows him to escape the threatening family situation. He is not aware of the purpose of this maladaptive strategy. This information has been lost in the forest of preoccupations with contamination and in the habitual rituals that make up the decontamination process. The phobic strategy serves another equally important purpose for James. It allows him to escape the potentially threatening activity of relating to women in a social and sexual manner. He states that: "I don't really have time to date; I'm too busy with my daily chores and my job."*

Similarities Between James and Fred

To the outside observer, James and Fred have very different personalities. Fred is involved in a constant struggle with his environment to achieve more tangible outcomes in less and less time, whereas James is fighting to continue his strategy of withdrawal and interpersonal seclusion. Yet, they are both very frightened individuals. They are threatened by an environment that they perceive as demanding, hypercritical, and potentially dangerous. The content of their thought processes vary considerably. James worries about being contaminated; Fred is preoccupied with achievement and work.

The meaning of their self-dialogues (i.e., statements to themselves), however, is strikingly similar. Both James and Fred mistakingly appraise their life events as dangerous, and, as a consequence, they both engage in numerous faulty thinking habits. A close analysis of the thinking component of their response systems readily reveals all the disordered strategies that are associated with maladaptive coping. Their physiological reactions, in turn, reflect this strategy. James and Fred are highly aroused individuals. Both of them are out of balance, and this lack of physiological equilibrium is beginning to take its toll.

In order to completely understand this apparent paradox—two behaviorally divergent styles with strikingly similar maladaptive response strategies—we must take a brief excursion into the field of learning theory. Our itinerary takes us through the laboratory of psychologists and other investigators who are interested in identifying the processes that shape and mold behavior in one direction or another. This excursion will give us an answer to the question: "What makes James and Fred behave differently when their basic underlying perceptions of the environment are the same?

PRINCIPLES OF LEARNING

Life demands a combination of behavioral responses. We talk some and then we listen. We gesture and assume certain postures. We move toward and away from important daily encounters. All of these responses involve coordinated movements of various muscles that are stimulated by the nervous system to produce speech, to make gestures and expressions, and to keep us moving in one direction or another. This is overt behavior.

Contrary to the other components of the Human Response System, this series of responses is readily observable to the outside observer. It is overt as opposed to covert, public instead of private. It is this component of the system that is subject to the scrutiny of other people "He doesn't act the way he used to." "Did you see how nervous she was?" "I don't like the way he said that to me."

It is difficult for the observer to realize that overt behavior is the outcome of numerous subtle, unobservable private responses. Behavior is effected by meticulously coded messages from the brain and by the workings of the nervous and endocrine systems. These responses help create a response style that characterizes one's interaction with the environment. The following discussion focuses on a sample of these human behaviors and the principles of learning that effect them.

Operant Conditioning

Because of its easy access to the outside observer, overt responses have been the behavioral psychologists' favorite subject of investigation. They have observed, studied, and systematically categorized it. Principles of behavior have been derived that are applicable to a variety of life circumstances. B. F. Skinner's[44] development of the principle of operant conditioning is one good example. The basic principle of operant conditioning is: animal and human behavior is under the control of various consequences in the organism's environment. If the consequences of a behavior increase the chances that the behavior will occur more often in the future, it is a reinforcer for that behavior. These reinforcements or payoffs from the organism's environment are systematically studied in order to predict the organism's behavior.

A classic example of the effects of reinforcement on behavior is the intense responding that is emitted when one is playing the slot machine in a gambling casino. The gambler receives a periodic pay-off (on a specific schedule of reinforcement) from the machine for pulling the lever. As a consequence, lever-pulling occurs at an exceptionally high rate. Less tangible consequences are common in life and include a mother reinforcing an infant's smiling with her attention and a supervisor reinforcing a worker's production by a pat on the back.

Less desirable behaviors are reinforced in much the same manner. Disruptive classroom behavior among children, inappropriate verbalizations in hospitalized psychotics, and poor job performance among industrial workers are a few of the behaviors studied by the reinforcement-oriented behavioral psychologists. The principle of reinforcement indicates that these behaviors are learned and maintained in an environment because they pay off in some manner.

The environment reinforces or pays off a variety of human responses that are clearly counterproductive. For example, married couples who are experiencing difficulty in their relationships often engage in negative verbal interactions that are sometimes reinforced by the environment. Blaming is one of the most frequently occurring verbal behaviors among partners who are seeking professional help for their relationship. The problems in the relationship usually have a long, well-established history before the couple arrives at the therapist's office.

One partner often initiates the session by placing the blame for the problems on the other partner. The blamed partner sits patiently for a short while, but quickly takes the offensive and also assumes the role of the blamer. The verbal assaults become quite intense. Each partner hopes that the psychologist will take his or her side in the battle. They hope that he or she will find the real culprit in the relationship, place the blame, and administer the appropriate punishment. One of the first tasks for the therapist is to convince the couple that a therapist is not a judge and subsequently to extinguish the blaming verbal behavior.

How does this behavior develop? An analysis of the roots of the blaming syndrome usually reveals a history of reinforcement for the behavior. Each partner has complained about the partner to friends, relatives, and colleagues. These people listen sympathetically, hoping to help the individual through the difficult period. The behavior pays off. It gets the partner some attention and provides emotional relief. This behavior pattern often competes with and replaces open communication between the couple. There is a higher payoff for complaining to concerned friends than there is for openly talking about the problems with one's spouse. The negative effect on the relationship can be profound. The behavioral psychologist believes that many other adaptive and maladaptive human behaviors are reinforced in this manner.

Classical Conditioning

Classical conditioning is another learning principle that was developed in the psychological laboratory. Investigators have learned that certain life

events easily elicit reflex-like, automatic responses. These naturally elicited responses will to be repeated under a variety of stimulus situations.
For example, a child can be easily frightened by a loud noise. It produces a
startle response in the child. The startle response will be repeated in the
presence of another stimulus that has been associated with the noise. A
stimulus that was not previously feared but that happened to be present
when the startle response occurred can now also elicit the startle response. The child may have been playing with an animal when it was
startled by the noise. The animal may subsequently be feared by the child
due to this accidental connection between the animal and the startle response. This is learning through association.

Adults also learn many responses through previous associations. Many
fears and avoidance responses are developed in this manner. We learn to
avoid situations that have previously been associated with unpleasant
experiences even if the current situation is different from the past one.
Spoiled food that made one sick in the past continues to induce nausea
even though the food is known to be unspoiled. Some people are continually frightened by mild outbursts of anger from friends and relatives because of the arousal generated by heated arguments of the past.

Instead of eliciting unpleasant emotional states, some conditioned responses enhance the pleasures of life. Vividly imagining a pleasant scene
from the past can produce many of the positive feelings that were experienced in the actual situation. Momentos from loved ones allow us to remember and sometimes relive the great moments of the past. These
responses occur partly because of our ability to learn through the association of one life event with another.

Operant and Classical Conditioning

Several principles of learning are involved in the development of phobias.
A phobia is an extreme irrational fear of a fairly specific situation. In reality,
the situation presents no danger to the fearful individual. Yet the phobic
person responds to the life event as if it was life-threatening. The case of
James, described at the beginning of this chapter, would be categorized
as a contamination or germ phobia.

The most prominent behavior observed when a phobic person confronts the feared situation is avoidance. They will go to great lengths to
escape this encounter. Claustrophobics will vigorously avoid enclosed
spaces. Agoraphobics are afraid of exposure to the openness of streets,
large shopping areas, and even large rooms. The stimulus situation (open
or closed spaces) elicits disordered and irrational thoughts and an acute
state of arousal in the phobic. These fear and avoidance responses have

been classically conditioned to the stimulus situation by various unpleasant experiences in the individual's past.

Avoidance behavior pays off for the phobic because it reduces the person's physiological arousal and creates a relatively greater feeling of comfort and relaxation. The avoidance behavior is strengthened and reinforced in this manner. The response will be repeated in subsequent encounters.

In addition to the discomfort-reducing pay-off, some phobias are further socially reinforced by the sympathy, concern, and attention given by concerned people in the phobic's life. Thus phobias are subject to at least two of the laws of learning: classical and operant conditioning. The phobic is classically conditioned to avoid situations that have been associated with unpleasant emotions and operantly reinforced to avoid the feared situation by a reduction in anxiety and an increase in sympathetic attention from concerned people.

Seligman's[17] work on child development and the phenomenon of "learned helplessness" has shed further light on the effect of complex principles of learning on the behavioral component of the Human Response System. Children learn to be self-sufficient and develop a sense of control and mastery over their environments because of an active interplay with mother, father, and other important people. By responding to a child in a consistent manner for behaviors such as crying and smiling, the mother teaches the child that its behavior counts. Seligman has shown that animals and humans who fail to learn this lesson become helpless in their attempts to cope with the environment.

The child becomes helpless when it learns that its responses have no effect on the environment. A child who is fed four times a day in an orphanage, regardless of the child's behavior, fails to learn that his or her behavior counts for anything. An animal who gets shocked no matter how much it works at escaping an aversive situation fails to learn that its behavior counts for anything. The same holds true for an adult who indiscriminately receives criticism for a variety of behaviors. The animal, child, and adult learn a sense of helplessness. The results of this sense of helplessness are a loss of motivation to respond and severe depression.

Modeling

People also learn from the behavior of others. We tend to imitate the behavior of other people particularly when we see them getting reinforced for their behavior. This is referred to as modeling. For example, children of parents who smoke are more likely to become cigarette smokers than children of nonsmokers. Children who observe other children engaging in aggressive behavior toward inanimate objects (e.g., toys) emit more aggressive behavior toward those objects when the opportunity to do so arises. This response is not limited to children. Adults are also subject to the effects of modeling but exhibit the tendency to imitate somewhat less than children.

LEARNED MALADAPTIVE BEHAVIOR PATTERNS: AVOIDANCE AND HYPERRESPONSIVENESS

The example discussed earlier—the phobic response—is a learned avoidance behavior that is clearly counterproductive. One that is equally maladaptive is the Type A Behavior Pattern. Whereas the phobic individual decelerates his or her responding when confronted with a threatening series of life events, the Type A accelerates his or her rate of behavior. In an article for the *American Scientist,* Psychologist David Glass discusses his research findings on the Type A coronary-prone behavior pattern.

> In contrast to B's, Type A's work hard to succeed, suppress subjective states (e.g., fatigue) that might interfere with task performance, exhibit rapid pacing of their activities, and express hostility after being harassed in their efforts at task completion—all, I would submit, in the interests of asserting control over environmental demands and requirements. I would also suggest that these demands must be at least minimally stressful, for the possibility of failure and loss of esteem was inherent in most of the experimental situations used in the validation studies. The coronary-prone behavior pattern might thus be described as a characteristic style of responding to environmental stressors that threaten an individual's sense of control. . . . Type A's are engaged in a struggle for control, whereas Type B's are relatively free of such concerns and, hence, free of characteristic Pattern A traits. [45, pp. 180–181]

In contrast to the phobic's avoidance behavior pattern, the Type A pattern may be termed hyperresponsive. It is assumed to reflect a concerted effort to assert control over the life event rather than to avoid it. The development of this behavior pattern of hyperresponsiveness, like the phobic response, involves a complex combination of the learning principles outlined previously. Richard Suinn, a psychologist utilizing behavior modification techniques for the prevention of cardiovascular disease, provides some insight into the anxiety-reducing and, therefore, reinforcing qualities of the Type A pattern.

> It was my assumption that the Type A person engages in activities which are by nature stress producing. Additionally, it was my premise that the Type A person finds it difficult to extinguish such Type A behaviors because such a

person feels anxious when such changes are attempted. In response to such anxiety, the Type A person tends to repeat overlearned Type A behaviors. [46, p. 13]

The struggle for control and the escape from an unpleasant state of anxiety certainly appear to be two of the complex factors that make up the Type A personality. The effect of adult models who exhibited the behavior pattern on the Type A individual's behavior is also quite profound. A society that places a strong emphasis on work and achievement provides numerous adult models for this behavior pattern. These models insure a constant exposure of Type A behaviors to developing children, adolescents, and young adults.

Positive reinforcement from these adults is lavished upon individuals who imitate the model's Type A behavior. As we have learned from laboratory studies, this combination of influences—the frequent exposure to models and the positive reinforcement for the modeled behavior—is a potent strengthener of human responses.

The cases of Fred and James: Examples of learned, maladaptive behavior patterns. *I began the comparison between Fred and James with the statement that they were both frightened individuals. Yet, we observed that individually they exhibited behavior that was quite divergent. Fred resembles many hard-working, driving individuals in our society. James' unusual behavior is not so readily observable. Less extreme variations of his cautious, compulsive life style are more common. At this point, you are better able to understand their unique characteristics.*

Fred and James have different learning histories. They have acquired a unique set of skills for coping with stressful life events. Their diverse strategies stem from years of unique learning experiences. They were positively reinforced for different behaviors. Fred was probably praised and rewarded for his aggressiveness, independence, achievement, and hard-driving approach to life. James was reinforced for being cautious, dependent, and passive in his relationship with the outside world. Their adult models were probably as unlike one another as Fred and James themselves are. Fred observed people in his environment getting paid off for reacting quickly and aggressively to every social and economic opportunity that came along in life. On the other hand, James observed his parents and other significant people coping with life in a cautious, apprehensive, and passive manner.

When Fred is presented with a series of stressors and frustrations he puts his system in overdrive. Under the same circumstances James sits back and is overwhelmed by a sense of helplessness and loss of control. Fred and James both experience a great deal of emotional upset, but their emotions are triggered by different circumstances and responses. Fred is more comfortable when he is goal-oriented. Therefore, work and working associates are sought out as a means of gaining satisfaction and well-being. Work is simply a means to the end of survival for James. He is more comfortable when he is alone in the solitude of his apartment. In this environment he is free to carry out his ritualistic behavior. Fred can't stand to be idle or alone even with a small group of family and friends. He cannot produce results in these environments, and production is the mainstay of his precarious state of equilibirum.

As a result of a complex set of learning experiences, each individual exhibits a divergent set of behaviors. Together, they represent a behavioral strategy for coping with activating life events. The respective strategies are triggered by demands from the environment. When the environment is perceived as harmless, the behaviors emitted by James and Fred are generally adaptive. Unfortunately, Fred and James rarely appraise life events in this manner. On the contrary, they often generate the "dangerous environment" hypothesis. As a consequence, they are chronically exhibiting maladaptive habits of living. The tolls that these habits take will be highly individualistic. Yet, in this respect, they do have another thing in common: Fred and James experience heavy doses of emotional upset, emotional disturbance, and perhaps a debilitating set of psychosomatic problems.

CREATURES OF HABIT

Human beings, along with most of their ancestors on the phylogenetic scale, are creatures of habit. We learn specific behaviors under a variety of environmental conditions and repeatedly use these same responses in coping with life. The overlearning of certain behaviors occurs quite rapidly and can be executed with a minimum amount of effort and conscious awareness. Hunt and Matarazzo, two psychologist who have conducted research on human behavior, have defined a habit in the following manner: *A fixed behavior pattern overlearned to the point of becoming au-*

*tomatic and marked by decreasing awareness and increasing depen-
dence on secondary, rather than primary, reinforcement.*[47]

One of the most common examples of the development of habitual
behavior is the process of learning how to drive. At first the novice driver is
conscious of every move that is necessary for starting, moving, and stop-
ing the car. The entire response system must be mobilized to concentrate
on shifting gears, turning corners, and parking. Very soon, however, the
responses become automatic and seem to move to another level of
awareness. The car can be driven without really thinking about it. The
system is no longer totally mobilized in order to meet the demands of
driving, and little effort is required. The behaviors are executed without
total concentration by the driver. In addition, the driver becomes less dependent on instructions, feedback, and reinforcement from the instructor
and relies more on internal signals for executing the response. Thus driving is overlearned and becomes habitual.

Studies with animals and humans show that responses that are learned
under one set of circumstances tend to be repeated under other circumstances. A newborn child enters this world with a definitive
response—crying. It is a natural behavior often elicited by the physician's
slap to the baby's rear. Subsequently, the crying response will be elicited
by other stimuli (when the child is hungry or in pain) and will operate on the
environment (particularly the mother) for attention. Crying will be repeated
because of the effect it has on the environment and because it is important
for the child's survival. The child does not have to learn a new response
every time it wants something from the outside world. That strategy would
not be very effective or economical. It has a very good habit—crying—that
gets the payoff very consistently.

From the time that you are an infant and for the remainder of your life
you are a creature of habit. You learn hundreds of responses that pay off in
some way. Without habits, you would scramble around randomly to cope
with your environment. It is obvious that the development of habits at all
levels of the Human Response System is a necessary prerequisite for
adequate coping and survival.

Unfortunately, the same process occurs in the learning of maladaptive
behaviors. It is often the case in life that too much of a good thing is bad for
you: too much food, too much work, even too many vitamins. The list is a
healthy one. The same holds true for habits learned by the Human Response System in its attempt to cope with a complex environment. Joseph
Danysh, in his book *Stop Without Quitting,* cites an extreme example to
illustrate this point about habits.

To appreciate the force custom exerts upon our habitual behavior, let us
consider some extreme examples. The Tierra del Fuegan who lives in a land

whipped by freezing antarctic gales wears no clothing save a certain cere- monial robe—a kind of half-cape—slung over one shoulder, which he wears always on the same side of the body regardless of which way the wind blows. When his bare side is exposed to those icy, antarctic blasts, wouldn't you think the Fuegan would have sense enough at least to turn the uncov- ered side away? Sense enough he may have, but independence sufficient to flaunt the custom of his fellow Fuegans he has not. [48, p. 89]

For a further example, take the habit of cigarette smoking. Everyone would agree that it is a bad habit. Yet, some people smoke habitually to facilitate pleasurable experiences, to cope with stress, to relax, and for a variety of other reasons. Witness the following series of human responses identified in my research project on cigarette smoking:[49]

1.   The smoker is confronted with a life event—important speech, tele- phone call, or meeting.

2.   Smoker engages in a self-dialogue: "I sure could handle this situa- tion better if I had a cigarette." "Cigarettes make me more relaxed when I'm tense."

3.   The smoker reaches for the same brand of cigarettes, placed in the usual location, and engages in the act of smoking in the same way that he or she has done in the past.

If you asked cigarette smokers about this sequence of responses, they would probably be unaware of the specific thoughts and behaviors that accompany the act of smoking. Cigarette smoking is a habit. It demands very little conscious attention. The strategy is initiated and completed in much the same way that it has been executed many times before. The consequence of this particular overlearned behavior is documented on the cigarette pack itself. We all agree that it is a poor way of coping. Yet there are 70 million smokers in the United States today.

OTHER LEARNED BEHAVIORS

The previous discussion focuses on extreme behavior patterns, the dire consequences of these maladaptive strategies, and the tendency for these strategies to become habitual. Most learned behavior patterns fall some- where between the extreme ends of the behavioral continium of Type A and phobic behaviors. Depending on various life circumstances, all of us are capable of exhibiting both hyper- and hyporesponsive patterns. Some situations elicit a hard-driving, active behavioral strategy. Others produce a passive and cautious sequence of habits. Our lives from one day to the next represent a curious mixture of excessive involvement followed by detachment, withdrawal, and then periods of balanced activity.

The following categories of behavior represent a sample of habits that can lead to emotional upset and disturbance. Each one of us can exhibit one or more of these and other behaviors depending on the environmental event that we are confronting at any given time in our lives. In small doses each one of the following behaviors can be adaptive. When they become overlearned, overused, and resistant to change, they can be maladaptive. Admittedly, the sample is small. You can make the judgement about other behaviors in your life that are comparable to these maladaptive responses.

Perfectionism

People learn to be perfectionistic as a strategy for coping with life events that are threatening. They hope to avoid failure, criticism, rejection, and other real and fantasized consequences by being perfect. There are many faulty beliefs that accompany this behavior pattern. These are discussed in Chapter 8. The behavior pattern itself consists of numerous habits that include compulsiveness, orderliness, and excessive cleanliness. The perfectionist cannot stand to make mistakes at work, home, or in social situations. Fallibility of any kind is energetically avoided by people who exhibit this behavior pattern.

Dependency

Dependent individuals often escape from making decisions on their own. They rely on other people for most of the important activities and decisions in their lives. Dependent individuals avoid responsibility. The dependent person looks to other people for excessive attention and support. This strategy often leads to an intense fear of being alone.

Cautiousness

Cautious individuals are fearful of taking risks. They often move very slowly in making any changes in their lives. Change itself is threatening. They often stay in unpleasant situations for long periods of time. They continue with bad relationships, marriages, and jobs in order to avoid the emotional experiences that accompany life changes. Their everyday interactions are characterized by excessive passivity, shyness, and often quick detachment from risky, social encounters.

Overindulgence

This category can include alcoholism, drug abuse, and overeating. Individuals who overindulge in one or more of these habits often do so as a strategy for coping with stressful life events. Life is generally quite stressful for these people, and they do not have adequate coping skills. As a consequence, they consume excessively in order to help them handle numerous activating life events. The rate of consumption of alcohol, drugs, and food increases as the pressure increases in the individual's life. The habits become so pervasive that they often preclude the learning of more adaptive coping skills.

These behaviors are not independent of one another. In fact, quite to the contrary, many of these habits reside together to make up a maladaptive coping strategy. The following discussion deals with the interrelationship that exists between maladaptive learned behaviors.

MALADAPTIVE HABITS OF LIVING: THE BREAKDOWN OF FEEDBACK

The driver of a car learns a set of responses that become habitual and can be executed with a minimum of effort and awareness. The information exchange and feedback to the response system regarding the adequacy of these behaviors are conducted much like the communication process that occurs at the physiological level of response functioning. The brain does not have to consciously instruct the heart to beat slower in order to reduce blood pressure. Under normal circumstances this exchange of information and feedback occurs automatically. The driver of a car does not have to consciously instruct the muscles of the legs and arms to shift gears and apply the brakes. The behavior is overlearned; it is a habit. The behavior, driving, would be disrupted if the driver had to be conscious of the results of all of his or her actions. The reduction of feedback in this particular habit is adaptive. This state of diminished feedback is characteristic of many learned behaviors that people emit on a regular basis such as writing, walking, and even speaking.

The ability of the response system to develop habits, to submerge behaviors to lower levels of consciousness, is adaptive in many cases. The very same tendency to habituate is at the core of many maladaptive responses. The feedback deficit that is adaptive in some human responses becomes destructive in others. The cigarette smoker, for example, suffers from a deficiency of information. The response has become so automatic that the smoker can light up, take numerous drags, and extinguish the cigarette with little awareness of this sequence of behaviors. The smoker's response system has lost its ability to provide the smoker with feedback about the consequences of the habit. The heat of the inhaled smoke, the discomfort in the lungs, and even the potent smell of the ashes are ignored. Smokers cannot profit from what their response systems are telling them. This immediate feedback is lost in the ritualistic chain of behaviors that join together to make up the act of cigarette smoking.

Behavior problems can be viewed as feedback problems. The Human Response System fails to profit from information and feedback about the adequacy or inadequacy of its own behavioral level of functioning. Phobic individuals are often aware of the irrational nature of their fears. Most phobics will confess that "there is nothing about enclosed spaces, open spaces, or germs to be afraid of." Yet, phobics fail to use this information in their own behalf when they are confronted with the feared situation. They continue to habitually behave as if the phobic object or situation was actually dangerous.

Phobics rarely give themselves the opportunity to obtain feedback about fearful events because they vigorously avoid a confrontation with them. James' fear of germs and contamination by objects from Arizona and California was clearly a distortion of his environment. This distorted set of perceptions prevented him from confronting his fears. These disordered thoughts completely halted environmental interactions that were crucial to adaptive functioning.

The Type A Behavior Pattern can be conceptualized in the same manner. Type A individuals fail to profit from the feedback provided to them by their response systems. The Type A habits errode interpersonal relations, they effect the normal homeostatic mechanisms of the body, and they even diminish the ability to be productive at work. However, the behavior pattern is perceived as the necessary means to the end of success, happiness, and well-being. The response system, subjected to and executing the Type A's incessant struggle with the environment, fails to adjust itself. The information that it is receiving about its own functioning is lost in a forest of hyperactive behaviors. It ignores this information until a complete breakdown of functioning takes place. A heart attack demands attention and usually gets it, even from a system engaging in a persistent and stubborn array of habits.

Fred avoids the threat of criticism and failure at work by excessive involvement in the work environment. James detaches himself from the danger of intimate interpersonal relations by preoccupying himself with the rituals of his phobia. Both individuals fail to confront their environment in an adaptive manner. Both engage in habits that diminish the knowledge of the results of their own actions.

Fred doesn't understand why he can't get along with his colleagues. James fails to see the connection between his severe anxiety and his compulsive behaviors. The things people say to Fred about his behavioral style don't make any sense to him. Likewise, James' severe emotional disturbance does not help him to change his behavior. The results of their actions only drive them further into their maladaptive behavior patterns. Both are in a state of feedback deprivation. The knowledge of results of their own actions fails to regulate their response systems in a positive direction.

The same feedback deficit is pervasive in many other learned behaviors. Perfectionists ultimately sabotage their own performance goals by becoming too perfectionistic. Dependent individuals falter in their quest for love and approval by becoming too dependent. The cautious person gets too cautious. The person who indulges too often to make it through a difficult and lonely night often overindulges to a dangerous level. Habits of living often become maladaptive because they become imbedded in the response system at a very low level of awareness. The system fails to profit from the knowledge of results of these habitual actions. A system deprived of feedback has only one alternative: It chronically repeats one self-defeating habit after another.

In Chapter 10, you revisit James, Fred, and other individuals who habitually engage in maladaptive behaviors. With your current level of knowledge of the Human Response System and some new ammunition for counteracting its problems, you should be able to give them some assistance, and in doing so, help yourself in the process.

10 SELF-REGULATION

Behavior

THE CASE OF RICHARD

Richard was always the kind of person you could depend on to accelerate the pace of a group's interaction. He could step into a serious conversation among several of his co-workers and immediately influence the group's behavior. The topic of conversation would change from work to personal and humorous anecdotes. He could find a humorous note in every serious discourse, and his presence would inevitably loosen up an uptight situation. Richard disrupted everyone's work, but most of his co-workers enjoyed this pleasant intrusion into their lives.

Everyone looked forward to Richard's arrival to work in the morning. Coffee was the first item on his morning agenda and socializing was second. Regardless of where each individual fell in the work hierarchy, everyone could depend on a significant exchange with Richard before the end of the morning. He would enter the coffee room, slap several people on the back, look them straight in the eyes, and make delightfully personal comments to everyone. Richard was a highly sensitive individual who maintained a close relationship with a large number of people. He was easily the best-liked person in his office.

No one in the office would ever admit that they had observed Richard engaging in a serious conversation. None of the staff would describe him as a hard worker. Richard was so relaxed and easy-going that he appeared to be fooling around even when he was seriously working. In reality Richard was extremely productive. Although he rarely took his high-level executive position too seriously, he was the Vice President of a very successful business. He was particularly intense about the human relations aspect of his job. Richard was a manager of people, and he spent a great portion of his time making sure that his employees were reinforced for their work and happy about the work environment. The company seemed to take care of itself under the type of atmosphere created by Richard and his managerial staff.

Richard's life away from work was a different matter. A number of circumstances were impinging upon his life in a negative manner. His marital relationship had been deteriorating over the last several years, and it had recently become an intensely destructive force in his life. Communication between Richard and his wife had come to a complete halt. They were living together but leading very separate lives. Neither of them were motivated to open the lines of communication or seek professional help for the benefit of the relationship. Richard sought his help and intimacy elsewhere. He had initiated a relationship with another woman in an attempt to obtain the attention and affection that he felt deprived of in the marriage.

The extramarital relationship provided Richard with short periods of intimacy and relief from a home environment that was becoming progressively more tense. Yet it was a source of stress in its own right. The secretive manner in which he conducted the relationship was certainly not conducive to happiness and emotional well-being. Most of his interactions with this woman added insult to a response system that had already been injured by frequent stressful encounters. Nevertheless, Richard was resorting to this alternative relationship more frequently in order to avoid the difficult confrontations at home.

Richard and his female companion went to great lengths to hide their ongoing relationship. In spite of this caution, their meetings were ended abruptly by an unexpected event. During one of their encounters she reluctantly informed him that her husband had recently become aware of their relationship. Richard felt devastated by the event. It was extremely difficult for him to handle the real and fantasized potential consequences of this occurrence. He feared losing the intimacy and support of the relationship at a time when it was necessary for his emotional survival. He feared the consequences of this discovery in his job and dreaded the thoughts of how his family would react. There was a growing awareness of the affair among the residents of the fairly small *community where he resided. His apprehensions grew stronger. They were substantiated when he received a calm, but serious phone call from her husband. During their brief conversation he threatened Richard with serious repercussions for his behavior.*

Richard began feeling alone and isolated. There was simply no place to turn to for relief. He stopped participating in a number of previously relaxing activities. He feared going out to the gym and the social club because he would encounter people who might confront him about the relationship. He felt progressively more uncomfortable at work because his boss, co-workers, and subordinates might be aware of the relationship. Richard no longer playfully engaged in social behavior at work. Instead, he withdrew to his office and shut himself off from this characteristically pleasant environment. His fears and apprehensions grew more intense as a result of this isolation. Richard became preoccupied with real and imagined consequences, and it became progressively more difficult for him to discriminate between fantasy and reality.

Richard was in a real dilemma when we first met. He was suffering from a severe anxiety reaction and was experiencing a number of psychosomatic problems. His most prominent difficulty was a feeling of dizziness that was precipitated by a variety of physical movements. Standing from a sitting position and moving quickly to the left or right caused him a great deal of discomfort. The dizziness was particularly debilitating to him as an active individual. Prior to this time he regularly participated in athletic events for exercise, social contact, and relaxation.

The problem that was most disturbing to Richard was his inability to function at work up to his own previous standards. He would spend a large portion of his time behind closed doors, performing routine tasks and worrying about his marital situation. He was not communicating with or supervising his people. Richard had withdrawn from his co-workers. Contact with them precipitated severe anxiety and dizziness in him. He spent a small amount of time dealing with the work situation and then withdrew to his office. In addition to the obvious emotional and psychosomatic consequences of this strategy, Richard was on the brink of losing his job.

It was not difficult to see that Richard appraised his environment as extremely threatening and dangerous. His strategy for dealing with this feared environment was to escape into the seclusion of his own thoughts and fantasies. The consequences of this maladaptive strategy were immediate and intense. Before I discuss the case any further, it is necessary for you to take another brief look at the disordered thinking habits discussed in an earlier chapter.

THE "DANGEROUS ENVIRONMENT" HYPOTHESIS REVISITED

A major point made in Chapter 7 is worth summarizing here. Humans readily perceive their environments as dangerous. This perception alerts the remainder of the response system for action. The fight–flight response is initiated along with other complex physiological responses. Thinking tends to become disordered, and the system is distracted from further constructive interactions with the environment. The behavioral outcome of this perceived threat is often approach and avoidance behavior. The cases of Fred and James illustrate two extreme example of these behavior patterns. They were labeled hyperresponsiveness and hyporesponsiveness, respectively.

It is important to remember that all of us, to a greater or lesser degree, exhibit these behavior patterns when we arrive at such an appraisal. The response is a natural outcome of a response system that is alerted and readied for action. At one time in our historical development as humans it was an adaptive response, and the negative effects of this excessive arousal pattern were dissipated in the struggle for survival. Today this response pattern has no obvious direction. It simply leaves the system upset and programmed for trouble.

As you read in Chapter 9, both maladaptive behavior patterns served to take Fred and James away from threatening situations. Fred was running away from imagined negative evaluations. He immersed himself in the world of work and excluded other activites from his life. James retreated to the safety of his apartment in order to avoid the failure that might stem from an active social life. The two quite divergent behavior patterns became strikingly similar when they were analyzed as maladaptive human responses to threatening life events.

ADAPTIVE EXPOSURE OR TAKING ANOTHER LOOK: COUNTERACTING THE "DANGEROUS ENVIRONMENT" HYPOTHESIS

One consistent theme emerges from our understanding of the Human Response System: the system functions adaptively when it engages in a direct, active interplay with the environment. It functions in a maladaptive manner when it retreats from these encounters. The emotional and psychosomatic outcomes of these retreats have been documented in numerous cases. An extremely important behavioral imperative logically stems from this analysis: Exposure to environments that are appraised as threatening is extremely adaptive. Put much more simply, you must take another look in order to effectively reevaluate an event that has been misperceived as dangerous.

We learn maladaptive behavior patterns in a variety of complex ways. One consistent process takes place with each learned response. It becomes habitual. It then takes on the major drawback of a habit: the automatic execution of the response with an accompanying loss of conscious awareness. Adaptive exposure or taking another look at an environment that has been defined as dangerous breaks up the links in the chain of habitual responses. It improves awareness and increases the chances for adaptive behavior change to take place. My work with Richard illustrates the execution of this strategy and its beneficial results.

Adaptive Exposure and Coping: The Case of Richard

There were numerous specific steps involved in helping Richard with the multiple aspects of his dilemma. The marital relationship had been deteriorating for several years, and interaction between Richard and his wife was more hostile with each encounter. The children were becoming more aware of the family problems and began reacting to the situation in their own destructive manner. The cumulative effect of these responses created a tense and volatile home environment.

Richard reflexively used an avoidance strategy in coping with the difficulties. He withdrew to the gymnasium, to another relationship, and to himself. His wife adopted essentially the same posture. These strategies culminated in a total loss of physical, verbal, and emotional contact with each other.

Destructive behavior patterns often have a tendency to generalize to other activities in one's life. Richard's behavior was no exception. He became progressively more withdrawn and isolated from work, and when his extramarital relationship terminated, he withdrew from numerous social and recreational activities.

Richard gradually cut himself off from the relationships with his wife, children, friends, and associates. He engaged in the superficial encounters required of him, but meaningful exchanges with significant people were minimal. This deprivation of interplay with his environment precipitated severe anxiety, emotional distur-bance, and subsequent psychosomatic problems.

A system that is not receiving information about its own function-ing cannot find adaptive solutions. It cannot regulate itself. It continues to repeat old habits in a cyclical fashion, never replac-ing old links in the chain of maladaptive behaviors with new re-sponses. My general objective was to systematically shape Richard back into interaction with his environment. He could profit im-mensely from taking another look at it. The adaptive strategy in-cluded the following specific responses: a series of open and honest talks with his wife, the resumption of an outgoing and assertive strategy at work, and an active engagement in social and recreational activities. All of these responses were to be made in spite of the real or imagined risks of failure and criticism.

Richard initiated the adaptive strategy by reducing his tendency to escape from the home environment. He stopped making excuses for coming home late and refused to allow himself to exit shortly after dinner to attend to "business matters." He stuck it out at home and endured the tension. Richard began talking to his wife about their marriage. At first it was extremely painful, but the encounters with her shed new light on the situation. He was sur-prised to find that she still had positive feelings for him and that she wanted to resolve the situation in a reasonable fashion. Through the opening of communication between them, Richard obtained new and valuable information about his own function-ing. The talks led to a consequence that he previously feared—a serious consideration of divorce as a viable alternative. In view of the exchanges between them and the new information they had obtained, it soon appeared to be the most adaptive solution to the problem.

Richard initiated his previous adaptive behavior pattern at work. He was surprised to find that people were not critical of him. Quite to the contrary, they were understanding and helpful. One specific important breakthrough for Richard occurred when we pinpointed a maladaptive habit pattern that he exhibited towards his boss, the President of the company.

Richard had become very detached from this previously rewarding relationship. As the circumstances surrounding his problems out-

side of work grew more complex, Richard became progressively more reluctant to pursue the relationship. He imagined that his boss was silently disapproving of his life style. The less contact that he had with this individual, the more negative fantasies he generated. He had an irrational fear of being criticized by his boss and perhaps even fired. The fantisized fear almost became a self-fulfilling prophecy: Richard detached himself from the President because he expected to be criticized and fired. In fact he was almost terminated because of the detachment itself and not because his boss disapproved of Richard's behavior.

The most adaptive strategy for coping with these fantasies was to increase the frequency and quality of contacts between Richard and his boss. He began increasing the number of scheduled and unscheduled visits with the president of the company. It was painful initially, but Richard remained in his presence for longer periods of time. He would go out of his way to drop into the President's office to ask for advice. The fears began to extinguish as the amount of contact significantly increased. Richard could once again maintain eye contact with his boss and generate a meaningful conversation. These new responses helped him obtain new information about his boss' true feelings of concern and support. The feedback from these interactions helped Richard regulate his own behavior and feelings at work.

Through these encounters Richard obtained information about himself and his environment that helped him through the crises. The same strategy proved to be effective for social and recreational activities. He increased the frequency of responses in these situations and once again found relief and relaxation from his efforts. Anxiety, emotional disturbance, and psychosomatic symptoms subsided with his new and adaptive strategy. Taking another look and re-entering a threatening situation paid off in terms of emotional well-being and personal effectiveness.

ALTERING THE HYPORESPONSIVE BEHAVIOR PATTERN: ADAPTIVE COPING IN A DEPRESSED INDIVIDUAL

Adaptive coping can be facilitated by placing oneself back into a direct confrontation with the environment. In many cases the return to emotional well-being is quite rapid. Other problems are more difficult to change because of the pervasiveness of the hyporesponsive coping strategy. The case of Laura, discussed in this section, illustrates this point. Laura was deeply entrenched in a strategy of living that was painfully maladaptive. Yet, she held on to it tenaciously. The strategy led to deep and profound depression.

The mask of depression covers a variety of behaviors that have been extinguished over a period of time. Depressed individuals often suffer from a behavioral deficit. They fail to emit behaviors that were previously a part of their human response repertoire. Responses such as initiating social contacts, engaging in pleasurable activities, and responding in an assertive manner have reduced in frequency. Other maladaptive habits such as social isolation have increased. Problems such as passiveness, dependency, and sleeping and eating difficulties are commonly observed in depressed individuals.

As Seligman has demonstrated in his research studies, depressed individuals have learned to be helpless. They believe that their own behavior makes no difference in terms of receiving positive outcomes from the environment. On the basis of numerous laboratory experiments on the phenomenon of learned helplessness, Seligman puts forth the following theory about the development and modification of depression:

> . . . the expectation that an outcome is independent of responding (1) reduces the motivation to control the outcome; (2) interferes with learning that responding controls the outcome; and, if the outcome is traumatic, (3) produces fear for as long as the subject is uncertain of the uncontrollability of the outcome, and then produces depression.

> The theory suggests a way to cure helplessness, once it has set in, and a way to prevent it from occurring. If the central problem in lack of response initiation is the expectation that responding will not work, cure should occur when the expectation is reversed. [17, pp. 55–56 From Helplessness: On Depression, Development and Death by Martin E. P. Seligman Copyright © 1975 by W. H. Freeman and Co. by permission.]

According to this well-substantiated theory, people avoid situations that have been previously associated with physical and emotional pain. If the situation is consistently unpleasant, the avoidance behavior becomes more or less permanent. The expectation of coping with the life event in the future is characterized by a sense of helplessness. The "what is the use of trying" attitude commonly expressed by depressed people stems from this perception of loss of control over environmental outcomes.

Reversing the expectation that responding makes no difference, according to Seligman, is a matter of forcing the organism back into the situation that it was previously avoiding. This approach is similar to the "taking another look" strategy discussed earlier. Exposure to situations that have become aversive is crucial for overcoming helplessness. A gradual confrontation with extremely stressful life events was the key to altering the life of a woman who had been depressed for a significant portion of her adult years.

The Case of Laura

Laura was a depressed woman who had learned to be helpless very early in her life. She consistently isolated herself from people because she felt helpless in their presence. In the past, her behavior failed to lead to any positive outcomes. Laura quit her job because she was asked to take on additional responsibilities. She stopped relating to the neighbors in her community because they often asked her to take responsibility for certain neighborhood functions. Laura was even threatened by her family because of their demands for attention and affection.

The following is a sample of the hyporesponsive behaviors that contributed to her sense of helplessness:

1. Waking up extremely late in the morning.
2. Failing to plan a daily schedule of activities.
3. Avoiding social encounters with the neighbors.
4. Refusing to interact affectionately with her children.
5. Passively relinquishing all social and family responsibilities to her husband.

Each hyporesponsive behavior was counteracted by an active response. She was instructed to:

1. Prepare an activity schedule each evening for the next day, wake up early, and stick to the schedule.
2. Schedule social encounters with friends.
3. Initiate affectionate responses towards the children.
4. Firmly express her opinions to her husband about the week's social and family functions.

The problem that was most bothersome to Laura was her intense loneliness. This occurred in the midst of an entire community of housewives that were ready and willing to engage in social contact. This problem became the focus of a new strategy of responding.

A number of maladaptive social habits were pinpointed once Laura forced herself into initiating interactions with other housewives. One particularly important habit occurred during neighborhood functions in the presence of other women. Laura desperately wanted to be involved in these functions. She was rarely in attendance because of the emotional discomfort that she experienced before and during the activities. Laura was painfully shy during these encounters, rarely smiling, kidding, or even speaking in the presence of other women. She was afraid that she just didn't have anything to say. She feared that other women would be critical of her because she wasn't an enthusiastic and dedicated housewife. This passive, inhibited approach to her interactions with other women made her apprenhensive before the functions. During the activities Laura was extremely nervous and inhibited, and a severe state of depression was quite common when she returned home.

The new strategy involved a series of new behaviors. Laura began increasing the frequency of smiling during the activities and started using her good sense of humor in an assertive way. She began relating humorous anecdotes about her role as a housewife. She assertively stated her desire to return to work on a full-time basis. Instead of being preoccupied with her own inner thoughts and worries, Laura concentrated on each woman's conversation and began inserting her own comments and opinions. She forced herself to express thoughts and feelings that she previously kept to herself.

The fear of sounding stupid had always inhibited Laura. She soon found that people listened to her and respected what she had to say. Laura had a significant difference of opinion from the other women when it came to their roles as housewives. Yet she found that they were interested in her ideas and were not exceptionally critical of them as she had imagined they would be.

Laura even took the additional risk of conducting a social activity at her own home. She organized it in a relaxed manner, and it turned out to be a pleasurable experience. This new behavioral strategy taught her many new things about herself and her neighbors. She used this information to regulate and control her feelings of depression. The depression diminished dramatically with the increase in the frequency and quality of her interpersonal contacts.

ALTERING THE HYPERRESPONSIVE BEHAVIOR PATTERN: ADAPTIVE COPING IN THE TYPE A INDIVIDUAL

The Type A Behavior Pattern and the hyporesponsive reaction, although quite distinct from each other behaviorally, are both examples of maladaptive coping. Whereas the hyporesponsive person is generally passive in coping with life's demands, the Type A individual engages in a series of hyperactive responses. The phobic and depressed individuals become less active, almost immobilized, when confronting threatening situations. The Type A individual, on the other hand, becomes excessively active.

Deficits in the knowledge of results of one's actions that are commonly experienced by the phobic, anxiety ridden, and depressed individual are also incurred by the Type A individual, except for just the opposite reason. The hyperresponsive behavior pattern is so chronically hurried that it fails to attend to information obtained from the interplay with life events. A system that is exposed to too much information can be just as debilitated as one that gets very little. Both have difficulty utilizing the exchange of information with the environment for behavioral adjustments. Self-regulation in terms of maintaining physical and emotional equilibrium is improbable.

The alteration of this behavior pattern involves the identification and modification of the maladaptive habits that make up the Type A strategy. Rapidly paced responses are slowed down. Tangible achievements are placed in their proper perspective, and time is set aside for meaningful and intimate interpersonal relationships. Hostility is monitored and diluted. The system is slowed down so that new, adaptive behaviors can replace old, maladaptive ones.

Richard Suinn[46] has conducted a program, Cardiac Stress Management Training (CSMT), to alter the behaviors identified as maladaptive and contributing to the high incidence of heart disease among Type As. The Type A behaviors he attempts to modify are: (1) an intense sustained drive to achieve self-selected, but poorly defined goals; (2) a profound inclination and eagerness to compete; (3) a habitual propensity to accelerate the rate of execution of many physical and mental functions; (4) a continuous involvement in multiple and diverse functions subject to deadlines; (5) heightened mental and physical alertness; and, (6) faulty cholesterol and fatty deposit removal, leading to the presence of obstructions in the blood vessels long after meals.

Suinn's program was an attempt to alter these Type A behaviors. The CSMT is a combination of Suinn's Anxiety Management Training and visio-motor, behavior rehearsal techniques. The Anxiety Management Training involves training Type As in relaxation and imagery techniques that are comparable to the ones discussed in this book. Visio-motor, behavior rehearsal relies upon relaxation and imagery training to get these individuals to practice adaptive non-Type A behaviors under the controlled conditions possible with the use of imagery. This approach increases the chances that Type As will change their behavior in real life situations. From comments obtained by individuals in the program, the preliminary effects of the techniques on the Type A Behavior Pattern are good. Data on blood lipid levels were also obtained from the Type A individuals. Both cholesterol and triglyceride levels were lowered for the patients that participated in the CSMT program. Further research is being conducted in order to confirm the preliminary favorable results.

Suinn's program, as well as others that have developed in the last several years, emphasizes the importance of changing habits in the reduction of the Type A Behavior Pattern. A similar approach is taken by Friedman and Rosenman.[8] In the final section of their book, *What You Can Do If You're Type A,* they provide guidelines and drills for changing this pattern of behavior. They state that: "unless you establish new habits meant to supercede and replace your old ones, you will not free yourself from the Type A illness." Here are a small sample of their drills:

A drill against hurry sickness:

Whenever possible, shy away from making appointments at definite times. Admittedly, almost all work-connected appointments must be made and kept at definite times, but your nightly arrival time at home should be elastic. Remember, the more unnecessary deadlines you make for yourself, the worse your 'hurry sickness' becomes. [8, p. 262]

A drill against hostility:

Begin to speak your thanks of appreciation to others when they have performed services for you. And do not do so, like so many hostile Type A subjects, with merely a grunt of thanks. Take the time to look the man or woman who has served you well full in the face and then in *full* and gracious sentences let him or her know how grateful you are. [8, p. 266]

A drill toward things worth being:

You must allocate time for your reading, for learning new avocations you have chosen to pursue, and for visiting museums, galleries, and theaters. There must be time for you to recall your past. This need not be carried out on a fixed schedule, but certainly should be frequent; the true enrichment of your life is possible only by bringing back into it the things and thoughts of your earlier life. [8, p. 270. Copyright © 1974 by Alfred A. Knopf, Inc. By permission.]

Behavioral drills for changing the Type A Behavior Pattern were used successfully in the case of Fred discussed in the previous chapter.

Hyperresponsive Behavior Profile: The Case of Fred

The Behavior Profile Inventory included in Appendix III was developed to assist individuals in identifying their hyperresponsive behaviors. An individual that completes the inventory can obtain a range of scores from 30 to 150. The general categories of the inventory are:

> 30 – 50: Mild hyperresponsiveness
> 51 –100: Moderate hyperresponsiveness
> 101 –150: Extreme hyperresponsiveness

In addition to providing a score that indicates a general trend toward excessive activity levels, the individual items provide target behaviors that are pinpointed in order to reduce hyperresponsiveness. You can turn to Appendix III and complete the inventory to obtain a general survey of your hyperresponsive tendencies.

The case of Fred discussed in Chapter 9 provides a good example of the use of the profile in a program oriented towards altering a hyperresponsive behavior pattern. As you would suspect from the description of the case, Fred's score was on the extreme end of the behavior profile (132). He scored high on the majority of items on the profile, so we studied each item closely in order to target specific Type A behaviors that needed to be modified. In many cases he was instructed to count and monitor these specific behaviors in order to facilitate his awareness of the frequency of these responses.

Fred returned to work shortly after his discharge from the hospital. I instructed him to count and monitor the number of hours he worked during the week. He compared this count with the amount of time that he spent in family, social, and recreational activities. The balance was overwhelmingly in favor of "time spent at work." One simple suggestion was for him to set a limit on his work hours. At a pre-determined time during the day, he would force himself to stop working and engage in another non-work-related activity.

This simple strategy was extremely difficult for Fred to follow. He failed several times in his attempts to disengage himself from the work environment. After many frustrating experiences, he finally succeeded in leaving work early and participating in other activities such as physical exercise and family functions. At first he experienced a great deal of anxiety about being away from the office. I encouraged him to stick with it, concentrate on his long-term objectives, and reward himself for his perseverance. In the distant past these recreational and social activities had been rewarding and relaxing. As he changed his work habits and persevered, they once again became a source of enjoyment.

Numerous other behaviors, such as his impatience, rapid pacing, irritability, thought preoccupations, and excessive strivings for achievement, were dealt with in this manner. Each behavior was counted and monitored, and suggestions for changing the responses were discussed. Fred would literally force himself to engage in the new habit by scheduling a time to do it and by contracting with his wife, children, and friends to carry through with the new responses. He would then endure the emotional upset that inevitably stems from breaking old, familiar habit patterns. His perseverance always paid off in terms of new feelings of exhilaration and well-being. The calm always came after the storm of emotional turmoil that followed the initiation of a new pattern of behavior.

Perhaps the most dramatic changes took place in the area of Fred's interpersonal relations. Prior to his hospitalization Fred spent very little time engaging in meaningful conversations with employees. The focus of his rapidly paced conversation was usually directed toward performance and work efficiency. He began spending extra time with each individual. Fred tried to get to know them at a personal level and asked each one for positive and negative feedback about his skills as a manager. At first he cringed at the thought of being criticized. Soon, however, he learned to cope with all of their reactions to him. Contrary to what he thought would happen, he found that their positive comments and feelings overshadowed their negative ones.

Fred was on the road to becoming an excellent manager of people. The second administration of the Behavior Profile, only

*several months after the first, showed that Fred's score was dra-
matically reduced. His score of 78 was only one minor index of his
new behavioral style.*

THE "SAVE-ENVIRONMENT" HYPOTHESIS: RISK TAKING AND ASSERTIVENESS

The previous discussions have focused on the maladaptive consequences of generating the "Dangerous Environment" hypothesis. Can humans learn a style of behavior that increases the chances of perceiving a safe environment? Research findings indicate that certain strategies of living facilitate a perception of safety and a sense of control over one's environment. Two behavioral techniques that enhance this style of living are risk taking and assertiveness. The acquisition of these response styles facilitates feelings of self-control and emotional well-being.

Risk-Taking

As you have observed from previous discussions, anxiety is a common emotion that is experienced by individuals who engage in both hyporesponsive and hyperresponsive behavioral strategies. Fear-prone and depressed individuals feel anxious because of their strategies of avoidance. Type A individuals experience anxiety, in part, because they can never accomplish all of their goals in the time allotted to these objectives. One major theme of this book has been that anxiety is a common warning signal of the human response system. It is feedback from a system that is faltering in its attempts to cope with life.

One major habit-changing and anxiety-reducing strategy that encompasses many of the adaptive responses recommended in earlier discussions is risk-taking. This behavioral skill involves systematically and regularly replacing old habits with new ones. The risk-taking principle is intimately related to the principle of adaptive exposure. Each time that you break one or more components of an old habit, you are taking a risk.

Each one of us has something invested in our habits. "I've done it that way for a long time." "It worked for me in the past." People have difficulty making changes. Breaking a habit involves taking a risk. Risk-taking involves an additional step. After breaking one link in the old chain of responses, an entirely new repertoire of responses is attempted in a bold and adventurous fashion. This principle can be stated in the following way: "Do something in threatening situations that is the exact opposite of what you feel like doing. Take a risk. Be adventurous! It is anxiety reducing and exhilarating. It helps you conquer specific, sometimes long-lasting fears and assists you in developing a less cautious, more adventurous approach to life."

The following risk-taking exercises have been successfully utilized by a number of people with divergent problems:

A man who was afraid of heights changed one link in the chain of the old habits by refusing to avoid the tall building he passed on the way to work. After doing that several times, he took a risk. He rode the elevator to the top of the building! The new response was difficult and anxiety producing at first. With practice, however, it became surprisingly natural and easy. The small victory he experienced from risk-taking in this manner had positive emotional consequences. His sense of accomplishment and self-control transfered to other life events.

A man that was shy and afraid to speak to attractive women changed one link in the chain of the old habit by talking at length to a very attractive female at work. Then he took a risk. He asked her for a date. Even though she refused his invitation, he learned something new about himself and the situation by emitting the new response.

The risk-taking strategy was used with a married couple that had sexual difficulties. Their sex life had become very dull. The frequency of sex had diminished significantly since the beginning of their marriage. I instructed them to observe the habitual chain of responses that took place before and during sexual activity. The couple was surprised to find that sex had become subject to a fixed behavior pattern. It always took place after 10:00 P.M. on the same evening each week. It usually took place in the same location. The couple prepared for bed in the usual way and dressed in the same evening wear. They made love in the standard position each time and said the same things to each other during each act of intercourse. They asked themselves after it was over: "Why are we so bored with love-making? It used to be so romantic and exciting."

When you look at it in this manner, it is not difficult to see the problem. Setting up a new chain of responses did wonders for a sex life that had lost its appeal. Some simple, but effective risk-taking sexual exercises included:

1. Picking a new time to make love—morning, afternoon, and so forth.

2. Changing the location of their sexual activity—on the sofa, on the floor, or in the kitchen.

3. Trying sex more than once in these locations.

4. Not changing into their evening wear. Making love in their clothes with only the necessary garments removed.

5. Reading a good sex manual and trying some new positions.

6. Talking differently to the partner during sex. Repeating profanities during the act of lovemaking.

Taking risks in this manner improved their sex lives dramatically. They discovered more creative ways to increase sexual excitement for each other. Previously, they would avoid communication (positive and negative feedback) about sex. After risk-taking, communication increased, and the anxiety generated by their cautious strategy diminished with each new experience.

The major objective in risk-taking is not an increase in the rate of interpersonal or vocational successes but rather the exposure to new information from situations that have been previously avoided. Even failure in these situations is an important experience. The system can use the information to regulate itself and to combat the emotional upset that stems from a cautious strategy of living.

Assertiveness: The Things People Say To Others

How does one get the most out of a life event once adaptive exposure and risk taking have occurred? The things people say to themselves have been emphasized as an important component of emotional well-being. Another important element of response system functioning is "the things people say to other people." Verbal behavior, and its accompanying gestures and postures, is an extremely important aspect of interpersonal relations. Within these person-to-person relationships, assertiveness is a major human response that can facilitate adaptive functioning.

Once the tendency to engage in maladaptive behavior is counteracted and you encounter the situation in a risk-taking manner, there are specific behaviors that can help you accomplish your objectives. Communicating interests, desires, and feelings in a firm, but nonaggressive manner in previously threatening situations will allow you to make the encounter an anxiety-free and productive one. As a consequence you will remain in the situation long enough to be rewarded by your experience. This increases the chances that you will want to return to the situation for further reinforcement.

Lange and Jakubowski, in their book *Responsive Assertive Behavior,* define assertiveness and distinguish it from nonassertive behavior.

Assertion involves standing up for personal rights and expressing thoughts, feelings, and beliefs in *direct, honest,* and *appropriate* ways which do not violate another person's rights. The basic message in assertion is: This is what I think. This is what I feel. This is how I see the situation. This message expresses 'who the person is' and is said without dominating, humiliating, or degrading the other person.

Assertion involves response—not deference. Deference is acting in a sub-servient manner as though the other person is right, or better simply because the other person is older, more powerful, experienced, or knowledgeable or is of a different sex or race. Deference is present when people express themselves in ways that are self-effacing, appeasing, or overly apologetic.

Two types of respect are involved in assertion: respect for oneself, that is expressing one's needs and defending one's rights, as well as respect for the other person's needs and rights. [50, p. 7 From Responsible Assertive Behavior: Cognitive, Behavioral Procedures for Trainers, by A. J. Lange and P. Jakubowski. Copyright © by Research Press, 1976. By permission.]

The relationship between risk-taking and assertiveness is extremely impor-tant. Once you decide to break an old habit and take a risk, it helps immensely to execute the new response in a manner that is palatable to your environment. Lange and Jakubowski provide an example of an asser-tive response in a simple situation that clarifies the meaning and potential positive effects of this behavioral strategy.

A woman was desperately trying to get a flight to Kansas City to see her mother who was sick in the hospital. Weather conditions were bad and the lines were long. Having been rejected from three standby flights, she again found herself in the middle of a long line for the fourth and last flight to Kansas City. This time she approached a man who was standing near the beginning of the line and said, pointing to her place, 'Would you mind ex-changing places with me? I ordinarily would not ask, but it's extremely impor-tant that I get to Kansas City tonight.' The man nodded yes; and as it turned out, both of them were able to get on the flight.

When asked what her reaction would have been if the man had refused, she replied, "It would have been okay. I hoped he would say yes, but after all, he was there first." [50, p. 8 From Responsible Assertive Behavior: Cognitive, Behavioral Procedures for Trainers, by A. J. Lange and P. Jakubowski. Copyright © by Research Press, 1976. By permission.]

In this example, the woman showed self-respect for her own need by asking the man if he would be willing to help her. Also, she respected the man's right to refuse her request and not fulfill her need.

The woman in this example took a risk—the risk of having her request rejected. The important connection between risk-taking and assertiveness is exemplified here. Once she decided to take a risk, the manner in which she communicated this response to the outside world became critical. She could have been passive, looking up to the man and pleading with him for help. He might have helped her in this situation, but she would have sacrificed her own self-respect for that pay-off. On the other hand, she could have been aggressive and demanded help. Under these circumstances she might have been rejected. On the other hand, if she won through force the victory would have occured under emotional circumstances. Instead, the firm assertive approach increased the chance of a pay-off with no sacrifice to her self-respect and emotional equilibrium.

Lange and Jakubowski discuss the alternatives to assertive behavior—nonassertiveness and aggressiveness.

> *Non-assertion* involves violating one's own rights by failing to express honest feelings, thoughts, and beliefs and consequently permitting others to violate oneself, or expressing one's thoughts and feelings in such an apologetic, diffident, self-effacing manner that others can easily disregard them. In the latter type of non-assertion, the total message which is communicated is: "I don't count—you can take advantage of me. My feelings don't matter—only yours do. My thoughts aren't important—yours are the only ones worth listening to. I'm nothing—you are superior."

> Non-assertion shows a lack of respect for one's own needs. It also sometimes shows a subtle lack of respect for the other person's ability to take disappointments, to shoulder some responsibility, to handle his own problems, etc. The goal of non-assertion is to appease others and to avoid conflict at any cost.

> *Aggression* involves directly standing up for personal rights and expressing thoughts, feelings, and beliefs in a way which is often dishonest, usually inappropriate, and always violates the rights of the other person. An example of 'emotionally dishonest' aggression is a situation where individuals who feel saddened by another person's mourning for the death of a loved one sarcastically degrade the mourner ('That's just what I like to see—a grown person sniveling like a two-year-old brat.'), instead of revealing their own sad and helpless feelings.

> The usual goal of aggression is domination and winning, forcing the other person to lose. Winning is insured by humiliating, degrading, belittling, or overpowering other people so that they become weaker and less able to express and defend their needs and rights. The basic message is: This is what I think—you're stupid for believing differently. This is what I want—what you want isn't important. This is what I feel—your feelings don't count. [50, pp. 9–10 From Responsible Assertive Behavior: Cognitive, Behavioral Procedures for Trainers, by A. J. Lange and P. Jakubowski. Copyright © by Research Press, 1976. By permission.]

Contrary to nonassertive responses and aggression, assertive verbal and physical behavior minimize the chances for anxiety and depression. Assertion involves a new behavioral strategy that is incompatible with these emotional upsets. Even if the individual fails to accomplish the desired goal by being assertive, the chances of repeating these behaviors in the future are increased.

A passive individual already assumes that the environment is dangerous. Given this assumption and the accompanying behavioral posture, the system generates the usual response to threat and danger—the anxiety response. The assertive person simply opens up, takes a risk, and responds to the environment with few assumptions about danger. The behavioral stance prepares the system for action. Anxiety in this case is minimal or absent. The firm and direct nature of the communication provides the response system with a face-to-face confrontation with the environment. Under these circumstances, it can accurately evaluate the impact of its responding. The passive individual never obtains this information and is left to his or her own negative assumptions about life events.

Assertiveness: Family and Social Relations

Many people avoid participating in family and social activities because they feel that expectations in the situation are overwhelming. They feel that they cannot cope with these life events. The following dialogue about family and social responsibilities took place between a client and myself: "I enjoy having friends over for dinner, but I feel a lot of pressure in the situation because I have to make sure everything goes perfectly. It's just not worth it." "I end up spending a great deal of time alone because I can't cope with the stress of these social events. I would like to spend time with my family, but I feel that the total responsibility for their well-being and happiness rests on me. That scares the hell out of me, so I just avoid being with them." These statements characterize the rigid expectations (and fear of subsequent loss of approval) in social and family situations that prevent the non-assertive individual from engaging in a potentially rewarding experience.

In these stressful situations, an assertive response to friends facilitates a positive experience: "I would love to have you over for dinner if you would each be willing to bring a covered dish and help me clean up afterwards." An assertive response to one's family includes these verbal responses: "I will go with you and the kids to the zoo for the afternoon, but I don't want the responsibility for all of you. I'd like for you to take responsibility for the youngest child. I will handle the next youngest, and Joey (the oldest son), can take care of his sister." The willingness to participate under altered circumstances (shared responsibility) and the assertive communication of these wishes to other people allows for a rewarding activity that might not have taken place otherwise.

These events and their solutions are relatively simple, but the frequency of their occurrence in family and social situations is quite high. The fear of admitting: "I can't handle the whole thing by myself," the fantasized repercussions of this openness (fear of criticism, loss of approval, and rejection), and the subsequent avoidance of events that demand this assertiveness contributes to many marital, family, and social problems.

The following case describes the use of the techniques described in this chapter in altering a fearful and passive strategy of living. This is the case of James described in the previous chapter. A brief review of James' case is presented in order to set the stage for you to understand the use of several behavioral techniques in altering a severely debilitating problem.

ADAPTIVE EXPOSURE, RISK-TAKING, AND ASSERTIVENESS: THE CASE OF JAMES

James came to see me for treatment because his life was becoming unbearably lonely. As James reflected on the twenty-six years of his life, he remembered being a loner, always isolated from the mainstream of events that took place around him. He was always somewhat uncomfortable around people, but his feelings of discomfort were now more intense than ever. James' life consisted of forty or more hours of work during the week. The remainder of the time he spent alone in his apartment. James had no close friends and had not been out on a date for six years.

My first contact with James was on the telephone. He spoke in a very nervous fashion, apologizing several times for bothering me at home, and criticizing himself profusely for not calling me at work. Self-criticism and the frequent use of apologies were part of his style of relating. It was difficult for me to set up an appointment with him because he was trying very hard not to inconvenience me. James' desire to be a "nice guy" got in the way of his ability to communicate his preferences to other people.

When I first met with him in my office, I reached out to shake his hand and noticed that he hesitated momentarily. James had his hands in his pockets. As he moved his right hand toward mine, he commented about the dryness of his skin and the deep red color that glowed from it. His hands were almost raw as if they had been rubbed and scrubbed incessantly for days. I later discovered that his hands gave away the true nature of his problem.

As you learned earlier, James had a severe contamination phobia. The focus of this fear was on the dirt and grime that can be found anywhere in the environment. Most of you are only mildly aware of this aspect of your life space. James and others that I have treated with similar problems were preoccupied with the fear of coming into contact with the germs that reside in dirt, garbage, food, and other people. The imaginery contamination that occurred because of this contact was capable of eliciting the irrational fear. Once the fear was stimulated by touching the contaminated object, James felt compelled to wash and clean incessantly until the germs were completely eliminated from the point of contact. Minimal emotional relief from this fear was acquired through the washing procedure. Consequently, the washing usually continued throughout the day because of the frequent exposure to the environment and its microscopic inhabitants.

James' contamination phobia was very specific and unusual. His fear of being contaminated was restricted to objects and people from Arizona and California. Anything from these two states, according to James, contained contaminating germs. Objects and people from other states were germ-free. His phobia-related behavior during each day of his life consisted of scrutinizing every object and person that came in close contact with him. He vigorously questioned their origin to himself. Were they from the two feared states? Labels on grocery items were read very closely. Newspapers, magazines, clothing, hardware, and other purchasable items were checked. Even his mailbox was contaminated because he once received a letter from California.

You remember James' refusal to have contact with his parents. They once visited Arizona and were now strictly off-limits to him. He had not seen them in three years despite the fact that they had been extremely close to him in his earlier years. They frequently urged James to return home during the holidays, but he steadfastly refused. They were not aware of the specific nature of James' problem, so he avoided contact with them through the use of a variety of excuses.

You would be quite surprised at the number of objects that come from these two states. I became acutely aware of this fact in the course of treating James' contamination phobia. He related the following incident to me that characterized the onset of contamination and the subsequent process of decontamination.

"One morning at work I was given an assignment to duplicate some prints that had recently come into our office. I removed them from the storage area and began working with them at my desk. I glanced at the corner of one of the prints and was surprised to find the words: "From Tuscon, Arizona." I was shocked. A feeling of anxiety rushed through me. I felt dirty and contaminated. My first urge was to rush to the bathroom to wash my hands, but I realized that my efforts to decontaminate myself would be futile. I had to work with the prints until my assignment was completed. There was no way to escape contamination. I would have to endure the feeling until I could get back to my apartment. By the time I arrived there in the evening I was drained of energy from the constant anxiety that I felt throughout the day. I quickly made up for my inability to wash at work. I washed my clothes, took several showers, and cleaned until I felt totally decontaminated."

How does an intense fear and avoidance reaction become attached to such an unusual set of stimuli? It is very difficult to identify all of the important historical antecedents to a fear such as the one described above. Some important facts were revealed during treatment: James was stationed in Arizona when he was in the Armed Services. It was a very traumatic period in his life. This was the first time away from his parents and the security of his hometown. At the base in Arizona he was suffering from a great deal of anxiety and was rapidly losing weight. James was sent to a psychiatrist for evaluation. The doctor recommended short-term hospitalization for evaluation and treatment. He was subsequently hospitalized at a base in California.

Shortly after that time, James was given a medical discharge from the service because of his psychiatric condition. He returned to his hometown for a short time in order to interview for a job. James obtained a position and was transferred to his job assignment in another city. Although he recalled an extraordinary concern for cleanliness as a child and adolescent, he pinpointed this move as the stimulus that precipitated the specific preoccupation with germs. This occurred approximately six years before he contacted me for treatment. James lived a reclusive life style during the major part of the six years prior to our therapeutic relationship.

There were two fairly distinct responses that James had to modify. The first was the phobic response itself. He had to break the habitual chain of responses that followed his exposure to the feared objects and people from Arizona and California. These washing and cleaning rituals reinforced his escape behavior and kept him in a constant state of fear and anxiety. Secondly, it was extremely important for him to increase the frequency of social behaviors. This strategy would facilitate adaptive exposure to other people by increasing the frequency of social contacts. It would also teach James to be less passive, cautious, and apologetic, that is, more risk-taking, in his interactions with other people. The development of a more adaptive strategy of living through the alteration of these two behavior patterns would reduce his reclusive responses and severe emotional disturbance.

My instructions to James regarding the phobic response were: "Don't engage in the same rituals each time that you are confronted with a 'contaminated' object or person. When you are exposed to objects or people from Arizona or California, don't wash immediately. Break this chain of responses by increasing the amount of time that you spend between exposure and decontamination. Relax and continue to do what you are doing for as long as you can. Then you may wash if you have to. Each time that you do this, try to increase the time period between exposure and washing. Monitor this time period on a graph and study the results each day in order to obtain feedback on how you are doing."

James brought items from Arizona and California into my office in order to practice these new responses under my supervision. Before each session, James would select items (letters, magazines, etc.) from the two states, slip his hands into a pair of gloves, and place the items into a box. He then brought the box into my office. I would remove the items from the box and gradually expose James to them–first touching his shoes and pants with them and then placing the objects in his bare hands. His anxiety level would increase dramatically as the objects touched his clothes and body. His immediate impulse was to try to use the office bathroom for washing. I would ask him to wait several minutes before doing so. He agreed and held the items in his hands until it was time to wash. We increased the time period between exposure and washing every session.

The new strategy had an immediate and dramatic effect on his anxiety level. The longer he waited to wash, the more his anxiety diminished. James progressed dramatically each session. After several sessions, he could be exposed to the objects and wait until the end of the session before washing. Soon he could wait until he returned home to wash. Eventually, he could go without decontaminating himself at all.

The same approach was used with objects in James work and home environments. He would force himself to wait longer periods of time between contamination and washing. He observed his improvement from day to day through his self-monitoring procedure. His improvement was equally dramatic at home. James was spending less and less time cleaning, washing, and worrying about contamination. The time was ripe for building in new adaptive social responses.

James was motivated to date but didn't know where to start. Given his previous decontamination schedule, there was little time for him to make friends outside of the work environment. Work was the only avenue for initiating new relationships. His previous interactions in the work setting were very routine "good mornings," "hellos," and "goodbyes." James engaged in very little meaningful conversations with anyone. I instructed him to take a risk: "You should initiate conversations with acquaintances at work and maintain social contact with them for longer periods of time. This will increase your chance of making friends and may eventually open up new possibilities for dating relationships."

James found through these interactions that he had a lot more to say to people than he previously thought. As he opened up to others, they began to interact with him more frequently. He was still nervous and apprehensive around people and tended to be self-critical and apologetic in his conversations but he was taking additional risks. As the frequency of these contacts increased, he gradually changed his general style of relating in the work environment. James received increasing amounts of praise and reinforcement from work associates and, most importantly, from himself.

Perhaps the most difficult task of the entire treatment procedure was to get James to become more firm and assertive in his interactions. On one occasion James had decided to take a risk and initiate contact with a friend about going out together for an evening of fun and relaxation. James approached this situation in a very cautious manner and behaved verbally in the following characteristic way: "I haven't been out in a long time, and I need to get back into socializing sometime soon. You go to a lot of different places, don't you? I never have been good at that." James' physical behavior correlated very closely to his verbal behavior. As he spoke to his friend, he looked down at the floor, shuffled his feet, and displayed very few facial gestures. His hands remained in his pockets during the entire interaction and his eyes never made direct contact with the individual. During this interaction, he was tense and anxious.

The chance for emotional arousal and discomfort was quite high because of James' passive and cautious strategy. When James failed to accompalish his goal of initiating a social engagement, the likelihood of returning for another try was decreased. The discomfort experienced in the execution of the strategy was too intense. Even when he accomplished his objective, the emotional arousal associated with his strategy was so punishing that he was reluctant to do it again.

The same situation was executed with a new more assertive strategy. James' verbal responses were: "I've been out of commission for a long time now, but I'm ready to get on with some fun and relaxation. I understand that you know about some good places in town. Would you like to join me Friday night for an evening out on the town?" James' physical responses were comparable to his verbal assertiveness. James looked at his friend directly and made good eye contact with him. He smiled and gestured with his hands while he was speaking. He stood firm and upright in a confident manner.

James and I frequently practiced conversations in which I would play the role of a friend or co-worker and he would play the role of a confident and assertive male. Apologies and self-criticism were taboo. I instructed him to sit upright and make eye contact with me. He would practice making firm gestures with his hands while speaking. He could say things that were positive and self-confident and the words came out in a firm manner. Even the tone of his voice changed. These new postural and verbal responses reduced his nervousness and apprehension around people. He became progressively more comfortable around them and began taking additional risks.

James asked several of the women at the office for dates. After several casual relationships, he developed an interest in one particular woman. Subsequently, he joined a social club associated with his church and participated in several social events each week.

Towards the end of our therapeutic relationship, several months would transpire between sessions. When he arrived for our final session, I was taken back by his new behavioral style and physical appearance. James had a new hair style and contact lenses. As he reached to shake my hand, he looked me in the eyes and firmly gripped my hand with his. I noticed something else that was quite different about him. His hands felt very smooth. They were normal in color, and his skin had recuperated from the dryness precipitated by years of washing and decontamination. Along with his assertive manner and the many graphs of his behavior that covered the walls of my office, they were the most dramatic signs of James' new strategy of living.

SUMMARY: FEEDBACK AND BEHAVIOR CHANGE

The critical interplay between the response system and the environment was jeopardized under the direction of a maladaptive coping strategy. If the human response system fails to respond, it loses the opportunity to profit from an important source of information: the knowledge of results of its own behavior. The response system performs, then, with a deficit of feedback. Fred was running too hard and too fast to learn from his own behavior. Laura was too cautious and withdrawn. Both experienced the unpleasant results of a feedback deficit.

Research has shown that a number of behavioral strategies are effective in producing changes in behavior. They directly attack the "dangerous environment" hypothesis by encouraging, sometimes forcing, a direct confrontation with the environment. Adaptive exposure prepares the response system for significant encounters with "threatening" life events. The new interplay between the response system and the environment facilitates the perception of safety. You can probably recall numerous instances of this phenomenon. A long-standing fear of yours was extinguished because you were somehow forced into a situation; one that you previously avoided with great vigor. The emotional consequences of this small victory were overwhelmingly positive.

During particularly stressful life events, well-intentioned friends have been known to urge one to "hang in there." There is an important element of wisdom in that suggestion. Learning thrives on the exchange of information between the response system and the environment. It is accelerated when one "hangs in there" in a risk-taking, assertive manner. The risk-taker and the assertive individual are acutely aware of the results of their behavior. They are not easily threatened because they consistently challenge their environment. The knowledge they obtain from this ongoing exchange allows them to regulate and control their behavior on a regular basis. They experience a wealth of feedback. They are always in a position to use this feedback in their own behalf. Emotional upset and disturbance are minimal. When they are present, they are transient positive and negative signals that facilitate regulation of response system functioning.

Imagine the sense of exhiliration that would follow regular doses of this risk-taking. All of us know people who are interpersonally adventurous. They make friends easily. They are not subject to long periods of upset. They maintain a constant, risky interplay with the environment and seem to get the most out of life. Richard, Fred, Laura, and James captured this strategy to some extent. In their own special way, each learned to vigorously confront life events that were previously avoided. The feedback obtained from these behavioral confrontations helped them counteract faulty appraisals and set the stage for subsequent positive interactions with a complex but basically safe environment.

11 HUMAN RESPONSE SYSTEM

Feedback

I have attempted to simplify a tremendously complex system. Even this approach to the Human Response System has turned out to be rather complex itself. Many conclusions about the system have been discussed, and I review them here in a summary fashion.

Life is full of events that people have to cope with in one way or another. The most difficult life events are the daily interpersonal relationships that we encounter in the struggle for happiness, emotional well-being, and survival. These include relationships of love, work, and play. People-oriented events are particularly difficult because they often arouse a sense of danger in us. This easily aroused perception of threat stems from our fear of losing love, approval, and support from an environment that we depend on for survival.

The response system reacts quickly to this appraisal. It responds with all of its human resources, as a whole, in order to cope with the danger. Coping responses can be divided into various components. The major components of the Human Response System are: thoughts, physiological reactions, and overt behavior.

People think. We have self-dialogues. We talk to ourselves about life's daily demands. A set of physiological reactions arouses us to meet the demands of an important event and relaxes us in order to return the system to a state of equilibrium. Our behavior acts on the environment. We talk to it, change it, and in turn are influenced by it. This behavior is oriented toward maintaining an active interplay with the environment for the sake of our physical and emotional survival.

The response system encounters numerous stressors that demand an adjustment in its functioning. These adjustments (stress responses) of the Human Response System are often maladaptive and occur at each level of human responding. Thinking can become disordered. Physiological reactions can be chronically aroused. And rigid behavior can occur at a high frequency. These coping responses can be emitted repeatedly with very little awareness of their negative impact on the system. They can become entrenched in the system and develop into maladaptive strategies of living.

The Human Response System transmits warning signals that reflect the maladaptive interplay with the environment. The signals include the stress emotions—anxiety, anger, depression—and the many variations of these unpleasant states. They can be utilized by the response system as barometers of the adaptiveness of its coping strategy. The feedback obtained from these signals can stimulate the modification of maladaptive coping activities into adaptive responses. This is the positive use of stress. When the system fails to respond and continues to engage in maladaptive habits, emotional disturbance and psychosomatic illness are the consequences.

Psychological investigators have developed techniques that attack the maladaptive strategy at each response component. The system can be returned to a state of equilibrium by eliciting a state of relaxation. During this lowered state of physiological arousal, the tendency to appraise life events as threatening and dangerous is significantly reduced. A relaxed system is more willing to take another look and reevaluate a misperceived set of life events. Various imagery training techniques have been used to facilitate continued exposure and concentration on feared situations. New self-dialogues are learned in order to conteract irrational thinking and to pump in new ideas, beliefs, and attitudes. Behavioral skills such as risk-taking and assertiveness facilitate a positive and continuous interplay with an environment that offers the physical and emotional pay-offs of life.

Feedback is a principle that unifies many of the findings of these psychological investigators. The ability of the system to regulate itself based on the knowledge of results of its own activities is important for adaptive coping. Maladaptive coping strategies are a function of the breakdown of this built-in feedback ability. The development of an adaptive coping strategy through the use of self-regulatory techniques is, in part, due to their feedback-increasing effect.

At the very beginning of this treatise on stress and the Human Response System, a curious fact was noted that deserves elaboration. The fact is: among human beings one can observe tremendous variations in self-regulatory and self-controlling abilities. The capacities range from a response system gone-astray in the case of Type A individuals to the tremendous feats of self-control exhibited by Eastern Indian Yogi. The remainder of us fall between these extremes. Yet when we are placed in special circumstances that increase our motivation to respond, we exhibit impressive gains in self-regulation and control.

The concept of feedback helped explain this enormous variability in the ability to control and regulate one's own responses. The system has the capacity to use information and knowledge of its own functioning for its own behalf. Evidence has been presented from the areas of child development, physiology, organizational behavior management, and biofeedback training to support the importance of this notion for understanding human functioning.

A concluding question arises from the presented data: Are all human emotional and psychosomatic problems a function of a breakdown in feedback? This question cannot be answered accurately at this time. New areas of research will inevitably identify other unifying concepts that facilitate our understanding of the Human Response System. At this stage in the development of self-regulation and self-control, we can be assured of the following conclusion: People can profit considerably from an increase in knowledge and information about their own response systems, self-regulation and self-control starts with becoming acutely aware of the feedback obtained from one's own emotions and response signals, and individuals can take a major portion of the responsibility for the adequate functioning of their own response systems.

The path has been paved for the discussion of feedback from a self-management perspective. The remainder of this chapter focuses on the use of the concept of feedback in understanding and modifying a diverse set of human responses including eating behavior, interpersonal relations and psychosomatic problems. The groundwork will be laid for answering the following question: How can you use feedback to achieve a maximum amount of self-regulatory ability? This answer will be provided in the final chapter of this book.

FEEDBACK AND THE HUMAN RESPONSE SYSTEM

Feedback is an integral part of our lives. We use feedback on a daily basis to regulate and control a diverse set of human activities, ranging from simple behaviors such as eating to the complex responses involved in interpersonal relations. A discussion of feedback and its relationship to a very basic human behavior—eating—provides a good example of the importance of this principle in our daily functioning.

When you sit down for a meal, you obtain a wealth of information from the immediate environment. This includes the appearance of the food, the smell, and particularly the taste of the food. Perhaps the most important information that contributes to the regulation and control of the eating response is the feedback you obtain from your stomach as you eat. When your stomach begins to fill up, your brain picks up that information and feeds it back to you. Regulation of the amount you eat is dependent on this information and feedback. James V. McConnell, a well-known behavior modifier, has discussed the physiology of eating behavior in an interesting article, "Feedback, Fat, and Freedom." He views the concept of feedback as an important variable for understanding this human response.

> Recent research has uncovered surprising information on the physiology of eating behavior and how this inherited body machinery may control weight, or fail to. Buried away deep in the centre of your brain is a small bundle of nerves called the hypothalamus. Although it is only about the size of your fingertip, your hypothalamus has a large influence on your emotions and your motivations. From laboratory experiments on white rats, and from studies of humans with various types of brain damage, we have recently learned that two tiny sections of the hypothalamus exercise important control over eating behaviour. One of these tiny bundles of nerve cells is called the feeding centre. If we place the tip of a very thin metal needle, an electrode, in the middle of a rat's feeding centre, we can stimulate or excite the nerve cells there by passing a weak electrical current through the needle. Whenever we do so, the rat begins to eat. Even if the rat has just consumed a large meal, it will start to nibble away on whatever is handy and will continue to eat until we turn off the current. If we keep the stimulation up long enough, we can make the rat grow quite fat. On the other hand, if we surgically remove this feeding centre from the animal's hypothalamus, it will often stop eating altogether—unless we coax it.

> Close to the feeding centre in the hypothalamus is another bundle of nerve cells that scientists have named the satiation centre. If we place an electrode in this part of the rat's brain, we can bring the animal close to starvation merely by stimulating this centre electrically each time the rat starts to eat. As soon as the current is turned on, the rat stops eating, no matter how starved it is. On the other hand, if we remove the satiation centre surgically, the rat goes on a nonstop food orgy. It will eat and eat until it gets so fat it can hardly move." [51, p. 35]

Notice that you are revisiting the structure of the brain—the hypothalamus—that plays such an important role in guiding the responses of the physiological component of the Human Response System. The hypothalamus has been discussed as one of the chief regulaters of homeostasis through its impact on the autonomic and endocrine systems. Here you are observing an additional role for this structure in the regulation of eating behavior. McConnell continues his discussion by integrating the notion of feedback into the functioning of the hypothalamus.

> Under normal circumstances, the nerve cells in the feeding centre and the satiation centre act as alarm mechanisms to let the rest of your brain know whether or not you need food. As soon as you have eaten and digested a meal, the sugar molecules in the food are picked up by your blood-stream and are passed along to all the cells in your body. These sugar molecules stimulate or excite the satiation centre cells much as does electrical current from an electrode. These same sugar molecules have a negative or inhibitory effect on the cells in your feeding centre. The higher your blood sugar level, the more the nerves in your feeding centre are repressed or turned off. On the other hand, when you starve yourself for a while, the opposite set of events occurs—the decrease in the number of sugar molecules allows the nerve cells in your feeding centre to become more and more excited. They feed this message back to the rest of your brain, saying, "Eat—eat—eat!" Meanwhile, the decrease in your blood sugar level inhibits or turns off the cells in your satiation centre, so they stop sending feedback signals to the rest of your brain saying you have had enough. [51, p. 36]

It is well known among investigators of eating behavior that obese individuals often fail to respond to the feedback provided to them by their stomachs. They continue to eat when they are physiologically full. In some cases they eat so rapidly that the exchange of information between the stomach and the brain is disrupted. The eating behavior gets out of control. According to McConnell:

> People grow obese not because they have damaged hypothalamic centres but because they have not learned to control the feedback these centres give them—and because their stomach muscles have been trained to react the wrong way at the wrong times. [51, p. 36]

Behavioral scientists are attempting to control overeating among obese individuals by teaching them to use the information and feedback that is provided to them by their response systems.[53] This strategy includes the following responses: monitoring daily caloric intake and weight, modifying the length of time required to complete a meal, and even changing the rate of chewing behavior so that one bite of food is swallowed before another is consumed. These responses increase the exchange of information between the obese person and the discrete eating responses. The new strategy allows time for the response system to process the feedback between the brain and the stomach. It ultimately facilitates control of the eating response.

FEEDBACK AND INTERPERSONAL RELATIONS

In the area of interpersonal relations feedback obtained from fellow human beings—friends, relatives, co-workers and even acquaintances—is critical for developing positive social relations, intimacy, social outlets, and good working conditions. People listen to what other individuals have to say about them and regulate their own responses on the basis of this feedback. A supervisor can strengthen appropriate work behavior by providing positive feedback to the worker on his or her performance. Along the same lines, a parent can reinforce a child's appropriate behavior by providing the child with feedback: "When you do that mother feels good about you. You really are doing well."

Negative feedback can have a tremendous impact on human relations. If someone says to you: "I don't like that particular trait about you. It really turns me off," you may choose to ignore the statement. On the other hand, you may obtain the same feedback from several significant people in your life and choose to utilize the information to alter the behavior in question. People are constantly exposed to information from the social environment that can be utilized to regulate and control responses to the outside world.

Psychologists and psychiatrists work with many so-called "defensive" individuals who place impenetrable barriers between themselves and their environments. They often ignore the information provided to them from their interpersonal relations. These individuals fail to respond to negative feedback and have difficulty communicating their own needs, preferences, and problems to other people. Defensive individuals tend to be uptight, detached, and extremely cautious in their interactions and have difficulty getting beyond shallow relationships. They have very few friends and are prone to a variety of interpersonal problems.

One of the most common approaches to reducing defensiveness is to increase the exchange of information between the person and the environment by encouraging self-disclosure and openness. One important component of the change is to desensitize "defensive" individuals to negative feedback. The individual learns to accept criticism and other unpleasant responses without automatically closing up and becoming tight. The person is then willing to encounter a variety of human interactions in a risk-taking manner. This sets the stage for self-disclosure, openness, and positive interpersonal relations.

FEEDBACK, LEARNING, AND HUMAN BEHAVIOR

Many psychological investigators feel that feedback is at the very core of all human endeavors. They are interested in systematically studying the manner in which it contributes to human functioning. Dr. John Annett, in his book *Feedback and Human Behavior,* has integrated the fields of cybernetics, information theory, and human learning. He has studied the influence of feedback on the learning process. Annett discusses the role of knowledge of results in controlling and changing behavior. He has investigated the learning process in a variety of tasks including simple hand movements, mathematics, and psychotherapy. According to Annett, knowledge of results is one of the most general features of all learning situations.

Dr. Annett discriminates between two types of feedback: intrinsic and extrinsic knowledge of results.

> We have seen how, at a very general level, the concept of feedback can be applied to the analysis of behavior ranging from the simplest of movements to complex problem solving tasks. A piece of behavior can result in muscular and other bodily sensations and changes in the externally perceived environment, including, of course, the social environment. The general term used since about the turn of the century for a variety of forms of psychological feedback is knowledge of results (KR). . . . In general, 'intrinsic KR' is that which is normally present and is not often subject to experimenter manipulation, whilst 'extrinsic KR' represents feedback being supplied by the experimenter or specially adapted by him. [52, p. 26]

Annett's book deals primarily with extrinsic, augmented knowledge of results or feedback; that is, situations where the experimenter takes some performance measure which is not normally available to the subject and feeds this information to him or her. In positioning tasks, for example, the subject "makes a simple blind movement or excursion from a point of origin, stops, and returns. The extent of movement is measured against a standard criterion and KR (knowledge of results) is given. Learning is normally measured in terms of the increase in movement accuracy." He documents the importance of extrinsic feedback on other human responses such as motor tasks, perceptual skills, and verbal learning. He concludes by stating that:

> The feedback concept is significant not simply because it suggests analogies between organisms and machines but because it suggests certain basic characteristics of the structure of behavior. Rather than being simply run off as a result of prior stimulation, behavior, both simple and complex, can be seen as governed by results *at all levels.* In a very general way, the feedback concept seems to be able to account for some of the complexities of behavior and especially with flexible and adaptive behavior. [52, p. 36]

Annett's distinction between intrinsic and extrinsic feedback is important for understanding the learning that takes place in biofeedback training. Biofeedback training can be considered an attempt to combine the effects of both extrinsic and intrinsic knowledge of results in order to ameliorate certain psychosomatic conditions. The biofeedback trainer provides extrinsic feedback in the form of visual and auditory displays of physiological responses in addition to verbal reinforcement from the trainer for results in a desirable direction. The subject learns to regulate and control these physiological functions as a result of this extrinsic feedback. This represents the first stage of biofeedback training.

The second stage of training involves the identification, by the subject, of intrinsic results. That is, what internal responses (responses within the system itself) take place that can be used to regulate and control physiological responses when extrinsic feedback (the equipment and the trainer) is absent? If the positive results are to transfer from the training situation to ordinary life circumstances, the intrinsic stage of biofeedback training is mandatory.

The alteration of essential hypertension or high blood pressure is a good example of the use of extrinsic and intrinsic knowledge of results. Studies[54] have been conducted that indicate that high blood pressure can be reduced through the use of biofeedback training. The subjects learn to modify their blood pressure with the assistance of information provided by various forms of blood pressure displays. Progressive reductions in pressure are reinforced by this knowledge of results or feedback. These results are extended to non-laboratory settings by teaching the subjects to control their blood pressure without the use of the biofeedback equipment. The subjects learn to identify internal cues that they can use as feedback for self-regulation of blood pressure. The biofeedback equipment is seen, then, as only a means to the end of self-regulation.

PERSONAL FEEDBACK SYSTEM

The results on self-regulation of blood pressure have been obtained with other responses such as muscle tension in tension headaches, skin temperature in migraine headaches, heart rate and rhythm in various heart disorders, and other psychosomatic problems.[15] These subjects are able to develop internal strategies for regulating and controlling responses at all levels of the Human Response System. In this manner, they have developed the use of a Personal Feedback System. McConnell summarizes his discourse on feedback by discussing the importance of developing such a system:

> Real freedom, then, comes from knowledge—from knowing your own biological and psychological needs, from learning the effects you have on others, from becoming sensitive to how the behaviour of other people actually influ-

ences you. But this kind of knowledge always involves the development of finely tuned feedback systems: you come to know your own body when you learn how to listen to its special language, and you best achieve your goals in life by becoming aware of the continuous interplay between you and your social environment. Only by learning the limits on your freedom do you gain control of your destiny. The behaviourist, working within this strict discipline, can claim a hopeful motto: 'Ye shall know the truth, and the truth shall make you free.' [51, p. 40]

Techniques such as biofeedback training, relaxation, assertiveness, and others that allow subjects to learn to regulate and control responses via intrinsic feedback are critical to people who are interested in modifying the stress proneness of their Human Response Systems. The focus of the personal feedback techniques in Chapter 12 is based on the notion that you can learn to dramatically increase the knowledge of results of your responses. Through this intrinsic personal feedback, you can learn to control and regulate your own response system.

Carl Sagan, in his book *The Dragons of Eden,* urges the use of the full potential of human intelligence for the future survival of mankind: "The coordinated functioning of both cerebral hemispheres is the tool nature has provided for our survival. We are unlikely to survive if we do not make full and creative use of our human intelligence." [55, p. 248]

Sagan's reiteration of Jacob Bronowski's[56] imperative for our civilization is equally applicable to all of us at a personal level: "Knowledge is our destiny."

12 SELF-REGULATION
Personal Feedback

THE CASE OF JOSEPH

Joseph called me one morning for an appointment. When I asked him to tell me the general nature of his problem, I was mildly surprised by the answer. Joseph wanted me to treat him for lower back pain. He had viewed a television documentary on this problem, and the narrator made several summary statements at the end of the program. The thrust of the narrator's conclusions was: "There are an alarmingly large number of adults who suffer from lower back pain. Very few experts agree on the causes of this problem, and a variety of treatment techniques are prescribed, ranging from simple exercises to major surgery. The majority of investigators agreed that the stress of modern living is a significant contributor to the problem of chronic lower back pain."

I saw Joseph early one morning for his appointment. He told me that the early mornings were the most difficult times for him. His back was stiffened by the evening's sleep in spite of the fact that he slept on an extra firm mattress that was recommended to him by a physician. This was one of numerous recommendations made by his doctors over the last eighteen years. Others included medication, special diets, a back brace, and a multitude of exercise programs. None of these prescriptions helped. Joseph was on the brink of giving up on the problem and resigning himself to endure the pain for the rest of his life. He wanted to try one more approach before making this decision.

Joseph was thirty-five years of age and had been experiencing lower back problems since he was seventeen. He had injured his back during adolescence while doing routine exercises. The prob-

lem was very minor initially. He rapidly recuperated from the intense pain that immediately followed the injury and remained quite athletically oriented during college and through his early twenties. The back problem only occurred when he stood for long periods of time or exercised too vigorously. Still, the pain was transient and only had a minor effect on Joseph's level of physical activity.

The problem grew progressively worse during his late twenties and early thirties. It was not uncommon for him to injure his back while playing tennis or moving and lifting furniture. Joseph would be incapacitated for several days after the injury, but he would return to his normal level of activity in a short period of time. Several months later another injury would inevitably slow him down again. This cycle repeated itself regularly during each year of his life.

In the past few years Joseph had become more concerned about the problem. The periods between major injuries got shorter, and he began having minor episodes of the problem on a weekly basis. The pain eventually became a part of his daily existence. He would awaken with it in the morning and fall asleep with it at night. Many daily events would aggravate his back and cause him to experience a moderate level of pain. Standing for long periods of time, sitting in uncomfortable positions, and particularly active work days were a few of the conditions that aggravated the problem.

If Joseph had walked into my office ten years ago, I would have been at a loss to assist him with his problem. My work with Paul and many other individuals who manifested their problems in a psychophysiological manner had paid off. Joseph's problem could be understood by looking at his Human Response System and its coping strategy.

I asked Joseph to describe his problem to me in detail. I wasn't surprised to find that he could not give me the specific details that I requested. He only paid attention to the problem when the discomfort was fairly intense. "I'm only aware of the problem when it causes me a lot of pain," he stated. He could not describe to me the specific series of events that preceded the onset of severe discomfort. Joseph didn't know when the pain started or *what precipitated it. Like so many maladaptive habits of the system, the responses that contributed to his back pain were executed at a very low level of awareness. They had become automatic. Joseph's maladaptive habits were discretely housed in his own response system.*

Joseph came to see me because he had a vague feeling that there was a relationship between his style of living and his chronic pain. He was willing to take some responsibility for contributing to his lower back problem. Yet, he was still quite surprised and somewhat confused by my analysis of the situation. After a detailed evaluation I arrived at several general conclusions about the development of his back condition.

Joseph responded to the initial back injury in the usual manner. He refrained from any strenuous physical activity until the pain in his back subsided. According to his doctor there was no major medical problem sustained from the injury, so he slowly resumed a regular pattern of physical activity.

The muscles in his lower back apparently became somewhat more vulnerable to injury as a result of the initial insult, and Joseph experienced additional discomfort every nine to twelve months. The pain was usually initiated by a variety of athletic activities that young people are prone to engage in, but it was never debilitating. It had only a temporary effect on his daily functioning. Joseph would curtail his activity for a short time and resume his normal routine after the pain diminished. The pain became a warning signal for his system to make a temporary adjustment in its level of responding. Up to this point there were no permanent changes in his response system as a result of the vulnerability of his lower back.

Because of Joseph's previous painful experiences he became somewhat sensitive about the back problem. Instead of strengthening his back through systematic use and exercise Joseph began pampering it. He was very cautious about activities that might aggravate the back pain and he even made certain adjustments in his posture and style of walking. In order to compensate for the vulnerable area he would bend in a manner that minimized the use of his back muscles. Joseph eventually developed a style of sitting, standing, and walking that put very little demands on his back.

These postural and behavioral changes further isolated Joseph's back from the remainder of the response system. Soon, his lower back began suffering from the consequences of this habitual strategy. It became weaker in relation to other muscles in his body, and thus became even more vulnerable to stress and injury. As a result the pain became more frequent and intense.

The relationship between Joseph's response style and the lower back problem was not clear to him. He was not aware that his own postural and behavioral habits contributed significantly to the chronic lower back pain. The problem was seen as an isolated event that was unrelated to other components of his response system. He was unaware of the specific contribution of his own responses to the vulnerability of his back. At this point, the only exchange of information and feedback between Joseph's response system and his back was the intense and debilitating pain that he experienced.

After some practice in pinpointing the relationship between various activities in his life and lower back pain, Joseph identified several maladaptive responses to life events that predictably caused intense discomfort. These included his responses to excessive pressures at work, the physical demands of standing or sitting for long periods of time, and tense social and family encounters. During these stressful life events the pain would gradually increase in intensity. Yet he would not attend to it until it was very severe. By this time, Joseph's control over the problem was minimal.

Joseph would focus on the intense pain and say to himself: "Why did it happen to me? I'm athletic and strong. It should not have happened. Why do I have to deal with this pain every day of my life?" The self-pitying and whining flavor of his thoughts immobilized him. These preoccupying disordered thoughts distracted him from making the connection between life events, his response style, and the back problem. They kept Joseph from taking responsibility for the problem and prevented him from doing something constructive about it.

At a physiological level Joseph's lower back was in fairly good shape. He had been to enough doctors to assure himself of this fact. There was no evidence of any disc problems. Rather, the periodic pain seemed to be due to muscle strain as a result of the stresses on muscles and ligaments that surround the vertebral column. The lower back muscles seemed to vigorously contract and stiffen up with even the slightest provocation. Stressful days at work were a nightmare for him. Joseph knew that by the end of the day he would be experiencing severe pain.

Joseph's posture and behavioral responses correlated quite well with his maladaptive attitude about the problem. He could be observed standing and walking in a stiffened manner, somewhat tilted toward the right side. He would bend over quite cautiously, failing to adequately bend his knees. He sat in a slumped manner because of the pain that he experienced when he sat upright. Joseph had developed a large number of maladaptive postural and behavioral habits that aggravated the problem in his lower back. By being excessively cautious in order to avoid the pain of various movement and stationary responses, he had developed a strategy that would assure a gradual isolation and weakening of a component of his response system.

An Adaptive Coping Strategy

Joseph's habitual approach to the problem created a very low level of awareness between his response style and the excessive muscular contractions in his lower back. The new strategy was based on increasing information and personal feedback to him about this connection. The exchange of information between his back and the remainder of his system was limited to his awareness of intense pain. So this is where we started. Joseph's first task was to monitor this signal by becoming acutely aware of the variation in the level of discomfort in his lower back.

The initial stage of the feedback process was direct and readily observable. The first step was to teach Joseph how to monitor his pain. Joseph and I designed a discomfort rating scale in order to specify the exact amount of discomfort that he was experiencing from one period of time to another. The scale ranged from zero to twenty-five. Zero to nine indicated mild discomfort, ten to fifteen indicated moderate discomfort, and sixteen to twenty-five was used for extreme discomfort. The range of twenty to twenty-five was reserved for debilitating pain; that is, discomfort that was extreme enough to restrict movement.

Seven discomfort ratings were obtained for each day. The ratings would be taken throughout the day: two in the morning, one at noon, two in the afternoon, and two in the evening. A great deal of flexibility was allowed in the rating system so that it would accurately reflect the variability of discomfort. For example, Joseph might choose to obtain four ratings during a morning that was particularly stressful for him, whereas the remaining three ratings could occur during the rest of the day. Maintaining a rigid schedule of observations was unnecessary. The critical component of the self-monitoring process was to produce a general increase in personal feedback.

Figure 12-1 includes a sample of the discomfort ratings obtained by Joseph on his lower back. A great deal of interesting information was obtained from these ratings. All of the information cannot be communicated in this discussion, but the most salient points can be summarized. Joseph was surprised to learn several interesting bits of data: His pain varied quite dramatically during each day; it was most intense in the mornings and least intense in the evenings. The pain was significantly reduced through the simple act of self-monitoring, and he could do things during the day that significantly reduced the intensity of his lower back discomfort.

As a result of this initial stage of self-monitoring, Joseph learned that there was a cause-and-effect relationship between his responses and lower back pain. He commented: "It's almost as if there are new connections between my brain and my lower back, connections that I never realized were there." The initial sense of control obtained by regulating his own level of back pain was a significant victory for Joseph. Joseph compared this experience to the feeling of immense self-control that overwhelmed him when he quit smoking.

The second stage in the personal feedback process was to utilize other feedback-facilitating techniques. The relaxation response was systematically used to increase Joseph's knowledge of the relationship between muscle tension and lower back pain. He was instructed to relax periodically when his lower back pain was above a rating of ten. Joseph learned an extremely valuable lesson from this exercise. During the twenty minutes of relaxation, he could reduce his discomfort from fifteen or above to less than

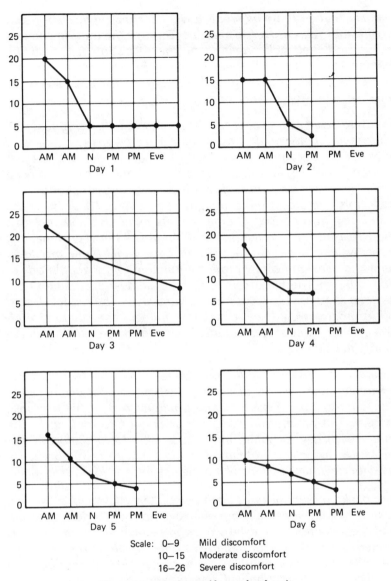

Scale: 0–9   Mild discomfort
          10–15   Moderate discomfort
          16–26   Severe discomfort

Figure 12-1. Ratings of lower back pain.

five. He learned to focus on his lower back during relaxation and significantly relax the tense muscles. Through the intense concentration and feedback provided by the relaxation response, he learned to control and regulate the pain. This response subsequently transferred to the daily life events that precipitated an increase in tension and discomfort.

The third stage of personal feedback involved changing Joseph's posture and behavioral style. During the previous two stages of treatment he became acutely aware of the pain induced by certain standing, walking, and sitting positions. Joseph began modifying these responses and observing the consequences of these new behaviors. He stood more upright and observed that he could stand for longer periods of time with little pain. He walked with a more relaxed gait and learned to discriminate between variations in his walking style. He sat with his back upright and shoulders high and felt significantly more comfortable for longer periods of time. The knowledge obtained from these new postural and behavioral responses led to a new postural style. The feedback paid off in progressively lower discomfort ratings. The cumulative effect of these three stages of personal feedback are reflected in the ratings in Figure 12-2.

Joseph is still engaged in the final stage of personal feedback. He no longer monitors his discomfort with a piece of graph paper. The self-monitoring has become a natural part of his response system. The process is somewhat analogous to looking in the mirror each day to obtain information about one's physical appearance. Joseph has obtained a mirror image of his back. He uses this feedback to control muscle tension and lower back pain.

The back problem has not been completely alleviated. However, Joseph has developed a comprehensive strategy for dealing with it and feels confident that he will soon resolve the problem. This strategy includes weight training in order to strengthen the muscles that were weakened by years of pampering, caution, and neglect. I'm sure that he will develop additional strategies on his own. Joseph has an ongoing communication with his response system through the development of a highly personal feedback system.

THE REMAINDER OF THIS CHAPTER FOCUSES ON THE BASIC steps involved in the development of this system.

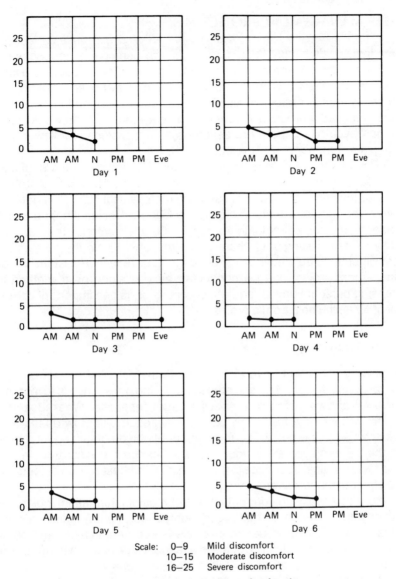

Scale: 0–9   Mild discomfort
        10–15 Moderate discomfort
        16–25 Severe discomfort

Figure 12-2. Ratings of lower back pain.

SELF-MANAGEMENT PROJECT

Some individuals simply know from their own personal experiences that they want to change something about themselves. Others obtain the feedback from significant people in their lives such as spouses, friends, co-workers, or health professionals. Perhaps through reading this book, you have pinpointed a problem in your response system that you would like to change. If you have, there are several systematic steps to follow in conducting a self-management project.

First I wish to reiterate an important point that I made at the beginning of this book. Your reading of this book may have alerted you to a problem that is serious enough to warrant seeking professional help. This does not prevent your use of the steps outlined below. Professional help and self-management are not mutually exclusive. On the contrary, they are intimately related. Taking your share of the responsibility in the helping process will undoubtedly facilitate changes in your response system. A self-management project can be conducted by you alone as a method for increasing personal growth and effectiveness or as one important component of obtaining help from a professional.

Self-Monitoring

The previous chapters have alerted you to the potential problems within your response system. The first step in modifying a response is to increase your level of awareness of a specific target response. When does this problem occur? How frequently does it manifest itself? How does it vary from one day to the next? The more information you obtain about a problem, the better off you are in your efforts to change it. It is still true, in spite of the technological advances in this area, that the best source of feedback from your response system is you.

Before you deal with your untapped sources of information, look briefly at an example of feedback that is commonly used by many individuals on a regular basis. The basic bathroom scale is used regularly by millions of people to monitor weight. The scale is a feedback device that informs them about their weight from one day to the next, from one year to the next, and even from one decade of life to another. It is a very convenient instrument that can be used in the self-management of weight.

As we all know the scale can be used to provide a dieter with continuous feedback about a particular weight reduction strategy. It is quite nice to have this mechanical device available for this project. However, if the scale became extinct, the dieter could do without it. Obtaining feedback without the scale's aid would involve slightly more work than the simple act of stepping on a scale, but the consequences would be well worth the extra effort. The alternative form of feedback involves no mechanical device at all. It simply demands the use of a calorie counter, a piece of graph paper, and a pencil.

The dieter writes down everything he or she eats each day. At the end of the day, the dieter converts each item of food into the number of calories consumed for that period of time. The total sum of calories consumed for each day is plotted on a piece of graph paper that has been set up for that purpose. The number of calories are represented on the vertical segment of the graph paper, and days of the week are represented on the horizontal portion. At the end of the week of calorie counting, there will be seven points on the graph.

The dieter can then determine daily weight loss by a simple calculation. The calories consumed for one particular day are subtracted from the number of calories allowed for a day (the number of calories one must consume in order to maintain weight at a constant level). This difference between consumption and daily caloric allowance is then divided by 3600 calories (the number of calories in one pound). For example, on "Day one" the dieter consumed 1000 calories. The calorie allowance to maintain the same weight for "Day one" is 2200 calories for a person that weighs a specific amount and has a normal activity level for that day (you can find out your own caloric allowance according to your weight by checking standard weight and calorie charts). The difference between allowance and consumption is 1200 calories. The dieter has lost one third of one pound on that particular day because 1200 calories are one third of the 3600 calories that are in one pound.

There are two advantages to this kind of feedback when compared to a weight scale. First, most used scales are slightly inaccurate, and they don't often reflect a weight loss early in the dieter's regime when accurate feedback is crucial. Second, the dieter gains much more information about eating habits from writing down each item of food and plotting the daily intake activity. The major point is that feedback can be obtained quite readily without the use of modern technological devices. In the case of calorie counting and plotting, this feedback strategy has proven to be very useful in changing eating habits and, consequently, weight problems.

This discussion on calorie counting has illustrated three important components of the *self-monitoring* process: pinpointing, recording, and graphically displaying human responses for the purpose of altering these responses in a desirable direction. The steps are discussed individually below.

Pinpointing. In the process of stress-watching you may have discovered one or more things about yourself that you would like to modify. It is important for you, at this point, to further pinpoint these problem areas for the purpose of using this information for self-monitoring and feedback.

The three components of the Human Response System are not equally receptive to self-monitoring. Thinking occurs at a very private level. Some-times these thoughts are even disguised from the thinker. Physiological reactions may go unnoticed for a period of time and only become evident after several reactions accumulate to produce one noticeable response. On the other hand, behavior is out there for everyone to see. If you are a cigarette smoker and wish to monitor your smoking behavior, you simply have to watch each cigarette that you smoke. You can count calories as a means of monitoring eating behavior and monitor ounces of alcohol for drinking behavior.

In spite of the relative difficulty of identifying private responses (e.g., thoughts and physiological reactions), it is important for you to develop skills in monitoring these responses. Human responses that usually re-main disguised and hidden from observation can be pinpointed. Heart rate is an example of a physiological response that is monitored for us by physicians but is rarely the subject of self-monitoring. In some instances it can be a valuable response to pinpoint and observe, particularly since an increase in heart rate accompanies many states of emotional arousal. In addition, heart rate is extremely simple to pinpoint (e.g., placing two fin-gers of one hand over the carotid artery in the throat) and monitor (e.g., counting the number of pulse beats occurring in a sixty-second period), because it corresponds directly to the rate of the pulse. In this manner, anyone can pinpoint heart rate and monitor it from one minute to the next, from one hour to the next, and from one part of the day to another. This has proven to be a valuable response to monitor for people who have an excessive increase in heart rate during stressful daily encounters. This information on heart rate can provide feedback to these individuals on the amount of emotional arousal occurring in a variety of activating life events.

There are literally hundreds of discrete human responses available for pinpointing and self-monitoring. Table 12-1 provides examples of these responses from each component of the Human Response System. This list is far from complete. Each one of you should be able to pinpoint other responses that are more relevant to your own particular response system.

The most important task in the pinpointing process is specifying the response clearly enough so that you can readily observe it. If you are interested in changing a discrete behavior—fear of speaking in a group— you must clearly specify the responses to be observed. For example, observing "reluctance to speak in social situations" is not as specific as

TABLE 12–1. Pinpointing Human Responses

Component of the Human Response System	Examples of Human Responses for Self-Monitoring
Emotions	
1. Anxiety	1. Ratings of anxiety level
2. Depression	2. Periods of extremely low moods
3. Anger	3. Outbursts of anger
Thinking	
1. Thought preoccupation and worries	1. Amount of time spent worrying
2. Thought distractions or loss of concentration	2. Attention span
3. Irrational thinking	3. Frequency of irrational thoughts
Physiological Reactions	
1. Muscle tension	1. Tension headache ratings
2. Cardiovascular	2. High blood pressure measurements
3. Gastrointestinal	3. Frequency of constipation or diarrhea
4. Neurological	4. Number of tics, spasms, or seizures
Behavioral Responses	
1. Hyperresponsiveness	1. Time spent at work
2. Hyporesponsiveness	2. Frequency of social activities avoided
3. Habit proneness	3. Overeating/weight

"amount of time spent talking during a four-hour cocktail party." Table 12-2 provides some practice in pinpointing responses. The first column includes several responses to be pinpointed. The second column indicates a nonspecific, unclear observation; and the third is a very specific pinpointed response.

As you can see from the Table 12-2, a variety of responses can be pinpointed, ranging from behavioral responses (cigarette smoking) to less specific physiological ones (tension headaches). In each case the method of observation is different. Some responses can only be observed through the use of ratings. Nevertheless, the point emphasized here is the need to specify the response as clearly as possible. In this manner, many responses that you previously thought were unobservable are now ready to be pinpointed for self-monitoring.

Recording. Once the response to be monitored has been pinpointed, the rate of occurrence of the response must be counted and recorded. The method of counting and recording varies from one response to another. For example, counting sheets are often used with cigarette smokers.

TABLE 12–2.   Specifying Responses to be Self-Monitored

Response	Nonspecific and Unclear	Specific and Observable
Lack of exercise	Number of exercise activities per week	Amount of time spent exercising per day
Cigarette smoking	Number of packs smoked per day	Number of cigarettes smoked per day
Over-eating	Pounds gained per week	Number of calories consumed per day
Fear of asking for a date	Number of male/female contacts and conversations	Number of telephone calls and other contacts where date is requested
Insomnia	Number of nights without sleep	Number of hours slept per night
Tension headaches	Number of headaches per week	Discomfort rating from 1 (no headache) to 10 (severe headache) per day
Lack of sexual enjoyment	Number of times sex was enjoyable	Pleasure rating from 1 (no pleasure) to 10 (extreme pleasure) during intercourse

These sheets are placed between the cellophane wrapper and the pack. Every time a cigarette is taken from the pack, the smoker indicates this response on the counting sheet. At the end of the day, the rate of cigarette smoking can be observed directly from the sheet.

Wrist counters have been used to count certain responses. The counter is worn on the wrist, and each time a pinpointed behavior occurs, the appropriate spot on the counter is depressed in order to register the response. Note cards be used in the same manner. The card is carried in a shirt pocket, wallet, or purse and used for counting when the pinpointed behavior is observed. The responses can be summed at the end of the period of observation. For example, the number of angry outbursts can be recorded by using note cards. Each time this response occurs, a mark is made on the card. At the end of the day the marks are tallied in order to determine the total number of angry outbursts for that day.

Rating and time scales can be used to monitor responses that do not occur on a discrete basis. Heart rate is a discrete response. At the end of one minute, you can easily determine the number of beats that have occurred. On the other hand, back pain and tension headaches are not discrete responses. At the end of an hour, you cannot easily identify the number of tension headaches or backaches that you have experienced. These two problems start at one point in time and then end at another point. They also start at one level of intensity (e.g., very mild) and vary to another level (e.g., very severe). In responses such as these, it is far easier to use time scales where you plot the length of time of a particular response (e.g., headache) and/or the intensity of the response (e.g., zero equals no pain, one equals mild pain, . . . , and ten equals severe pain).

The case of Joseph discussed at the beginning of this chapter provides an example of the recording of a non-discrete response—lower back pain. You recall that a rating scale was used in order to record the variability of this response. The scale was made up of twenty-five points: 0−9 indicated mild pain, 10−15 indicated moderate pain, and 16−25 indicated extreme pain. The scale and a single day's recordings are duplicated in Figure 12-3. Joseph was asked to make seven recordings of the intensity of his pain each day. The seven recordings were spread throughout the day: two in the morning, one around lunchtime, two in the afternoon, and two in the evening. This style of recording allowed him to observe the variations in the intensity of the response each day.

Displaying. The recorded responses must be displayed in order to achieve maximum feedback. The most frequent form of display is the use of a graph. The graph usually contains the days of observation on the horizontal portion of the page and the frequency of occurrence on the vertical portion of the page. For example, if you are graphing cigarette smoking behavior, the vertical line of the graph would contain the frequency of occurrence. On "Day one," a point would be placed at the

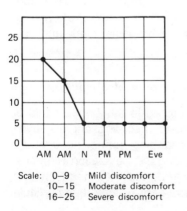

Scale: 0−9   Mild discomfort
10−15   Moderate discomfort
16−25   Severe discomfort   **Figure 12-3. Rating of lower back pain.**

appropriate frequency (e.g., twenty cigarettes). On "Day two," a second point would be placed indicating the frequency for that day (e.g., twenty-five cigarettes). The two points are then connected to indicate a trend in cigarette smoking. It is increasing, decreasing, or remaining the same. This type of display is referred to as the line graph.

Joseph's recordings in Figure 12-3 illustrate the use of a line graph. The vertical portion of the graph indicates the intensity of the pain (0-25), and the horizontal portion indicates the times of the day (morning, noon, afternoon, and evening). A line was drawn from one recording to another to determine the trend in the observed response (back pain).

Other graphic forms of display are available such as the bar graph, where the points are not connected but a line is drawn from one point to the bottom of the graph. Regardless of the type of display used, it is extremely important to use some form of display in order to obtain the maximum amount of information from the self-monitored response.

Once the line graph or bar graph has been constructed, it should be placed in a location that is readily available to you, the observer. You want to be able to observe and analyze the data on a daily basis, perhaps even several times per day. If you are monitoring the number of calories consumed per day, the best location for the graph is directly on the refrigerator door. On the other hand, your graph of ratings of the pleasure of sexual intercourse would most likely be found somewhere in the bedroom. The display of back pain or tension headaches is best executed by carrying the graph in your briefcase, pocket or purse so that it is always available. The most appropriate location is one that maximizes feedback.

USES OF SELF-MONITORING

Self-monitoring can be used for two purposes: to monitor the changes in human responses as a function of the application of a new strategy (e.g., observing changes in weight as a function of a special diet), and as a specific strategy for change in its own right.

Monitoring the Effectiveness of New Response Strategies

The effectiveness of the new strategies outlined in this book should be monitored. This can be executed by pinpointing, recording, and displaying the response that you are interested in changing during the use of a specific strategy. For example, if you are using the Relaxation Response to change a tension headache problem, you can monitor headache discomfort on a daily basis. In this manner, you can evaluate this particular strategy—relaxation—for altering your headaches. If the monitoring shows that headaches have not reduced in frequency and discomfort over a significant period of time, a change in strategies is warranted.

If you choose to use a new thinking strategy for changing your irrational ideas during performance-type situations (e.g., speaking to large groups), you may want to monitor the frequency of irrational thoughts several hours before and after the performance takes place. The effectiveness of this new strategy can then be evaluated by comparing the frequency of irrational thoughts from one performance situation to the next. In the same manner, a new behavioral strategy (e.g., a change in time utilization) for changing a Type A Behavior Pattern might include self-monitoring of hours spent at work, hours spent in leisure activity, number of appointments scheduled in one day, or all three responses. In summary, feedback is an integral component of the strategies outlined in the chapters of this book. Each treatment strategy can be accompanied by a self-monitoring program.

Monitoring as an Independent Strategy

As you learned in the first section of this chapter, some responses can be altered through the use of self-monitoring alone. The pinpointing, recording, and displaying of information about a particular response can serve as a potent strategy for change. The feedback and reinforcement obtained from observing the variations in a particular response can have profound effects on that response. For example, some smokers have been known to quit smoking simply because they have become more acutely aware of the real, not estimated, frequency of their cigarette smoking. In addition, the sense of control the smoker obtains from observing a slight reduction in cigarette smoking from one day to the next is a powerful incentive for further changes.

One of several tenable explanations for explaining the potent effect of feedback on human responses is the inherent reinforcement people obtain from observing changes in their own response. It is powerfully reinforcing to observe the control of one's own behavior. As Seligman has pointed out in his research on learned helplessness, the perception of control, that is, the knowledge that one's responses make a difference in terms of outcomes, is a basic requirement of human beings. The perception of control can be inherently reinforcing. Self-monitoring and feedback facilitate this sense of control and provide the opportunity for self-reinforcement to take place.

Other important sources of reinforcement are available as a function of self-monitoring. Social reinforcement can be obtained by displaying the record of your responses to significant people in your life. They can provide you with additional reinforcement for response changes. Tangible reinforcement can also be available. After you meet a designated goal in your project you can allow yourself to purchase a special tangible item that you could not previously justify. Social and tangible reinforcement can add to the inherent reinforcement of self-monitoring.

THE SECOND STAGE OF PERSONAL FEEDBACK: USE OF OTHER FEEDBACK-FACILITATING TECHNIQUES

The self-monitoring technique represents the initial stage of the Personal Feedback process. It helps you become acutely aware of information that is emanating from a problemed component of your Human Response System. The second stage of personal feedback consists of maintaining this communication on an ongoing basis. In this stage other feedback-facilitating techniques are utilized.

Behavioral technology has provided the response system with a variety of effective response-altering techniques. Each one contributes to the adaptive functioning of the entire system. Each in its own way facilitates feedback in one or more components of the response system. Relaxation induces a return to physiological equilibrium through facilitating knowledge of results of response functioning. Rational and ordered thinking encourages the learning of new thoughts, beliefs, and attitudes by pumping new information into the system. Habit-changing behavioral techniques reinforce an active interplay with the environment to assure that an ongoing exchange of information takes place.

The second stage of personal feedback involves coordinating the self-monitoring process with these behavioral techniques. The case of Joseph illustrates the integration of self-monitoring, relaxation, and changes in postural and behavioral responses. The positive consequences of personal feedback take place when the knowledge of response functioning consistently leads to a modification of the problemed response. Through the self-monitoring process, Joseph became acutely aware of the maladaptive responses that predictably led to severe back pain. He became so well-trained in this monitoring process that he could think about his lower back, provide himself with a rating of his lower back pain, and alter the intensity of the pain through an immediate response. A rating of 20 provided Joseph with distinctly different information from a rating of 15. The critical stage of the personal feedback process took place when a rating (e.g., 15) stimulated his use of a behavioral technique (e.g., relaxation). Subsequently, the new response—relaxation—predictably produced a new result: a reduction in back pain (e.g., from 15 to 5). *In summary, knowledge of response functioning led to a new response that subsequently produced a new positive effect. This is Stress Watching and Stress Management at its most effective level.*

A PERSONAL FEEDBACK SYSTEM: THE FINAL STAGE—A NEW STRATEGY FOR LIVING HAPPILY, EFFECTIVELY, AND WITH A MINIMUM OF EMOTIONAL UPSET

The self-monitoring and behavioral component of developing personal feedback are not ends in themselves. They are means to the end of utilizing knowledge of results of your own human responses for self-regulation and control. The final outcome of all of the techniques outlined in this book is the development of a Personal Feedback System. Each technique, in its own way, facilitates the personal feedback of one or more components of the Human Response System. In various combinations, they can be utilized to redirect human responses that have gone astray from the goal of response equilibrium.

As part of a *Personal Feedback System,* the technology outlined in this book is directed toward facilitating human functioning by reducing emotional upsets and disturbances and by increasing personal awareness and effectiveness. I have attempted to synthesize the current state of scientific knowledge for you. The technology of human behavior is changing rapidly, and new findings will undoubtedly refine the data presented here. Each individual is ultimately responsible for deciding on the particular combination of responses that will make up his or her strategy of living. Thus it is important for you to remain open to new developments in the area of human behavior in order to continue to provide your Human Response System with new information.

The final case discussed in this book illustrates the profound effects of the development of a personal feedback system. In this case, a long-standing and debilitating problem was dramatically changed in a relatively short period of time. This individual's problem was relatively unusual, and it may be somewhat difficult for you to identify with it. Nevertheless, like several of the cases presented in earlier chapters, the problem and its resolution illustrates an important point about human behavior and its modification. The use of an extreme example of human response system malfunctioning will teach you something about your own human vulnerabilities and strengths.

There were two critical treatment components that made up the personal feedback strategy utilized in this case: (1) self-monitoring of levels of tension and (2) the Muscular Relaxation Response.

THE CASE OF DORIAN: THE PROFOUND EFFECTS OF A PERSONAL FEEDBACK SYSTEM

I first met Dorian after he had been in the county jail for eighteen days. He was sent by the court to the state psychiatric hospital for an evaluation. The judge wanted to determine his receptivity and motivation for treatment. Dorian was an exhibitionist. He had been in legal trouble for this behavior a number of times in the last ten years. He was twenty-eight when I met him, and the last ten years of his life were blemished by a series of personal crises. Each crisis was precipitated by unusually strong urges that over- whelmed Dorian, took over his sense of rationality, and pushed him to engage in irrational and dangerous behavior.

Dorian was a handsome young man with a very pleasant smile and charming personality. Even during the stress of the evaluation of a problem that was very embarrassing to him, he maintained his sense of humor. He kidded with the hospital staff and charmed all of them into enjoying his company.

Dorian was athletically built. He was a physical education major in college, and shortly after graduating he became a coach for a local high school in his hometown. He taught several classes of tennis and was very well-liked by his fellow teachers and by the students. Dorian's career as a coach ended abruptly when several of the high school girls reported to the principal that Dorian had ex- posed himself to them.

The incident that led to his incarceration and hospitalization was fairly typical of the pattern of behavior that almost always culmi- nated in Dorian's exhibitionistic response. Dorian was working as a driver's education instructor for a company that sold driving lessons. He had done extremely well with the company and was in line for a managerial position. On one typical afternoon he was working with a woman with an intense fear of driving. She was making progress under Dorian's guidance. They stopped by her house to pick up her checkbook on the way back to his office. Dorian was waiting in the car in front of the house when the woman's teenage daughter came out to the front porch. She hesi- tated for a moment and then returned into the house. Dorian got one glimpse of her and immediately bolted from the car. He ran around to the back of the house to search for an inconspicuous entry, entered the house through the back door, and encountered the young girl. Several minutes after explaining his presence there, Dorian exposed himself. He left the premises and returned to the front of the house to find the woman waiting in the car. They returned to his office. Dorian was arrested the next day and escorted to the county jail.

From the public's standpoint exhibitionism is a frightening and disgusting behavior. The exhibitionist is feared and hated. The individual is often lumped in the same category as the rapist and child molester. The reaction is understandable, but the belief on which it is based is usually far from the truth. The exhibitionists that I have treated never touched or assaulted the people to whom they exposed themselves. On the contrary, I have frequently found them to be quite passive. Although Dorian was outgoing and personable, he was intimidated by women and felt insecure and apprehensive in their presence. This anxiety was, in fact, a major component of his problem.

I evaluated Dorian and found that he was extremely motivated for treatment. He was as confused as anyone about his behavior. After the exhibiting response occurred, he became extremely ashamed and depressed. He would promise himself that it was the last time, that he would never do it again. Yet, when the situation arose, he would respond reflexively as if he was programmed like a computer to make predictable responses under specific stimulus conditions.

Dorian described the sequence of events to me that typically occurred prior to and following his exhibitionistic behavior. He emitted the following responses in one way or another many times during the previous ten years of his life: "I was working in the store at the mall. It was a particularly busy day of selling, and I felt under a great deal of pressure. The day seemed endless. It was the weekend and business was heavier than usual and I knew that I had to work an extra few hours in the evening. I felt a great deal of tension throughout my body, but particularly at the back of my neck and shoulders. My threshold for anger was lowered. Customers became progressively more irritating to me as the day passed into the evening. I couldn't seem to shake this feeling of tension and irritability.

"It was time for a coffee break. I walked out of the store to the coffee shop when I noticed two teenage girls walking towards me.

They had apparently finished their shopping and were leaving the mall through the back exit. My heart started pounding, and I became very excited. This rush of emotions overwhelmed me and the tension in my body seemed to diminish by comparison. I felt exhilarated and I knew what I had to do.

"The two girls had to pass by a vacant part of the mall in order to reach their destination. I rushed quickly to the back section of the mall and entered a store that had recently been vacated. It was dark there and no one would notice me. I situated myself in the corner of the store and waited for them to pass. The closer they got to me the more nervous and excited I became. When they were close enough to see me I exposed myself to them.

"Sometimes I want people to see me and sometimes I don't. This time I did. I even made some noises to attract their attention. When they saw me, I became even more excited and turned on. I realized the danger of getting caught, but it really didn't matter to me at that point. They moved on hurriedly. My mission was accomplished. I felt free and relaxed for a short time after that experience.

"Later that evening I became severely depressed and felt ashamed about what I had done. The fear of getting caught preoccupied me. I was miserable and afraid."

Dorian experienced a chain of reactions that was common among the exhibitionists that I have treated. There was a build-up of stress and tension during a specific life event, sexual urges were triggered by a specific stimulus (usually young females), and tension and anxiety was released through the exhibiting response. The final reaction was characterized by a profound emotional disturbance that included feelings of guilt, depression, and fear.

Does this chain of responses represent the results of a maladaptive strategy for coping with stressful life events? The scientific investigation of sexual deviations is making inroads into this and other questions. My work with these individuals leads me to believe that the problem is a consequence of a maladaptive response strategy. Somewhere along the developmental history of these individuals, they have learned to cope poorly with stress. The reason for the sexual manifestation of the maladaptive re-